Hiking the Blue Ridge Parkway

HELP US KEEP THIS GUIDE UP TO DATE

Every effort has been made by the author and editors to make this guide as accurate and useful as possible. However, many things can change after a guide is published—trails are rerouted, regulations change, techniques evolve, facilities come under new management, etc.

We would appreciate hearing from you concerning your experiences with this guide and how you feel it could be improved and kept up to date. While we may not be able to respond to all comments and suggestions, we'll take them to heart, and we'll also make certain to share them with the authors. Please send your comments and suggestions to the following address:

Globe Pequot
Reader Response/Editorial Department
246 Goose Lane
Guilford, CT 06437

Or you may e-mail us at: editorial@falcon.com

Author Randy Johnson is also happy to hear from readers. Please visit his website, where you'll find multimedia features about hiking and more information about Randy and his books: www.randyjohnsonbooks.com.

Thanks for your input, and happy trails!

Hiking the Blue Ridge Parkway

The Ultimate Travel Guide to America's
Most Popular Scenic Roadway

Third Edition

Randy Johnson

GUILFORD, CONNECTICUT

FALCONGUIDES®

An imprint of Globe Pequot

Falcon and FalconGuides are registered trademarks and Make Adventure Your Story is a trademark of Rowman & Littlefield.

Distributed by NATIONAL BOOK NETWORK

Copyright © 2003, 2010, 2017 by Rowman & Littlefield

Photos by Randy Johnson unless otherwise credited

TOPO! Maps © 2017 National Geographic Partners, LLC. All Rights Reserved.

British Library Cataloguing-in-Publication Information available

The Library of Congress has catalogued the earlier edition as follows:
Johnson, Randy, 1951–
    Hiking the Blue Ridge Parkway: the ultimate travel guide to America's most popular scenic roadway / Randy Johnson—1st ed
        p. cm. — (A Falcon Guide)
    ISBN 0-7627-1105-1
        1. Hiking—Blue Ridge Parkway (N.C. and Va.)—Guidebooks 2. Blue Ridge Parkway (N.C. and Va.)—Guidebooks.
    I. Title II. Series
    GV199.42.B65J64 2003
        917.55—dc21

                                    2002041646

ISBN 978-1-4930-2460-5 (paperback)
ISBN 978-1-4930-2461-2 (e-book)

∞™ The paper used in this publication meets the minimum requirements of American National Standard for Information Sciences—Permanence of Paper for Printed Library Materials, ANSI/NISO Z39.48-1992.

Printed in the United States of America

To past and present Appalachian families—the people who know
how much you have to love the mountains to live there.

And to the men and women of the Blue Ridge Parkway—who
help the rest of us appreciate why it's worth the effort.

Contents

The Hikes

The North-Central Blue Ridge
Mileposts 0.0 (I-64 at Shenandoah National Park, VA) to 121.4 (US 220 at Roanoke, VA)

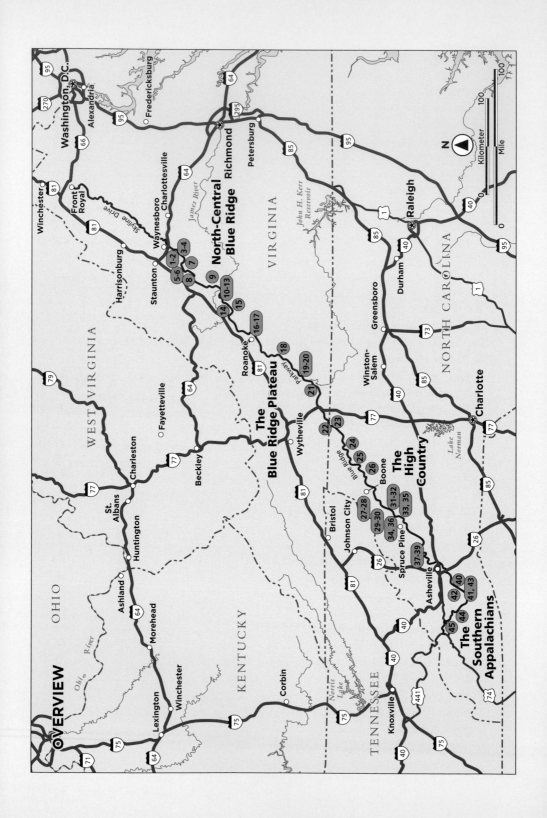

The High Country
Mileposts 276.4 (US 421 at Deep Gap, NC) to
384.7 (US 74 at Asheville, NC)

The Southern Appalachians
Mileposts 384.7 (US 74 at Asheville, NC) to
469.1 (US 441 at Great Smoky Mountains National Park, NC)

Foreword

As we pass the 2016 centennial anniversary of the National Park Service, never has the importance of the Blue Ridge Parkway been clearer to me. The 469-mile route is much more than a road. It is one of the most biodiverse places in the temperate world. It is a living history museum protecting and passing on the stories of Appalachian culture, music, and life. It is a wondrous landscape brimming with outdoor adventures waiting to be experienced.

Still, the Parkway struggles to maintain a delicate balance between beauty and prosperity. In addition to welcoming more visitors than any other National Park unit (over fifteen million in 2015), the Blue Ridge Parkway is the number one economic engine for the communities that border a route that stretches from Shenandoah National Park to Great Smoky Mountains National Park. In 2015, visitors spent more than $952 million in the region. Add in factors such as jobs provided and the total impact is $1.3 billion.

Behind the economic impact on local communities, the often hidden critical issue is how the National Park Service keeps up with the sheer task of managing the country's longest linear park and its throngs of annual visitors. The Parkway currently has more than $516 million in deferred maintenance needs. Restaurants and lodging buildings stand shuttered because of shortfalls in funding. Crumbling infrastructure and vacant staff positions can be seen and felt by the visiting public.

As you explore this national treasure, you can't help but notice the greatness that exists, but also note the greatness that could be. Then act. Through the many organizations that support the Parkway, including the Blue Ridge Parkway Foundation, you can give, volunteer, and become a voice for the protection of this spectacular place.

Randy Johnson's one-of-a-kind, updated guide, *Hiking the Blue Ridge Parkway*, introduces you to many of the destinations you can explore in and around the Parkway. His rich descriptions and vivid color photographs will give you a glimpse of what awaits you out on the trail—and help you plan the perfect Parkway trip.

After experiencing the Blue Ridge Parkway, you'll go home changed for the better. Let's all cherish that experience. Better yet, let's share it with future generations, the people who will care for our public lands into the next one hundred years—if we just show them the path.

Carolyn W. Ward, PhD
CEO of the Blue Ridge Parkway Foundation
Editor, *Journal of Interpretive Research*

How to Use This Guide

When the first edition of *Hiking the Blue Ridge Parkway: The Ultimate Travel Guide to America's Most Popular Scenic Roadway* appeared in 2003, I set out to break the mold of the Blue Ridge Parkway trail guide. The only existing book on that topic ignored great hikes just off the Parkway and contained virtually no maps or photos.

Today, you hold in your hands the thoroughly updated, single-volume solution for the serious Parkway explorer. This book not only features the hikes and facilities of the Parkway, but also the best trails in the national forests and state parks that line the 469-mile scenic road.

This book also includes best-kept-secret suggestions from an award-winning travel writer who has actually lived beside the Parkway for decades. Rich chapters feature each segment of the Parkway, with recommendations for where to stay, eat, and explore. With easy "leg-stretcher" trails everywhere along its length, taking a walk is the perfect Parkway pastime and a big reason why my "expanded hiking guide" concept earns its subtitle as "the Ultimate Travel Guide" to the Parkway. It's the perfect travel format for every Parkway visitor. It will boost even a casual motorist's appreciation of the surrounding scenery—and may even entice you off the beaten path.

Instead of featuring one hike in a location (as many FalconGuides do), this unique volume overviews entire trail systems, offering diverse hiking options. But no book *can include all the trails* on and along the Parkway, so I've chosen great hikes and world-class walks for all kinds of people—the experienced and outdoorsy, families, and people with disabilities, too. Unlike competing guides that require readers to patch together hikes from listy, disconnected chapters of trail data, here hikes are recommended in easy-to-follow text that brings all the trails together in one spot. This book doesn't waste space on "hikes to nowhere" that few will take.

To get the most out of this book, refer often to the final section, the mile-by-mile Parkway Mileage Log that includes all the overlooks, entrances and exits, interpretive sites, museums, visitor centers, and craft shops along the way—all keyed to numbered mileposts you'll see dotting the roadside. The log details everything from the location of picnic tables to the subject of roadside exhibits, with mileages to adjacent towns and attractions.

While the Mileage Log keeps you on track with your trip, it also directs you inside the book for detailed, engaging write-ups on featured hikes. The index and table of contents also guide you inside the book.

But keep in mind, the Mileage Log also includes many roadside or nearby trails that appear only in the log—so don't forget to scan the log at your location for additional options.

Since the first edition of *Hiking the Blue Ridge Parkway*, others have emulated my concept, but none achieve as thorough a reference as this book. This brand-new, thoroughly updated third edition is packed with full color photos and maps—and designed for anyone who visits the Parkway, the most popular unit of the national park system and a premier portal to the Southern Appalachian experience.

Eighty-plus years later, hybrid and electric cars are passing this historical marker where the Parkway started at Cumberland Knob in 1935. This one bears the colorful North Carolina license plate that supports the Blue Ridge Parkway Foundation.

Introduction

Hiking the Blue Ridge Parkway

With the passing of the Blue Ridge Parkway's eightieth anniversary in 2015, there has never been a better time to explore what travel writers call "America's most scenic highway." Stretches of road elsewhere in the United States may indeed be spectacular, but nothing matches this manicured, uniquely uncommercialized half-a-thousand-mile thoroughfare through the lofty heart of America's first frontier. That makes the Parkway a globally recognized icon of the American road.

Scenery aside, the 2008 completion of the Parkway's main visitor center in Asheville and the recent finalization of the Blue Ridge Music Center near the Virginia–North Carolina state line are reminders that the experience just keeps getting richer for visitors.

A Parkway vacation—tackling the length of the roadway from the southern end of Shenandoah National Park in Virginia to Great Smoky Mountains National Park in North Carolina—is a singular experience, a dazzling juncture of earth and sky.

Most of the time spent in the Southern mountains—in a car or on foot—involves either going up or coming down. But the Parkway follows almost continuously along the crest—truly a skyline traverse.

At the Parkway's 45 mph speed limit, the drive could be completed in eleven hours. But the point of this book is that it shouldn't. With vistas beckoning from dozens of overlooks, and trails everywhere, this is a motorized wander that surely should be given at least a week.

The Parkway is a place of raw springtime, where deep winter gives way to a season of hoarfrosted trees and rich earth-toned forests full of snow-flattened leaves. You dip down from cloud-shrouded, winter-whitened branches to suddenly open views that stretch for miles into valleys unseen only moments before. The bite in the air takes your breath away.

As spring progresses, your car sails through a lime-green swale lit by a pale beam of sun. Overhead, a cold-shadowed summit towers through the trees. This is when everything bursts into shades of green and pink and one of the world's most diverse natural environments explodes into bloom. The Parkway becomes the perfect place to play Aaron Copland's *Appalachian Spring* on the car audio system.

Summer is a delicious time on the Parkway—a season of golden high-altitude light and refreshing breezes. The sunniest days elicit rich forest aromas, from the fecund pungency of galax spread beneath a grove of lower-elevation oaks to the perfume of spruce and fir warming in a rare still day on the summits. During this short, poignant pause in an otherwise harsh climate, it's cool enough to induce a summer-colony subculture. Long before the Parkway was built, now century plus–old inns attracted sweltering flatland Southerners to these heights. New resort communities prosper in the same tradition.

Autumn brings brilliant clarity and color, with crystal-clear days alternating with misty highland rains. Winter brings moody fogs that randomly hide and expose eerie, ghostlike forests and sudden vistas. Winter can be stunningly beautiful—when Parkway travel is possible. Snow and ice blast these heights, forcing closure of many of the gates one sees at many road crossings on the Parkway.

Whatever time of year you motor the Parkway, you'll marvel at ever-changing perspectives. A chasm suddenly yawns in a curve—and is gone. As you pass an overlook, a father and son stand silhouetted against the sunset.

The Parkway isn't literally a national park, but it is a unit of the National Park Service—and the nation's most visited one at that. More than half the population of the United States lives within a day's drive of the Parkway. Average annual visitation hovers below twenty million, but in 1988, twenty-five million toured the road.

Best of all, this national treasure has trails along its entire length, making the Parkway a perfect destination for hikers. Indeed, a drive on this high road is a motorized metaphor for the trail experience itself. The Parkway is an Appalachian Trail for autos. But don't just settle for looking through the windshield—getting out of the car is a must.

Be on the road early or late and you'll likely have to stop and sit amazed behind the wheel as a herd of deer gambol across the road. Ravens soar with the air currents above evergreen-covered summits. Peregrine falcons, reintroduced at Parkway-adjacent sites since 1984, now nest and dive all along the road. Flocks of turkeys, also successfully reintroduced, prefer trailside Parkway meadows. Groundhogs munch everywhere; the Parkway's handcrafted stone walls (some recently restored) seem to be their favorite seats.

There's culture as well. Since our nation's earliest westward migrations, the fertile valleys to the east and west of the Blue Ridge Mountains have filled up with farms, towns, and eventually cities. A relative few of those newcomers, Scots-Irish and Germans among them, settled into the very highest elevations of the Blue Ridge and adjacent ranges. Long traditions of music and crafts were practiced in these storied hollows.

Luckily for today's hikers and motorists, early mountain farms, cabins—even a mill—have been preserved at key places along the Parkway, and they impart a sense of what life on the heights must have been like. These exhibits incorporate some of the Parkway's shorter, tamer trails, but they're deeply insightful and worth a wander. Noteworthy stops include the Mountain Farm Trail at Humpback Rocks (Milepost 5), Trail's Cabin at Smart View Picnic Area (Milepost 154.5), the Johnson Farm at Peaks of Otter (Milepost 85.9), and Mabry Mill (Milepost 176.2).

Handcrafts were essential for survival in this "land of do without." A rich tradition of crafts comes to life in a variety of places on and adjacent to the Parkway. Don't miss the Northwest Trading Post (Milepost 258.7), the Parkway Craft Center in Moses Cone Park (Milepost 294), and the Folk Art Center near Asheville, North Carolina (Milepost 382).

The Parkway's craft centers and mountain lifestyle exhibits are just the beginning. Skilled crafters often demonstrate their skills at the Parkway's various craft centers. Reenactors at the lifestyle exhibits depict the kinds of domestic and commercial activities it took to wrest a living from a harsh climate and primitive facilities. If you make time for these programs, an amazing part of America's past will come to life for you.

The National Park Service also tries to remind Parkway travelers of the past by leasing lands along the road for farming and other traditional activities. And while you surely will see vacation homes perched in plain sight of the road (Who wouldn't want a perpetual Parkway view?), organizations such as the Blue Ridge Parkway Foundation (www.brpfoundation.org) and Friends of the Blue Ridge Parkway (friendsbrp .org) purchase land and scenic easements to preserve the Parkway's viewshed. These groups also fund a wealth of special improvement projects, some noted throughout this book. The Foundation and Friends update visitor centers and other facilities, and turn out volunteers to maintain trails. The Foundation also runs a fun program to document your "End-to-Ender" drive of the Parkway, share trip stories, and earn a certificate and car sticker. Please join one of these groups. And if you live nearby, sign up for the Blue Ridge Parkway Foundation's Parkway license plates in North Carolina, or the Friends of the Blue Ridge Parkway's plate in Virginia.

Life on the Parkway

With all these attractions, many visitors slow down and take weeks to tour the Parkway and meet the "who's who" of significant Appalachian summits that line the route. That means visitors need places to stay and eat, and there are enticing resort areas and rustic rural destinations not far from the Parkway, but the high road comes through.

Most Parkway facilities are open from April to late October. Some are staffed earlier and later than others—there's a wide range of elevations and weather conditions on this lofty road that affect facilities. Best bet: check the Parkway's "Operating Hours and Seasons" web page (nps.gov/blri/planyourvisit/hours.htm).

Picnicking is a quintessential Parkway experience. Choose from eleven formal picnic areas with restrooms and hundreds of picnic tables at dozens of overlooks (noted in the Mileage Log). You can also park on the grass and spread a blanket on the roadside—just pick a spot that will support your car and be well away from traffic.

Camping is another must-have experience, and the Parkway's eight campgrounds—an average of one every 59 miles—offer 625 tent sites and 317 RV slips. All the Parkway's campgrounds charge a daily rate for "first-come" campers. And you can reserve a campsite in advance for a slightly higher rate at all campgrounds except Crabtree Falls (www.recreation.gov or call toll-free: 877-444-6777).

At press time, Mount Pisgah is the only campground with showers (loop B and C), but the Blue Ridge Parkway Foundation is fund-raising to add showers and other upgrades at Price Park Campground. Major campgrounds can have camp stores with firewood and basic supplies for sale (charcoal, starter fluid, snacks, flashlights, batteries, ice, canned goods, etc.), but don't expect a wide selection.

Backpack camping is permitted (and requires a permit) at only three sites on the Parkway (Rocky Knob, Virginia, and Doughton Park and Price Park in North Carolina). In the near future, those options may increase with the opening of campsites along the Parkway on the Mountains-to-Sea Trail in North Carolina. Luckily many trails in this book connect to national forest and other lands where camping is widely permitted.

There are also commercial campgrounds just off the Parkway, as well as nearby campgrounds run by the USDA Forest Service. These are concentrated in the national forests at the northern and southern ends of the Parkway and include Sherando Lake and Cave Mountain Lake in Virginia and Black Mountain and Davidson River in North Carolina. And North Carolina's Mount Mitchell State Park offers the East's highest tent camping.

Like many national parks, the Parkway has overnight lodging options besides camping but in recent years a number have been shuttered for lack of concessioners willing to invest in and operate the facilities. The Parkway is attempting to address the situation but it may take time, so check the Parkway's website for the latest. Peaks of Otter Lodge north of Roanoke in Virginia (the only year-round lodge) and Pisgah Inn south of Asheville in North Carolina are successful concession sites and good bets for longevity. Among other overnight facilities that have been closed in recent years are Rocky Knob cabins (built during the Depression by the Civilian Conservation Corps) in Virginia and Bluffs Lodge in North Carolina. Again, the Blue Ridge Parkway Foundation is orchestrating costly repairs to prepare Bluffs Lodge, its coffee shop, and camp store for again serving visitors.

Peaks of Otter Lodge and Pisgah Inn have full service restaurants, and there's a restaurant at Mabry Mill and a snack bar at the Northwest Trading Post, but in a situation similar to some lodging sites, other Parkway eateries have been forced to close. Among the snack bar/restaurants closed as this book went to press are eateries at Otter Creek in Virginia and dining spots in North Carolina near Bluffs Lodge in Doughton Park and at Crabtree Falls near Mount Mitchell. Keep in mind that the restaurant at Mount Mitchell State Park continues to be successful.

The facilities above are referenced in the travel introductions to each section of the Parkway and in the Mileage Log.

The Climate

A mix of serious seasons reigns on the ridgetops. Dramatically different microclimates emerge with each bend of the road.

Summer on the Parkway comprises June through September. June forests are fully leafed out—except on the very highest summits, where it remains spring till late in the season. Rhododendron crowns that last stage of spring with a high-altitude bloom of legendary appeal. Target the third week of June for the best bloom at the loftiest elevations.

July is when temperatures peak along the Parkway. That differs from the rest of the South, where August and even September bring the hottest days. By August, temperatures along much of the Parkway are heading down the road to fall.

The hottest summer days at the lowest elevations—principally in Virginia—can be hot, up to the low 90s. On the higher parts of the road, summer temps climb to the low to mid-70s; the hottest days will reach the low 80s. But those days are rare. On the very highest peaks, summer days can be downright chilly. Add misty conditions, and temperatures can stay in the 60s and even 50s. Summer nights often dip to the mid-50s and mid-60s. The coolest summer nights can drop to the upper 40s at higher elevations.

Expect rain through the summer months. The loftiest peaks are home to a kind of temperate rain forest. You will encounter sunny periods principally after cold fronts that yield refreshing mountain temps, but generally summer is a time for daily thunderstorms and, possibly, sustained periods of wet weather. September usually ushers in a change—by late in the month, the highest areas are drying out and showing the foliage of fall.

May and October, the months when Parkway facilities routinely open and close, can bring hoarfrosted trees and cold. Even light snowfall is possible, especially at the

With so many entrances and exits, the locations for these distinctive Parkway access signs are chosen carefully. This one is near Linville, North Carolina (Milepost 305.1).

highest elevations. Normally May sees spring in full bloom, with warm days and chilly nights (consult appendix A for a bloom calendar of plants along the Parkway). October brings peak foliage color—from the 10th to the 15th of the month at the heights and during the last two weeks of the month in most other places.

April and November—the months before Parkway facilities open and after they close—can be beautifully clear and cool. Expect April to be the rainiest month, but the volatility of late-winter weather often quickly replaces rain with shine. The year's best long-range views are November's reward—with low humidity, infrequent rain, and no leaves to block the vistas. A November "Indian summer" can be one of the best times on the Parkway. But April and November are, respectively, the latest and earliest months when snow is expected. Both months have received substantial accumulations at the heights and atmospheric dustings lower down.

March and December are fickle. The Parkway's heaviest snowfalls can occur in March, when the first of spring's substantial rains run into the last of winter's cold. Outside of that, March is often clear and cold—perfect hiking weather. December is drier, but snow becomes more likely as fall gives way to winter. The highest peaks have a 50-50 chance of seeing a white Christmas.

Winter is the Parkway's truly quiet time. The peaks are often snow covered for weeks at a time from January through mid-March—to the delight of cross-country skiers. Even when snowless, trails and waterfalls are often covered in ice. Temperatures can dip well below 15°F at night and stay below freezing during the day. High winds, arctic temperatures, and deep snow can make the Parkway impassable. Expect gates to block Parkway access points during those times (in late fall and spring as well).

Virginia's Peaks of Otter Lodge (Milepost 85.9) is open and may be one of the region's best winter holiday bets. The Parkway is plowed in the vicinity of Moses Cone Park and Julian Price Park south of Blowing Rock, North Carolina—a nearly 7-mile section with particularly enticing winter trails for Nordic skiing. Snow doesn't stay all winter; coverage fluctuates with the weather.

Note: The weather described above is what you can expect on the Parkway itself. An easy way to check weather conditions on the high road is to visit the Parkway weather website that was launched in 2013 with support from the Blue Ridge Parkway Foundation. The site features weather observations and forecasts for many sites along the road (brpweather.com/). Also log on to www.weather.com for updated forecasts according to Parkway-area zip codes.

Being Prepared

Practical Cautions on a Lofty Road

It's refreshing when a road can be a natural experience—but tackle this trip with particular caution. The Parkway is a driving challenge for many "flatlanders"—an unrelenting combination of curves and grades for every one of its 469 miles. Stick to the 45 mph speed limit, and note that it is 35 mph in a handful of places.

Wildlife should be your first concern. Be especially alert at dusk, dawn, and after dark. Driving during daylight hours is best—for views and the safety of the many animals that live along the road.

Sheltered and exposed parts of the Parkway pose their own respective hazards. In warmer months dry pavement can suddenly become wet in a shady curve. That can mean a sudden change to snow or glare ice in colder months, hence the "Beware of Sudden Icing" signs. Parkway fatalities often occur under just these conditions and signs denote these high collision areas. The growth of motorcycling on the Parkway has led to many signs that specifically warn bikers about tricky curves. Take these signs seriously. Fog also necessitates slower speeds. You'll never see it denser than on the Parkway. Such weather hazards explain why signs urge motorists to avoid the Parkway in fog, snow, and ice. In the worst winter weather, motorists have been stranded and even died on the Blue Ridge Parkway.

Taking the above concerns seriously doesn't mean that you should delay the motorist who shows up on your rear bumper. Bear in mind that locals drive these roads every day and know every curve. The Parkway is often the best way for locals to get to work, so just pull over at the next overlook. The almost endless supply of these effortless on-and-off options gives visitors no excuse for blocking traffic. Please be especially conscious of this if you're driving an RV. Also of interest to RV owners, the Mileage Log includes the minimum height of the Parkway's more than twenty tunnels.

Selecting a Trail

The uniqueness of the Parkway creates an unusual mission for this guide. A Parkway road trip between Shenandoah and Great Smoky Mountains National Parks can be a seamless experience of the Southern Appalachians, and this guide is designed to provide that opportunity.

How many times have you crossed a park boundary only to have your trail guide say, "See the guide to _____ National Forest for that hike"? The Parkway is bordered by state parks, national forests, and private wildlands throughout its length. There are countless trail options, and if you miss the best of those options, you haven't made the most of the Parkway. This guide covers the Parkway as well as the best off-Parkway hikes along the route—often lesser known and less crowded. (However, it's not possible to include all trails.)

When deciding on a Parkway hike, first match the trail to your level of ability. Luckily, the Parkway's famous leg-stretcher trail philosophy means that many of its trails—dozens, in fact—are easy ambles to a great view or secluded spot. You can just pull off the road and go. Signs tell you which trails are very short; so does the Mileage Log in this guide.

Hikes in this guide are listed—and described—as easy, moderate, or strenuous.

Easy: Generally, regardless of length, an easy trail has a graded or benched treadway, meaning that the tread has been excavated, like a mini road grade, for predictable footing. An easy hike is relatively level, with a grade that's gradual and consistent.

Moderate: A moderate trail, besides often being a longer hike, may involve a rougher, rockier treadway and fluctuations in the rate of rise, though the climb is usually gradual.

Strenuous: Strenuous trails are longer and steeper overall or in places, require substantial exertion, and often have uneven footing or involve the use of ladders or climbing over rocks.

When a trail is said to "slab around a peak," it means that it avoids a summit, generally keeping to a gradual grade at one elevation. For instance, the Nuwati Trail on Grandfather Mountain (rated easy) is considered untaxing because of gradual grades. Nevertheless, the text mentions that the trail has rocky footing, a fact that hikers will need to consider.

Trail entries often use the term "loop" to describe a hike—a route that resembles a circle—but there are at least two different types of loops. A lollipop loop is a single trail that leaves a trailhead, splits some distance away, then returns to the split (forming that circle) and then to the trailhead—a frequent occurrence on the easiest Parkway paths. Others are actually a "circuit" hike—a route that originates on one trail but turns onto different trails on the way back to roughly the same starting point. Many longer hikes on the Parkway and adjacent to it are circuit hikes.

This book suggests lollipop loops and circuits wherever possible. On a high-elevation, linear park like the Blue Ridge Parkway, many possible hikes are out-and-back treks that descend off the ridge and require a slog back up. The most egregious of these are not included here to concentrate on the kinds of hikes people enjoy the most. Also, between the Mountains-to-Sea Trail along the Parkway in North Carolina, and the Appalachian Trail on the northern Parkway in Virginia, it's often possible to just stroll away from your car on an out-and-back "hike to nowhere." The Mileage Log is a good reference for these trail crossings. Even if one of these strolls isn't really a great hike, they make it easy to just set off into the woods.

Trail entries also specify the elevation gain in a given hike—that, after all, is where most people truly feel the effort. In many places trailheads are the trail's low point, often where a trail reaches a road. On the Parkway, the trail often descends first then climbs back to the trailhead.

Mileages are given for most hikes, often with "about" appended to them. This is done where seemingly reliable data conflicts with the author's own experience or other information, such as park brochures or official publications. All mileage information should be considered a best estimate. Certain kinds of terrain make it difficult to measure with certainty a trail's exact length. In addition, the varying levels of experience that hikers bring to a trail can make mileage information less meaningful. Trail descriptions and ratings are often more valuable than simple mileage figures.

I often suggest ways for inexperienced or less physically fit hikers to sample longer, more strenuous trails. Most entries, for instance, suggest places to turn around or alternative routes that avoid the most difficult terrain. Still, a person in very poor condition could find an easy-rated trail to be a challenging hike, so the trail descriptions

The colorful, fanciful TRACK Trail signs dispense engaging, educational brochures designed to help adults introduce kids to the outdoors. The Parkway may be the premier venue for the TRACK Trail vacation.

in this book are subjective. If you are overweight, do no regular exercise, or are unsure of foot, expect an easy hike to be moderate and a moderate hike to be strenuous. The nice thing is that with consistent exercise, your personal rating system can match—or exceed—the ratings in this book.

There are a lot of new trails in this book, and the growing network of easy, interpretive TRACK Trails are ones to be on the lookout for. Based on an idea from the Blue Ridge Parkway Foundation, many easy paths have been outfitted with brochure racks containing a broad assortment of general and site-specific educational materials intended to help families stay fit while learning about the outdoors. Many TRACK Trails are available along the Parkway (including one at Price Lake for paddlers where boats are for rent!), so check the index and be sure to take a hike. Visit kidsinparks .com/ to download brochures in advance and then track your hikes online to win prizes.

Don't Forget the Net

Nature-loving hikers also tend to be people who are comfortable with the Internet. If you're online, definitely check out the exploding trove of hiking information to be found on the World Wide Web. The richness starts with individual home pages for national, state, and private parks; you'll find information, maps, directions, and even the latest campground rates.

Turn to appendix B for a listing of Internet sites of interest to Parkway travelers.

What to Carry

The shortest, easiest nature trails in this book require that the hiker carry nothing other than a camera or binoculars. But hikers who venture more than a mile into fields or forests will want to carry a few essential items. A small backpack or fanny pack is big enough for the essentials:

- a water bottle or hydration system
- a snack or extra food
- spare clothing and other protective items (raincoat, sunscreen, insect repellent, sunglasses, and a hat)
- a small first-aid kit (bandages, antiseptic, extra-strength aspirin/acetaminophen, moleskin for blisters)
- this guide—or the relevant photocopied pages/map
- the recommended hiking maps
- any trail permits required by managing agencies

The ultimate item you'll want to carry isn't in your pack but in your head: knowledge. The information contained here is timely and extensive, but no single trail guide can do it all. Explore the variety of resources available to those who enjoy the outdoors, including FalconGuides and other books on survival, route finding, mountaineering, and backpacking. To be truly prepared, take courses in first aid and CPR.

Maps

A National Park Service strip map of the Parkway, available at Parkway headquarters and visitor centers, provides the perfect main map for your trip. Laminated commercial versions are also now available. That map plus the highly detailed and accurate trail maps in this book should be all you need. The Parkway also publishes its own stylized and less detailed trail maps of many of the major developed recreation areas.

These are often referred to in the text as the "handout maps" that are available at the local visitor center, campground, etc. If you want to be sure you can find these, download them before your trip from the Parkway website (nps.gov/blri/index.htm). Choose "Plan Your Visit">"Things to Do">"Hiking"> then click pages for trails in Virginia or North Carolina and choose your hike. I've also included links for those maps in the text under the locations where they're available. Nevertheless, other maps, notably USGS topo quads and especially US Forest Service maps of backcountry and wilderness areas beside the Parkway, are recommended for many hikes. (See appendix B for additional resources and links to USFS sites that sell the maps.)

Clothing

Choose clothing that is comfortable and protective.

Any summer outdoor activity on the Parkway might seem to call for shorts and T-shirts, but when choosing hiking clothing, the best policy is to be prepared for the worst weather the season and place can deliver. This means being flexible, dressing in layers, and being prepared for rain and wind. Luckily, the latest trail shirts and pants (the latter with zip-off legs) are virtually weightless, dry fast, have antimicrobial properties that eliminate odor, and are even sun protection formula (SPF)-rated.

The best choices for outer garments are waterproof and breathable jackets and pants made of synthetic fabrics. They're expensive but highly recommended. In spring, fall, and especially winter, your outer layer is the first line of defense. Under that, wear more layers—how many varies by season. Synthetic fabrics that are warm even when wet are the best choices. Look for polypropylene T-shirts, long underwear, pants, and zip-up or pullover pile jackets.

Major insulating garments are definitely necessary in severe winter weather. The choice for insulation is, again, synthetic materials that won't lose their insulating value when wet, although waterproof fabrics are bringing down back into vogue.

Footwear

On the Parkway's easy trails, you'll need only a sturdy pair of walking or running shoes. But on moderate or more difficult hikes—or even easy hikes with rocky footing—you'll want a good pair of hiking boots.

The newest-generation boots are lightweight and relatively inexpensive, boasting waterproof fabrics and various kinds of nonskid soles. They add comfort, safety, and enjoyment to any hike and are a worthwhile purchase for even a casual hiker.

Serious winter hikers will need more than a lightweight three-season boot. And those who walk wilderness or primitive trails may need to cross streams without the aid of bridges. Rather than avoid these trails, carry a pair of aqua shoes, which slip over bare feet, or sport sandals for wading. They also make great in-camp wear.

Weather Dangers

It is not enough to own the proper clothing. Be sure to put on your high-tech garments before you become thoroughly wet or chilled.

Hypothermia results when lack of food and/or exposure to severe weather conditions prevent the body from maintaining its core temperature. Hypothermia can occur at any time of year—at temperatures well above freezing—with the dramatic cooling effects of wind and rain. To prevent it, stay dry and protected with the right clothing—especially a hat, since up to 70 percent of heat loss can emanate from your head. Don extra layers when you stop for a rest, before you get chilled. And remove layers before you get sweaty, starting with that hat. Adequately fuel yourself with food and water, drink plenty of fluids (in winter, simply breathing robs you of moisture), and nibble energy foods (such as trail mix, sandwiches, and hot soups). Set up camp early to accommodate any inexperienced or less physically fit members of your party.

The best way to treat hypothermia is to stop it before it starts, but you may not be able to. Do not ignore such symptoms as uncontrollable shivering and, later, slow and slurred speech, stumbling gait or clumsiness, and disorientation. Take immediate action to shelter and refuel anyone with these symptoms—including yourself.

Frostbite. Frozen flesh can result from severe cold, and its first sign is reddened skin. Next, the frozen site—often toes, fingers, or portions of the face—will turn white or gray. The best prevention is to stay warm so that your extremities receive the blood flow they need. If you can avoid it, do not venture into extreme conditions or exposed areas where windchill factors are below minus 20°F. In severe conditions hikers should monitor one another's faces and suggest shelter when the need arises. Do not rub frozen skin or slap frozen extremities together. When an area with severe frostbite begins to thaw, expect severe pain; use aspirin or acetaminophen to ease the pain on the way to medical assistance.

Lightning. In summer a hiker's major danger is lightning, especially on exposed mountaintops—and the Parkway is full of them. At the first rumblings of thunder, move off ridgetops and seek shelter in a group of smaller trees rather than under one tall one. Rest in a low, dry area (but not a gully or near a pond, where water can conduct the current). Avoid overhangs or small caves where ground current might pass through you. In a lightning storm you're better off sitting in the open below surrounding high points and atop a low-lying rock that is detached and thus insulated from the ground. To further insulate yourself, crouch low or kneel on top of your pack or sleeping pad.

Heat stroke and heat exhaustion are warm-weather equivalents of hypothermia. The Parkway isn't known for hot hikes, but be sure to carry and drink plenty of fluids, especially if you're sweating heavily. Avoid hiking in the hottest part of the day, and cool off by slipping into one of the trailside pools often mentioned in this guide's hike descriptions. (**Note:** Swimming is prohibited in Parkway waters.) If you feel dizzy and drained, heat exhaustion may be the culprit. Relax, drink fluids, and let your body recover. Heat stroke is a more extreme—and dangerous—condition. Rather than being damp and drained, you'll be dry and feverish, signs that the body has given up the attempt to cool down by perspiring. Immediately cool the affected person with cold, wet compresses. Administer water, and seek medical attention.

Trailside Pests

Winter weather largely eradicates the Parkway's most bothersome bugs, reptiles, and plants. But spring, summer, and fall are different matters.

Bees. Do everything you can to avoid contact with concentrations of bees. Be cautious around fruit and flowers, and be on the lookout for nests hanging from limbs, in hollow trees and logs, or on the ground. And don't act like a flower. You can't avoid sweating, which attracts some types of bees, but don't entice them with perfume or scented body care products.

As long as you're not allergic, most stings are minor and easily treated. Simply scrape an imbedded stinger out with a knife blade. (Don't squeeze it out, which releases even more venom into your bloodstream.) A paste made of water and unseasoned meat tenderizer that contains papain (a papaya enzyme) can neutralize bee venom; baking soda paste does not.

Some stings are not so simple. A person who is allergic to bee stings or is stung many times can suffer anaphylactic shock—even death. Around a hundred people a year die from bee stings in the United States. An over-the-counter antihistamine that contains diphenhydramine (such as Benadryl) can help control mild allergic reactions. Serious toxic reactions and anaphylactic shock can either set in immediately or after some delay. If you know you are allergic to bee stings, always carry an epinephrine syringe bee sting kit—and be sure your companions know where it is and how to use it.

Ticks. The Piedmont and coastal forests of Virginia and North Carolina are favorite warm-weather habitats for ticks. Hikers on the Parkway's highest mountains are less likely to find ticks, especially where spruce and fir forests prevail. Ticks can carry Lyme disease and Rocky Mountain spotted fever—potentially deadly diseases. North Carolina is infamous for the latter. Both diseases can take up to two weeks to gestate before symptoms develop. Among the signs are arthritis-like joint pain, high fever, and/or a circular rash.

The best defense against ticks is three-pronged: First, at the lowest Parkway elevations, use a tick and insect repellent that contains N, N-diethyl-3-methylbenzamide, more commonly known as DEET. Second, whether you use repellents or not, wear long-sleeved shirts and long pants and avoid walking through tall grass, brush, or dense woods. Third, frequently check yourself for ticks, especially at night and when you finish a hike. Focus on armpits, ears, scalp, groin, legs, and where clothes, such as socks, constrict the body. It takes awhile for ticks to attach and transmit disease, so you have a good shot at preventing infection if you find them early.

If a tick becomes embedded in your skin, use a bit of repellent, rubbing alcohol, or a hot, extinguished match to encourage the tick to back itself out. If you must use tweezers to remove a tick, grasp the head to avoid squeezing toxins into the wound. And don't hesitate to pull a little bit of your skin out with the tick so that mouthparts do not remain to cause infection.

Flies. In spring (mid-April to mid-June), hikers on the Parkway's higher elevations can be troubled by the same tiny black flies that pester North Country hikers in Minnesota and Maine. More often hikers here see common houseflies and horseflies; the latter are particularly vicious at the coast. The best defenses are to use insect repellent, keep food and garbage covered or stored elsewhere when picnicking and camping, and cover your body. The newest trick is to reduce the use of chemicals and buy and wear the new Buzz-Off treated clothing, the first bug-banning technology to get the EPA's nod.

Mosquitoes and gnats are prevalent, especially on cool mountain evenings. Again, the Buzz-Off garments are effective, or use repellent with DEET.

Poison ivy, poison oak, and poison sumac are all found everywhere on the Parkway except the highest peaks. All produce contact dermatitis—rash and watery blisters that appear twelve to forty-eight hours after skin rubs against the plant resin. The outbreak usually runs its course in ten days, but isolated cases can be severe or cause allergic reactions. Learn to identify these plants ("Leaves of three, let it be"), and be wary of wading through brush in shorts.

If you realize that you just touched one of these poisonous plants, remove and isolate contaminated clothing until it can be washed at home. Flush the affected skin with water but no soap—your skin's natural oils will protect you temporarily. Cover rash areas with calamine lotion. See a physician if face, genitals, or more than 25 percent of your body is affected. Preventive creams you can apply before exposure are also available.

Snakes rank high on the list of hiker fears, but these animals play their role in nature, and only two venomous types are found in the Blue Ridge: timber rattlesnakes and copperheads. Snakes are not a problem on the Parkway's higher peaks.

The best way to avoid being bitten is to be observant—and be able to recognize poisonous snakes *before* they can bite. Rattlesnakes and copperheads are generally heftier than nonvenomous snakes and have triangular or arrow-shaped heads and vertically slit pupils (versus tube-shaped heads and round pupils for nonvenomous snakes). Don't reach blindly behind logs and rocks, inspect wooded sites before you sit, and watch where you step. Luckily, of the 20,000 people bitten by venomous snakes annually in the United States, fewer than 15 die. The venom of these two species is also relatively slow acting, almost half of all bites don't transmit venom, and antivenin is widely available in local hospitals.

If bitten, be able to report what kind of snake bit you. Observe your wound: The bite of a pit viper includes two or more prominent fang marks, while a nonvenomous snakebite usually leaves two rows of indentations and no big holes. If possible, use a commercial snakebite kit within three minutes of the bite. Immediately remove all watches and rings that may cause constriction from swelling. Do not make incisions with a knife or try to suck out the venom. Do not use tourniquets, cold water, or ice packs, which increase the possibility of gangrene. Instead, loosely splint and immobilize the affected limb, and mark on the victim with a pen the time and spread of swelling. If you are within twenty minutes of the trailhead, carry the victim (or permit the person to walk slowly, with frequent rests) to a vehicle for immediate transfer to a hospital. If hiking alone—not necessarily a good idea—walk as calmly as possible back to your car for help. Hikers who are far from a trailhead should send a companion for help and wait for emergency personnel to return with antivenin.

Bears. Most other animals in North Carolina are harmless to hikers. The exception is the rarely seen black bear. Most of the time, a backcountry glimpse of one of these reclusive mammals includes its rear end sprinting away. If you have a sudden encounter with a nearby bear, especially a mother with cubs, steadily and calmly back away. Leave the area. Do not turn your back on the bear. Do not run or climb a tree, since this may provoke a chase—and you cannot outrun a bear. Stand your ground if charged; bears often bluff.

The most problematic locations for bear encounters are popular campsites, where bears forage through garbage. There they can be aggressive, especially if you approach

Whether this bear was washing his hands or staking a claim, the signs and sights of bruins have brought bear-proof trash cans and food storage strategies to the Parkway and adjacent lands.

while they are enjoying food. Stay away. The best defense against such encounters with bears—and with skunks and other animals, even mice—is to keep your food away from camp. Safely hang bagged food by tossing a rope over a tree limb, tying on your food container, running the food into midair away from the trunk, and tying the other end where you can reach it. Bear-proof food canisters are another great way to deter bruins. Generally bears are much more of a problem in Shenandoah and Great Smoky Mountains National Parks than along the Blue Ridge Parkway. But problems with bears seem to be on the rise at Parkway campgrounds and picnic areas, many of which now provide bear-proof trash receptacles. National forests line the Parkway for miles, and bears can be an issue in places like North Carolina's Shining Rock Wilderness where 2016 policies prohibit camping at Graveyard Fields and require the use of bear canisters.

Waterborne pests. The other animal threat is a microscopic one. Ingestion of waterborne pests can cause a variety of backcountry infections. Perhaps the best known is *giardia lamblia*, but an E. coli infection can be deadly. Hikers have even contracted Type A hepatitis from drinking untreated water in the "wilderness." Unfortunately, even pristine-looking streams may contain these and other disease-producing agents. All hikers should carry water from treated sources, carry commercially bottled drinks, or filter the water they use. Boiling water for at least five minutes (before adding food or flavoring) will kill the tiny protozoan that causes giardia, so campers can often prepare hot foods with water from streams and springs. Boiling can cause drinking water to taste flat, so pour boiled water back and forth between clean containers to restore its oxygen content, or add flavorings. Better still, carry a portable backpacker's water purifier. Do not attempt to disinfect water with halazone, chlorine, or iodine.

Zero Impact

Everyone's heard the dictum "Take only pictures, leave only footprints." Well, even footprints cause soil compaction and erosion in many of the popular wilderness areas that line the Parkway. However, damage to the environment can be minimized.

Zero-impact hiking and camping starts with an effort to minimize any evidence of your presence. That starts with staying on defined trails and restricting your outings to a small party of people. Intelligent strategies for protecting trails, such as not shortcutting switchbacks, also reduce the likelihood that you'll brush directly through poison ivy or step on that snoozing copperhead. Groups of four to six hikers can more easily find campsites and deal with emergencies and don't disturb other hikers' wilderness experience. Whatever your party's size, try to keep your noise level down, especially when camping in the vicinity of others. Noise travels far after dark; there's no excuse for loud conversation or rowdy behavior after 9 p.m. At developed Parkway campgrounds, be sure to notice the signs that specify quiet times and restrict the use of RV generators.

Littering is the number one trail pollution problem. The dictum "Pack it in, pack it out" has become the basic backcountry credo. Too many people lug food and drink into the woods in heavy containers, then leave the bottles and cans behind when they're empty. Pack properly, using lightweight plastic, and you won't be tempted to jettison the refuse. Bag trash immediately to avoid attracting bugs and animals, and consider picking up litter left by others.

Everyone generates waste in the woods, so proper disposal is another element of zero impact. Where restrooms are available, use them before hitting the trail. When hiking or camping, use proper methods of disposal to keep urine, feces, soap, and garbage out of water sources. To make a "cat hole" for body waste, use a small trowel to remove a cap of sod (keep it intact) and dig a hole at least 6 inches deep in organic soil (damp but not wet) at least 200 feet from surface water, trails, campsites, or other places where people congregate. This is your "toilet." Use natural wipes such as leaves, or pack out toilet paper in a plastic bag. After using your pit, mix soil into the waste to hasten decomposition, then cover with the sod cap. When urinating, avoid hitting plants; try to go on mineral soil or sand. Choose a sunny spot to hasten evaporation.

Camping impacts the environment in ways that hiking does not. Hikers who intend to camp should read up on clean camping: How to choose a campsite, the safety and environmental benefits of carrying a camp stove (where allowed), and many other topics are addressed in several fine publications. A touchy topic for campers is how to keep your body and equipment clean without polluting streams and lakes. Some camping purists choose not to bathe in the backcountry; others wouldn't camp if they couldn't get clean. The best way to wash and not pollute nearby drinking water is to carry a large pot or bucket of water at least 200 feet from the water source. Lather minimally with biodegradable soap, and rinse; dilute and disperse any suds on the ground with more water. To brush your teeth, go the same distance away and use the smallest amount of paste and water possible. Disperse by spitting, and rinse away residue with water. Visit the Leave No Trace website for more (LNT.org).

Hiking with Pets

Woodsy forays with Fido are fun. There's nothing like sharing the exercise and camaraderie of the great outdoors with your favorite friend. But be aware that dogs can be a headache for other hikers and for park managers, so restrictions apply. Pets are allowed on Blue Ridge Parkway trails and in campgrounds, but they must be leashed at all times.

Sadly, not everyone out there loves dogs (or, at the very least, your dog). It can be frightening to see an unleashed animal charging down a trail at you, especially if you're a parent with children or another pet owner with your own dog on a leash. Many national parks actually prohibit dogs because their territorial instincts can complicate life for wildlife populations already trying to survive in shrinking natural areas. While out of sight of their owners, unleashed dogs can trample fragile plants, dig up animal dens, even kill wildlife, and leave their scent (not to mention piles of poop, sometimes on the trail).

There are real virtues to using a leash. Many dogs get permanently lost in wild areas, severely injured in encounters with wildlife, or hurt in falls.

Hiking with Kids

Hiking is a wonderful way to instill a love of the outdoors, an enjoyment of physical fitness and exercise, and less tangible values of environmental and personal responsibility in young people.

You don't have to wait until a child is ten years old to take him or her out into the woods. Many of the hikes in this guide are great for kids—the leg-stretcher trail philosophy makes the Blue Ridge Parkway particularly well suited to children. On the Parkway, even a short walk can lead to high adventure.

Now's the time to take your child or grandchild on a hike, and the Parkway is the perfect, approachable place to do it. This young fella is enjoying winter on the Price Lake Trail (Milepost 297.2).

Trail descriptions highlight paths suitable for toddlers (on their first unaided woods walks), family hikes, beginner backpacking trips, and saunters with the elderly and physically challenged. Sample some of these, but don't expect to make the entire hike or reach that intended campsite. Be flexible with tiny hikers—let them set the pace.

Many parents purchase sophisticated child-carrier packs that include a pouch for kid items. These increase your mobility, but remember to duck below tree limbs and other obstacles. Also, children often fall asleep in these packs, and few have a way to stabilize a sleeping tyke's head. Be prepared to use a scarf, pillow, or other items to cushion a napping child's head, and be sure to work out the system in advance.

Cool-weather hiking with children poses more challenges. Since children in carriers aren't active, it is easy for them to become cold, especially in winter. Don't overdo winter hikes. Carry hot drinks or soup in a thermos. Be aware that just bundling a child in urban-style outerwear may not keep her or him warm. There is no substitute for effectively layered, high-quality clothing. Foam-lined, heavily insulated boots with polypropylene or wool socks and substantial mittens should also be basic requirements. A word to the wise: Children who have a bad experience will not be enthusiastic about hiking in the future.

Focus on comfort and safety at any time of year. In warm weather, such items as sunscreen, hats, insect repellent, topical anesthetic for bug bites or sunburn, and snacks and drinks are the ingredients for a successful family hike.

Trail Etiquette

You can enhance your safety and limit human conflict in the outdoors just as you can limit impact on the environment. Conflict between recreationists occurs in many ways.

Camping can be a touchy topic—hence the rule that Parkway campers observe quiet time between 10 p.m. and 6 a.m. Serious campers cope with darkness by going to sleep; when nearby tenters build a giant bonfire and party until midnight, the result can be unpleasant.

Avoid such conflict in the backcountry by choosing your sites according to your preferences. Choose an isolated campsite if you are a wilderness purist. A car-accessible campground may be more appropriate if you're taking the neighborhood kids on their first camping trip. With a little forethought and consideration, you can minimize conflicts between you and other Parkway recreationists.

Trails have their own particular form of etiquette. Unless it's unsafe to do so, step aside when other hikers approach, even if you have the right-of-way. Be diplomatic at all times. If the chemistry in a given situation is negative, be the first to back down and move on.

Criminal violence is rare on trails, but instances of robbery and rape make news. Be friendly but reasonably wary. Do not hike alone; if you do, don't flaunt expensive equipment or jewelry, and don't hesitate to say you're with a group of friends not far down the trail. Backcountry users have much in common, and the camaraderie of the woods can cause some people to treat everyone they meet as though they were old friends. But it is far better to keep an urban sense of security about you—which means not leaving your pack and other gear unattended and not volunteering information about yourself or your belongings.

Don't leave valuables in your vehicle. The number one crime associated with hiking is the trailhead auto break-in. When your trek begins at an isolated trailhead, consider parking at a nearby business and arranging to be shuttled. At the very least, lock valuables out of sight in the trunk.

Always let a responsible party know where you are going and when you'll return. Religiously comply with hiker registration and user permit systems, which exist at many places on the Parkway and at parks and preserves along the way. These function as a safety net and, where fees are collected, support the maintenance and management of the trails you've come to enjoy.

Enjoyment is, after all, what trails are all about. There's the exercise, the good times you share with those who accompany you and those you meet, and the scenic views, both vast and intimate. Sadly, today's nature lovers often find themselves spending a lot of time in cars. Fortunately, the American fascination with being "on the road" finds its ultimate expression on the Blue Ridge Parkway, where trail after trail makes it easy to turn a road trip into an unforgettable encounter with the outdoors.

These unbiquitous Parkway residents enjoy a true hibernation in winter. For the sake of groundhogs and so many other wildlife species, please take the 45 mph speed limit to heart.
HUGH MORTON

MAP LEGEND

81	Interstate
221	US Highway
43	State Highway
———	Blue Ridge Parkway
———	Local/County/Forest Road
— — —	Unpaved Road
— · — ·	State Boundary
▬▬▬▬	Featured Route on Trail
▬▬▬▬	Featured Route on Road
- - - -	Trail
‖‖‖‖‖	Boardwalk
▭	National Park/Forest
☺	Amphitheater
⌣	Bridge
△	Campground
▲	Campsite
⌓	Cave
✝	Cemetery
⛪	Church
—	Dam
⚲	Gate
⊠	Mine
▲	Mountain/Peak
Ⓟ	Parking
⌣	Pass/Gap
⛩	Picnic Area
□	Point of Interest
⛑	Ranger Station/Park Office
⛭	Restroom
⬈	Scenic View/Overlook
⌂	Shelter
⊙	Spring
⊥	Tower
①	Trailhead
⊢⊣	Tunnel
?	Visitor/Information Center
≋	Waterfall

The North-Central Blue Ridge

Mileposts 0.0 (I–64 at Shenandoah National Park, VA) to 121.4 (US 220 at Roanoke, VA)

The northernmost 120 miles of the Parkway is the perfect introduction to the Blue Ridge. Motorists starting on this section approach the mountains as people have for

Blooming azaleas are a frequent springtime sight on the sharp spine of the northern Blue Ridge. The Great Valley makes a stunning backdrop for this scene near Raven Rocks Overlook.

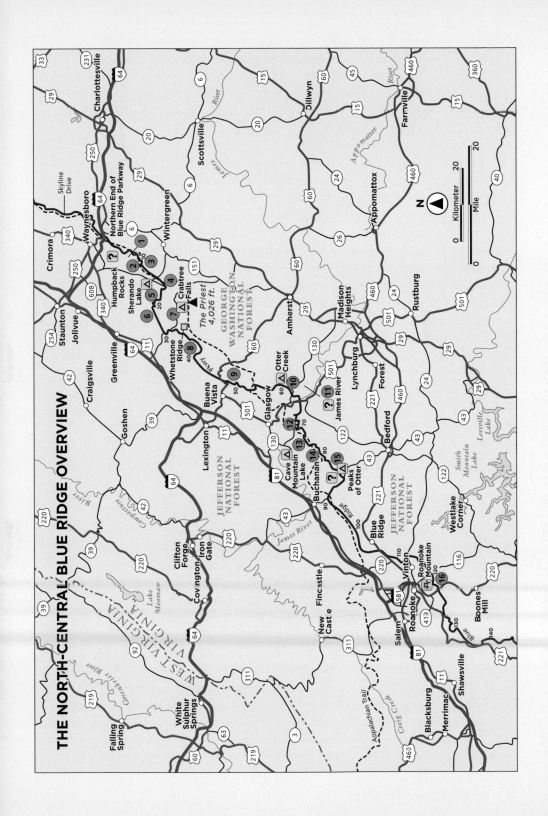

centuries. This is the Blue Ridge at its most definitive—the Appalachians, rearing sharply above the Piedmont to the east and the Shenandoah Valley to the west.

Indeed, the ridge seems sharper here than it does in Shenandoah National Park, just north of the Parkway. (*Travel tip:* The 100 miles of Shenandoah's Skyline Drive is a nice prelude that turns the Parkway's 469 miles into a nearly 600-mile mountain experience.)

From Rockfish Gap (Milepost 0) to US 220 in Roanoke, Virginia (Milepost 121.4), the dramatic spinelike ridge offers what some other sections of the high road don't—views from towering forested peaks into valleys checkerboarded with farms. These summits are largely unsettled; national forests wrap the Parkway corridor in multi-hundred-thousand-acre woodlands. In the evening these dark shapes bulk mysteriously against the twinkling of valley towns far below.

The ridge is high and airy until Otter Creek (Mileposts 55–64), when the Parkway dips through intimate forests to its lowest point—the James River, at 650 feet. Then up it climbs again, past the James River Face Wilderness and the high road's northern high point—3,950 feet, near Apple Orchard Mountain. Next are the Peaks of Otter's famous summits. From there it's a long scenic slide into the Roanoke Valley.

The Parkway's homage to the culture and history of the Southern highlands includes wayside exhibits and visitor centers. That starts immediately at Humpback Rocks Visitor Center and on the Mountain Farm Trail (typical late-1800s mountaineer farm). Don't miss this cultural side of the Parkway—trails are integral to its interpretation. Major interpretive sites include the James River Water Gap canal exhibit and Peaks of Otter's early-twentieth-century mountain farm and mid-1800s inn, Polly Wood's Ordinary.

Parkway service sites include a restaurant at Peaks of Otter Lodge (but sadly, no longer at Otter Creek). The lodge is also a highly regarded, spectacularly scenic spot to spend the night (even in winter, if you like to hike in the snow or cross-country ski). Campgrounds are available at Otter Creek and Peaks of Otter.

The USDA Forest Service Sherando Lake Recreation Area is a premier base for campers near the start of the road. Just across the Parkway from there, Wintergreen Mountain Resort represents the upscale end of the recreation and lodging experience. It's one of the South's premier ski areas and usually rated among the country's top tennis and golf resorts (with its own extensive trail system).

Anchoring the north and south of this section of the Parkway are cities worth a pause. The shaded sophistication of Charlottesville is on the north end, with the University of Virginia and an up-and-coming wine-producing region named for Thomas Jefferson's nearby home, Monticello. Also don't miss colonial fare at historic Michie Tavern, James and Dolly Madison's Montpelier, and the upscale Boar's Head Inn. Near Lynchburg, Jefferson's octagonal summer home, Poplar Forest, is also open. At this section's south end, the historic rail town of Roanoke has enticing urban amenities, including a historic downtown farmers' market, the Virginia Transportation Museum, and the O. Winston Link Museum of classic railroad photography.

Take the time to sample other cities and towns along this part of the Parkway—great attractions are within easy reach. There's the Frontier Culture Museum in Staunton. Civil War history saturates the Shenandoah Valley, and Virginia Military Institute is just one of Lexington's attractions. Other sites honor George C. Marshall, "Stonewall" Jackson, and Robert E. Lee. There's historic downtown lodging at The Georges, a classic B&B that pairs two stunning historic downtown hostels.

Natural Bridge, which Jefferson once owned and George Washington once surveyed, is near the town of the same name. The offbeat free attraction Foamhenge—yes, a life-size replica made of foam—is just to the west on US 11. Bedford, just east of Peaks of Otter, is the site of the National D-Day Memorial. The town lost more soldiers per capita during the invasion of France than any other place in the country.

The first section of the Parkway will leave you wanting more of these mountains. Luckily, there's 350 miles to go.

Check appendix B for a wealth of relevant websites and contact information.

From the crags of Humpback Rocks, this father and son peer down on the Parkway.

1 Humpback Rocks Recreation Area

Mileposts 5.8–6.0

Just 5 miles south of the Blue Ridge Parkway's first milepost, the Humpback Rocks Recreation Area provides a perfect introduction to the cultural and natural riches of this linear park. An interpretive trail through a hardscrabble farm explores the rustic life led by mountaineers up to the turn of the twentieth century. Don't miss the "1850–1950 Life along the Blue Ridge" exhibit at the small visitor center (where water and restrooms are available). The fascinating display emphasizes how the nearby Howardsville Turnpike and more distant canal on the James River (see that entry) created surprisingly diverse occupations and access to urban consumer goods for mountain residents in this area. Just across the road, a short, steep trail lifts hikers to Humpback Rocks and truly awe-inspiring vistas that stretch north and south along the Blue Ridge, east to the Piedmont, and west into the Shenandoah Valley. There's also a small picnic area.

Option 1: Mountain Farm Trail

An eye-opening glimpse into the rustic lives led by nineteenth-century Appalachian mountaineers who lived near what is now the Parkway.

Parkway mile: 5.8
Distance: 0.5 mile out and back
Difficulty: Easy (wheelchair accessible)

Elevation gain: Negligible
Maps: *USGS Sherando*; Parkway handout map, available at the visitor center

Finding the trailhead: Park at the Humpback Rocks Visitor Center and take the paved sidewalk south (left when facing the building). GPS: 37.972483 / -78.899333

The Hike

What a difference a century or so makes. The cabins and outbuildings of the re-created William J. Carter farm—plus interpretive plaques, seasonal programs, and costumed interpreters—give startling insight into the lives of Appalachian families. This pioneering lifestyle still existed in some places when the Blue Ridge Parkway was built in the mid-1930s. The 1890s farm found on the Mountain Farm Trail isn't the original; it was re-created in 1950 using period structures. Nevertheless, it is an authentic setting explored by a very easy trail.

Buy the trail's inexpensive booklet at the visitor center and take the paved sidewalk that becomes a gravel lane. On the left, you first reach a cabin and chicken house and then a "gear loft," where the family stored their "plunder" (supplies and equipment). Past those structures and across the lane, a contorted barn is surrounded by a stone-walled pigpen. Farther on, a springhouse channels cold water through a sheltered food storage structure. Beyond that is "kissin' gate"; pass through and you're in "Coiner's deadenin'," grass-covered meadows under the towering crag of Humpback Rocks. Here mountaineers cleared fields the slow way—by girdling trees to kill them and planting crops between the leafless giants (which were later felled).

You can walk beyond the gate, gradually rising to Humpback Gap and trailhead parking for the Humpback Rocks Trail. Retrace your steps, or park at the gap and take both trails from one central spot.

The Mountain Farm Trail presents a stunning selection of historic structures.

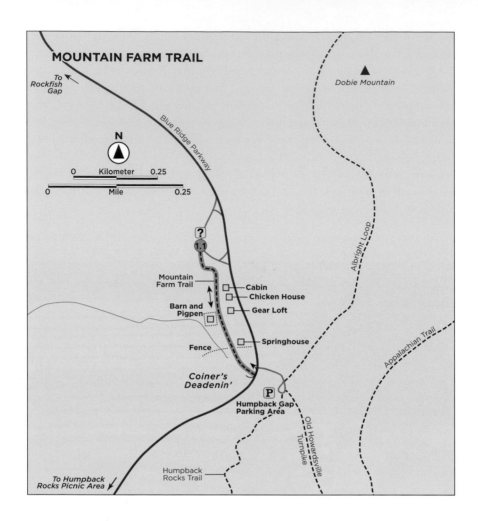

Option 2: Humpback Rocks Area Trails

A short, steep hike and a longer circuit from Humpback Gap reach superb panoramic views at Humpback Rocks. Other circuit hikes in the area include the new Albright Loop and an overnighter to an Appalachian Trail shelter. From Humpback Rocks Picnic Area, you can take the Catoctin Trail leg-stretcher and an Appalachian Trail (AT) hike to Humpback Mountain.

Parkway mile: 6.0 (Humpback Gap) and 8.5 (picnic area)
Distance: From Humpback Gap Parking Area, 2.0-mile out-and-back hike to Humpback Rocks and 3.6-mile circuit using the Appalachian Trail. Other circuits: 3.4-mile Albright Loop and 5.5-mile overnight backpack to an Appalachian Trail shelter (10.0 miles from the Parkway near Milepost 0). From Humpback Rocks Picnic Area, the Catoctin Trail is 0.5 mile

round-trip; using the AT, Humpback Mountain is 4.0 miles round-trip and Humpback Rocks is 6.0 miles round-trip.
Difficulty: Strenuous; easy for Catoctin Trail
Elevation gain: Approximately 720 feet to the rocks

Maps: *USGS Sherando*; Parkway handout map of Humpback Rocks area trails available at the visitor center or online at nps.gov/blri/planyour visit/humpback-rocks-trails.htm

Finding the trailhead: The Humpback Gap Parking Area has three entry points for these hikes (GPS: 37.968476 / -78.896530). On the south end of the lot, by the big orientation sign, the blue-blazed trail leads directly to Humpback Rocks. From the north end of the parking area, the blue-blazed trail leads to the Albright Loop hike, the AT, and on to the Paul C. Wolfe Shelter. From the middle of the parking area, the Old Howardsville Turnpike connector also reaches the AT. The Catoctin Trail and AT hike to Humpback Mountain leave the middle of the back loop of the Humpback Rocks Picnic Area, at Milepost 8.5 (GPS: 37.945449 / -78.926161).

The Hikes

Humpback Rocks

The classic Blue Ridge Parkway hike to Humpback Rocks is no easy leg-stretcher. Nevertheless, the effort is rewarded with some of the best views in the northern Blue Ridge. The basic hike is a strenuous, 1.0-mile climb to Humpback Rocks, a massive greenstone outcrop at 3,080 feet. The rocks jut west but offer expansive views of the patchwork of farms on both sides of the Blue Ridge—the Shenandoah Valley to the west and Virginia's Piedmont to the east. Please follow these descriptions carefully— rangers say people often get confused in a few spots. I've personally met hikers here who have failed to find the rocks after even a few tries.

The blue-blazed trail to the rocks was once a punishing part of the white-blazed Appalachian Trail. Since then the AT has been substantially rerouted to bypass the rocks. The now nicely graded, gravel trail still ascends steeply, but there are benches along the way.

At 0.5 mile the steep, gravelly trail with wide steps crests and flattens out and continues straight beneath the towering crags of Humpback Rocks. At that leveling off spot, too many people turn left where the old trail used to go. That extremely steep ascent was closed in the early 1980s, but it still confuses some people; even hard core hikers should avoid this old route. Bear right, actually straight, on the "new" trail with great uphill views. The trail soon ascends a set of wooden steps then switchbacks a half dozen times over increasingly rocky turns to a gap and a signed junction at 0.9 mile. Take a left and in 0.1 mile reach the cloven crags of Humpback Rocks. The best photos may be from the left crag of people on the right crag.

Caution: When you leave the rocks and enter the woods, don't bear left or you'll get sucked down the old trail. Enter the woods from the rocks and bear kind of right to reach the signed junction—and be sure to turn right there to go back down the trail you came up for a round-trip of 2.0 miles. Parkway rangers report that some

There is no better perch for sunset than the summit of Humpback Rocks. Bring your shades.

hikers miss this turn back down the mountain and unknowingly continue on toward the AT and beyond. Searches and unplanned overnight hikes have resulted.

Humpback Circuit

To make a counterclockwise circuit out of the hike to Humpback Rocks, don't turn right back down the mountain, but go straight at the signed junction to reach the AT in 0.2 mile. Turn left onto the AT at about 1.2 miles. Descend on the AT; there's a spring beside the trail on the left 0.8 mile below the junction, about 2.0 miles into your hike. Continue descending on the AT. At 3.4 miles the trail jogs left on an old road grade that is actually part of the Old Howardsville Turnpike.

This atmospheric avenue is fern fringed and quiet now. Built between 1846 and the mid-1850s, the road long linked the farms of the Shenandoah Valley on the west with the Rockfish Valley and the James River canal system on the east. (Check out where the canal breached the Blue Ridge on Parkway trails near Milepost 63.) The old road actually crosses the Parkway between Mileposts 4.0 and 5.0. Coming from that direction, wagon masters used to track their progress by sighting Humpback Rocks. If you hop off to the right of the trail on this section, you can see how artful rock work underlies the grade. When the AT bears right off the trace, go left at the sign, staying on the blue-blazed old turnpike (which has become a designated trail

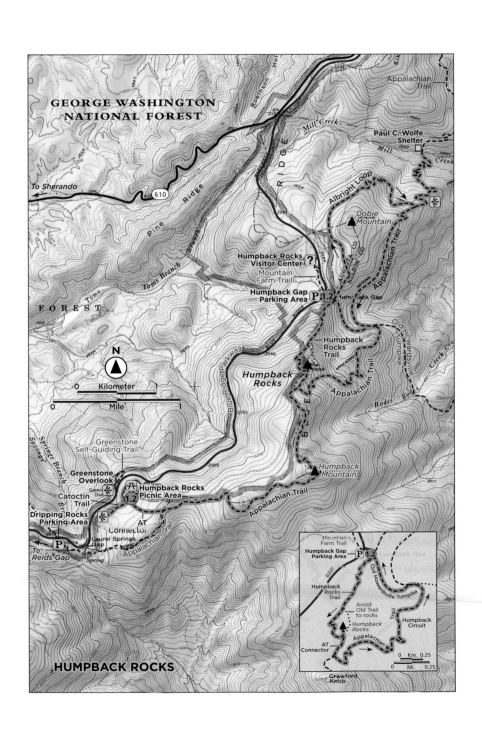

GEORGE WASHINGTON
NATIONAL FOREST

Appalachian Trail

Paul C. Wolfe Shelter

To Sherando

Pine Ridge

Albright Loop

Dobie Mountain

Humpback Rocks Visitor Center

Mountain Farm Trail

Humpback Gap Parking Area

Humpback Rocks Trail

Humpback Rocks

Appalachian Trail

Old Howardsville Turnpike

FOREST

Toms Branch

N

Kilometer
0   1

0   Mile   1

Blue Ridge Parkway

Humpback Mountain

Greenstone Self-Guiding Trail

Greenstone Overlook

Humpback Rocks Picnic Area

Catoctin Trail

Dripping Rocks Parking Area

Laurel Springs Gap

To Reids Gap

AT Connector

Appalachian Trail

HUMPBACK ROCKS

Mountain Farm Trail

Humpback Gap Parking Area

BRP

Humpback Rocks Trail

Avoid Old Trail to rocks

Humpback Rocks

Old Howardsville Turnpike

Appalachian Trail

Humpback Circuit

AT Connector

Appalachian

0   Km.   0.25
0   Mi.   0.25

Crawford Knob

since the first edition of this guide). You'll reach Humpback Gap Parking Area in 0.2 mile, for a 3.6-mile hike.

If the 3.6-mile circuit to the rocks appeals to you, my suggestion is to reverse the above direction. That way, the climb to the rocks is far more gradual and you see far fewer people. But use caution. Leave the gap on the old trace and continue when it joins the AT, but keep a sharp eye out for when the AT turns right to climb toward the rocks. This is another place where novices are drawn left and can end up lost down in the drainage. Hike the circuit in this direction, and the spring is on the right. Then it's all right-hand turns at junctions back to your car. Turn right off the AT at 2.7 miles; go right at the next junction to the rocks. Leaving the rocks, again go right at that intersection to reach the parking lot at 3.6 miles.

Albright Loop Circuits

At busy times, you'll encounter fewer people by heading north out of Humpback Gap on the 3.4-mile, moderate Albright Loop trail, named for an Old Dominion Appalachian Trail Club AT maintainer and field guide editor. The trail was created by adding a new trail west of Dobie Mountain. Keep in mind, in 2015, the trail across Dobie Mountain that created the Dobie Mountain Loop was closed due to erosion.

The blue-blazed trail leaves the north end of the parking area and goes left at 0.3 mile where the old Dobie Mountain Trail went right. Slab the summit and follow old road grades on switchbacks down to a junction with the AT at 2.0 miles. Go right on the AT (immediately passing where the now closed Dobie Mountain Trail used to go right). Check out Glass Hollow Overlook on the left, and at 3.2 miles, leave the AT and go right on the Old Howardsville Turnpike to the parking area for a hike of 3.4 miles.

The Albright Loop also can be used to create a nice 5.5-mile overnight circuit to the Paul C. Wolfe Shelter, where there's a privy, porch cooking area, and a waterfall and swimming spot not too far downstream on Mill Creek. Camping isn't permitted on the Parkway except at designated sites, and this is one of those places (tent sites exist too). Take the Albright Loop left and then left again on the AT at 2.0 miles. There's a nice view east at 2.2 miles. Cross Mill Creek at 3.1 miles; the shelter is just beyond, at 3.2 miles. Return on the AT with a right on Old Howardsville Turnpike at 4.7 miles to reach the parking area at about 5 miles.

Another nice overnighter to the shelter uses the more northerly section of the AT. Just south from the developed area where I-64 passes under the Parkway near Shenandoah National Park, the AT goes left off the Parkway through a break in the guardrail. It's 5.0 miles to the Paul C. Wolfe Shelter for a 10.0-mile round-trip.

Picnic Area Options

For a few more great hiking options, drive south on the Parkway to Humpback Rocks Picnic Area (Milepost 8.5). Two trails start on the outside loop of the picnic area. To the right, the easy 0.5-mile Catoctin Trail leads to a nice stone wall–encircled view of the Shenandoah Valley. Humpback Mountain and Humpback Rocks can also be reached from here. Take the blue-blazed side trail to the left that reaches the AT in 0.2 mile. (Off to the left, notice the remnants of stone walls that you'll also see in the picnic area.) A left at the AT reaches Humpback Mountain in about 2.0 miles (4.0 miles round-trip). If you continue past Humpback Mountain to Humpback Rocks, it's a 6.0-mile round-trip, with a lot less elevation gain than the hike from Humpback Gap—and much more solitude.

Raven's Roost Overlook near Humpback Rocks shows off the pastoral beauty of the Shenandoah Valley.

2 Greenstone Self-Guiding Trail

Milepost 8.8

Take this twenty-minute self-guiding loop trail to learn about the geology of the northern Blue Ridge and see how mountaineers used their most abundant resource—rock—to wrest a living from harsh surroundings.

Parkway mile: 8.8

Distance: 0.2-mile loop

Difficulty: Easy

Elevation gain: Negligible

Maps: *USGS Sherando*; no Parkway map available

Finding the trailhead: Park at the end of the overlook near the woods. (GPS: 37.947341 / -78.927691)

The Hike

This engaging self-guiding interpretive trail explains the natural setting and alerts you to the telltale signs of human habitation that are a stirring subtext to the Parkway experience.

The Mountain Farm Trail's extensive living-history exhibits at Milepost 5.8 re-create the picturesque side of the rustic Appalachian lifestyle. The Greenstone Trail imparts an anthropologist's insight into how to detect the evidence of a former mountain farm.

The overlook's interpretive sign explains that "hog-walls" were scattered throughout many places in the mountains. Built in the early 1800s and maintained in winter by slaves from lower-elevation plantations (Jefferson's Monticello is only 40 miles away), the walls penned nearly wild hogs that otherwise were permitted to roam the mast-covered slopes, becoming "free-range" delicacies. Before you hit the trail, look over the front of the overlook. Whether by accident or sensitivity, the builders of the Parkway spared the hog-walls below, and the Park Service's vista maintenance crews periodically expose them to view.

Pass the trailhead sign and go right along the gravel path. A sign describes the ubiquitous green rock of the overlook and the general area—Catoctin greenstone—as an ancient lava flow, evidence that volcanoes once existed in the region. Were the lava to liquefy today, notes the sign, it would fill the Shenandoah Valley. Undulating along over occasional steps, the trail bears left around the end of the loop and across a dome of greenstone. Mountain laurel and Virginia pine cling to this steepening side of the ridge.

Pause at the sign that describes how tremendous earth forces 200 million years ago uplifted the lava, sandstone, limestone, and shale of the area, transforming it into ridges and peaks. Between Mileposts 20 and 60, the shale and limestone are

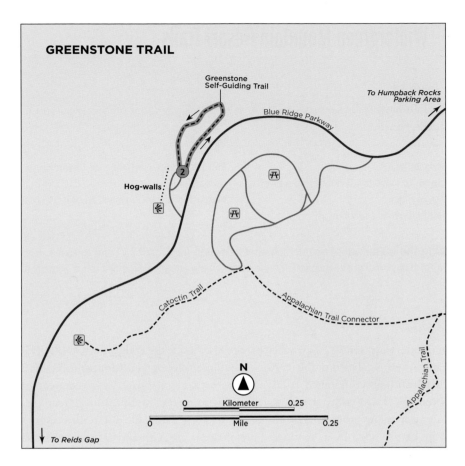

GREENSTONE TRAIL

Greenstone
Self-Guiding Trail

To Humpback Rocks
Parking Area

Blue Ridge Parkway

Hog-walls

Catoctin Trail

Appalachian Trail Connector

Appalachian Trail

N

| 0 | Kilometer | 0.25 |

| 0 | Mile | 0.25 |

To Reids Gap

particularly visible in road-cuts—a favorite haunt for geology students touring the Parkway. At that sign, look to your right and behind, just below where the trail crosses the crag, and you'll see another hog-wall—this one quite disheveled—arcing down through the rough woods. The sure of foot could go down and, being careful not to dislodge or alter the rocks, explore this high-mountain holding pen from centuries ago.

Swinging right, squeeze between a pine and a crag and emerge onto an open ledge with great views of the Shenandoah Valley. The vista here, on the nearby Catoctin Trail at Humpback Rocks Picnic Area at Milepost 8.5, and at the clifftop Raven's Roost Overlook at Milepost 10.7 showcase the outstanding pastoral scenery that recommends this first part of the Parkway.

An interpretive sign notes that you'll see all three types of rock along the Parkway—igneous (greenstone and lava), metamorphic (quartzite and schist), and sedimentary (limestone and sandstone). The trail climbs through a crag, to the right, and back into the parking lot.

3 Wintergreen Mountain Resort Trails

Milepost 13.7

This environmentally sensitive resort near the Parkway takes preservation and good hospitality seriously.

Parkway mile: 13.7
Distance: 0.3 mile to 12.0 miles on a diverse system of trails
Difficulty: Easy to strenuous

Elevation gain: Negligible for Shamokin Springs Trail
Maps: The resort publishes its own trail map.

Finding the trailhead: Leave the Parkway at Reids Gap (Milepost 13.7) and go east 1 mile on VA 664, then take the second left into the resort's main entrance. (The first left is actually the exit.)

The Hikes

Environmentalists weren't happy when private land beside the Parkway across Black Rock Mountain was purchased in the 1970s and became Wintergreen Mountain Resort. The Appalachian Trail was rerouted as a result (but it's still hiked today as a Wintergreen trail).

Not that it will satisfy the most ardent environmentalist, but Wintergreen's lodge and condominium accommodations and its status as a ski, golf, and tennis resort may actually be exceeded by its renowned preservation program and 30-mile trail system, a then refreshing approach I featured in a 1980s issue of *American Forests* magazine. More than 6,000 of the resort's 11,000 acres will remain as wilderness or forested open space by restrictive covenant. Wintergreen actually gave 3,000 acres of land to the Blue Ridge Parkway—and the resort's best roadside views are Parkway-style overlooks, one above the ski area. The resort's protected acreage includes the summit location of the Mountain Resort where most trails are located, but it plummets far below into the Stoney Creek parcel near the village of Nellysford where other hikes are popular.

Accommodations range from lodge-style studio rooms in the slope-side Mountain Inn to condominiums and single-family homes, all with access to resort dining spots and recreational and spa facilities linked by a resort-wide shuttle bus service.

The respected Wintergreen Nature Foundation offers diverse interpretive programs—a highly regarded annual Wildflower Symposium in May and Virginia's Natural History Retreat Weekend in September—from its interpretive base in a stunning structure near the resort's spa. Staff naturalist Doug Coleman was given a key role from the start in keeping the "green" in Wintergreen. Development is carefully sited, and sensitive plants are rescued beforehand. The foundation is now independent of the resort and undertakes added preservation efforts, such as 1,400 acres of easements recently protected on nearby Crawford Knob.

THE PLUNGE 2 MILES ↑
TO BLACKROCK + BRIMSTONE TRL.

Wintergreen's trails range from long and gradual to short and steep, like this path to The Plunge.

THE APPALACHIAN TRAIL

Each spring, hundreds of people hoist heavy packs and strain down a misty trail, intent on accomplishing the most difficult task of their life: trekking between Georgia and central Maine along the Appalachian Trail (AT). When regional planner Benton MacKaye first proposed an Appalachian Trail in 1921, he labeled the idea "an experiment in regional planning" aimed at preserving the East's wilderness.

Within two years of MacKaye's first article proposing the AT, the major trail organizations, including fledgling groups in the South, had endorsed the plan and built the first sections of the trail in New England. In 1925 a meeting held in Washington, DC, formally created the Appalachian Trail Conference, Inc., forerunner of today's Appalachian Trail Conservancy.

With railroad imagery fostered by MacKaye, the trail's "main line" from Georgia to Mount Washington in New Hampshire was intended to link various "branch lines" that would funnel jaded urban workers into the refreshing green corridor. Today, North Carolina's Mountains-to-Sea Trail is becoming a bona fide "branch line" indeed. "The path of the trailway should be as 'pathless' as possible," MacKaye maintained. In the late 1920s, that's exactly how it was.

In reality, the AT was built largely out of existing trails in the North and through unexpected devotion from trail clubs and the Forest Service in the South. Energetic Southerners helped build other sections, too: The Potomac Appalachian Trail Club completed the trail through Maine to Mount Katahdin.

During AT construction, nearly 600 miles of the Skyline Drive and the Blue Ridge Parkway were built, claiming dozens of miles of the AT's early route. Many trail clubs opposed building those roads. Luckily, the Civilian Conservation Corps (CCC) was enlisted to revise the route and build some of the three-sided lean-to shelters that line the trail. Nevertheless, Appalachian Trail Conference chairman Myron Avery called the scenic roads a "major catastrophe in Appalachian Trail history."

In one case, Coleman went to bat for a thirteen-acre spot scheduled for home development, and the Shamokin Springs Nature Preserve was born. Shamokin Springs is a popular trail in a rare Blue Ridge resort that other developers would do well to emulate. Here are just a few of many possible hikes for Parkway visitors who make Wintergreen a base of operations.

The Plunge (GPS: 37.945449 / -78.926161) is only about a 0.5-mile round-trip, but it is a steep, rocky hike on the way down and even tougher coming out. Nevertheless, it ends with a spectacular view of the Rockfish Valley. The deep clefts of Wintergreen's protected open space make up a good portion of the 160-degree view. Most people complete the hike in forty-five minutes to an hour.

The trail in any form became a symbol. Long before wilderness preservation was achieved in the East, die-hard hikers built the trails by following ridgetops and linking dwindling remnants of a wild heritage. By 1937 the first version of the trail was complete. Thousands of catastrophes—from hurricanes to commercial development—have claimed portions of the trail. But each time, a new generation of trail enthusiasts has stepped in and carved the path anew. As Myron Avery observed, the AT was the trail of which it could never be said, "It is finished—this is the end!"

In 1968 the AT became the first National Scenic Trail under the landmark National Trails System Act, which gave control to the Appalachian Trail Conference. It also authorized the acquisition of 1,000 miles of trail in private hands, by eminent domain if necessary. But acquisition of land was slow. After pressure from the trail community, an Appalachian Trail bill passed Congress in the late 1970s that has substantially sped up land acquisition along the route. Today, almost all of the path is in public ownership.

Maintenance of the path never wanes and is accomplished through the efforts of thirty-one organizations affiliated with the Appalachian Trail Conservancy. The conservancy boasts 40,000 members and thirty affiliated clubs. Many times each year, volunteers toil long hours in the task of maintaining their portions of the footpath and any of nearly 300 overnight shelters on the route. All told, about 6,000 volunteers work more than 200,000 hours each year on the path. Though four million people take to part of the trail annually, only 150 to 200 hikers a year complete the trail. Fewer than 10,000 have accomplished the feat since the trail's inception.

Almost a century later, MacKaye's proposal has had the philosophical impact he'd hoped for. More than perhaps any other recreational facility in the world, the Appalachian Trail symbolizes the power of nature to work wonders for those who take the time to wander in the woods.

Shamokin Springs Nature Preserve features a 0.3-mile loop trail through an amazingly diverse area (GPS: 37.931599, -78.947702). A braided stream is the focal point of this trail, and you meet it over and over as you cross and recross the many streamlets that eventually form Stoney Creek, the primary stream that flows through the resort's lower acreage. Grab the interpretive guide at the trailhead.

Take Grassy Ridge Drive and park at Wintergreen's Discovery Ridge Adventure Center below the Mountain Inn. A few loop trails here make memorable hikes. Follow the Grassy Ridge Trail beyond the center, and the 0.8-mile Hemlock Springs Trail heads left to follow a scenic stream that includes a loop at the bottom. Or at the bottom of Hemlock Springs, go north on Cedar Cliffs South Trail. At the junction

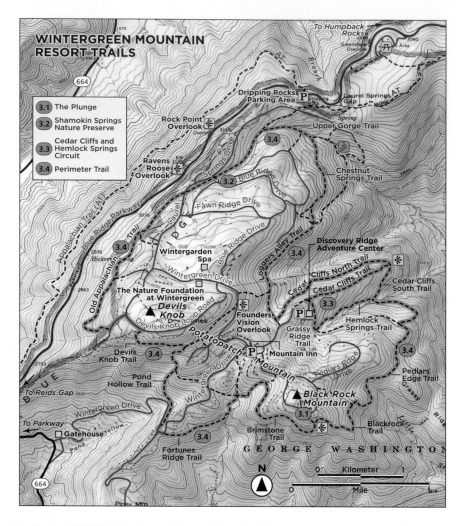

with Cedar Cliffs Trail, a short side path heads right to an awesome view of Shamokin Gorge. From there climb back up Cedar Cliffs and go right to take Grassy Ridge back to the center.

There's even a perimeter trail route that circuits a 13-mile loop around the mountaintop part of the resort. Designed to explore many different habitats and ecosystems, this trail is quite difficult in places and includes some truly rigorous hiking. Avid hikers are rewarded by forest and ridge walking, distant views, and intimate settings beside rushing mountain streams.

4 Three Ridges Wilderness

Milepost 13.7

Virginia's 4,600-acre Three Ridges Wilderness was designated in 2000. The great circuit hike it affords follows the Appalachian Trail as it swerves east of the Parkway and up and over Three Ridges, at 3,970 feet. The route descends from the peaks then skirts 1,000 feet higher than the AT's southerly trailhead on VA 56 to turn right on the Mau-Har Trail and loop back to the Parkway. The oddly named Mau-Har Trail uses the first syllable of the names of the two backpacking shelters you pass, Maupin Field and Harper Creek.

The shelters make nice out-and-back day or overnight hike destinations—Maupin Field is less than 2.0 miles from either of its trailheads, and Harper Creek is 2.6 miles. From the VA 56 trailhead there's a nice, secluded waterfall hike near the shelter on Campbell Creek. The route described below takes in the entire circuit, starting on the AT from the north. The shelters and their adjacent campsites are arranged best that way for either a one- or two-night camping trip. And, very important, the elevation gain is far less taxing than it is from the south.

Three Ridges Wilderness Circuit

One of the best backpacking loops on the northern portion of the Parkway, with a number of nice views, plentiful campsites, a waterfall, and two overnight backpacking shelters and adjacent campsites (each pretty accessible for easy out-and-back overnighters).

Parkway mile: 13.7
Distance: 13.5-mile circuit and a variety of shorter out-and-back day hikes
Difficulty: Strenuous

Elevation gain: 3,495 feet
Maps: *USGS Sherando*; Appalachian Trail Conference: Pedlar Ranger District, George Washington National Forest

Finding the trailhead: There are two Parkway trailheads for this circuit hike. Park in the gravel trail parking slip on VA 664 just east of Reids Gap at Milepost 13.7 (GPS: 37.901307 / -78.985323) or beside the gated fire road at Milepost 15.4 in Love Gap (GPS: 37.883837 / -79.009581). To get to VA 56, exit the Parkway at Milepost 27.2 and go east on VA 56; parking is on the right at 11.2 miles (GPS: 37.838294 / -79.023215). The trail crosses the Tye River on an impressive suspension bridge.

The Hike

The white-blazed Appalachian Trail leaves the meadows of Reids Gap at 0.2 mile and climbs gradually, then steeply to a ridgetop campsite on the left at 0.8 mile. There's a

At nearly 4,000 feet, the peaks of the Three Ridges Wilderness bulk over Virginia's western Piedmont.

nice view just across the trail to the right. The AT dips off the ridgetop and switch-backs to a T junction with a fire road at 1.7 miles. The fire road from the right makes a great alternative route to this campsite for Parkway backpackers who want an easier path to a quick overnighter. The fire road goes west 1.5 miles to Love Gap and is much more gradual than the AT from Reids Gap.

At this junction the AT goes left along the fire road. Straight ahead, where a sign directs hikers to as many as twenty designated campsites in the vicinity, a trail leads 100 yards to Maupin Field Shelter and the headwaters spring of Campbell Creek behind it. The blue-blazed Mau-Har Trail, your return route, leaves just south of the shelter and crosses then follows Campbell Creek down to the AT on the other side of Three Ridges.

Going left on the road, the AT immediately passes another trail to Maupin Field Shelter on the right that also passes a privy. The AT quickly leaves the old road and continues over Bee Mountain (3,022 feet) at 2.0 miles. It dips off the summit and climbs to the right of the ridgeline to commanding clifftop views from Hanging Rock at 3.7 miles. The Priest dominates the vista to the southwest. The trail contin-ues up across the forested double summit of Three Ridges at 4.2 miles then, at 4.4 miles, switchbacks steeply off the peak. It passes a number of views, then Chimney

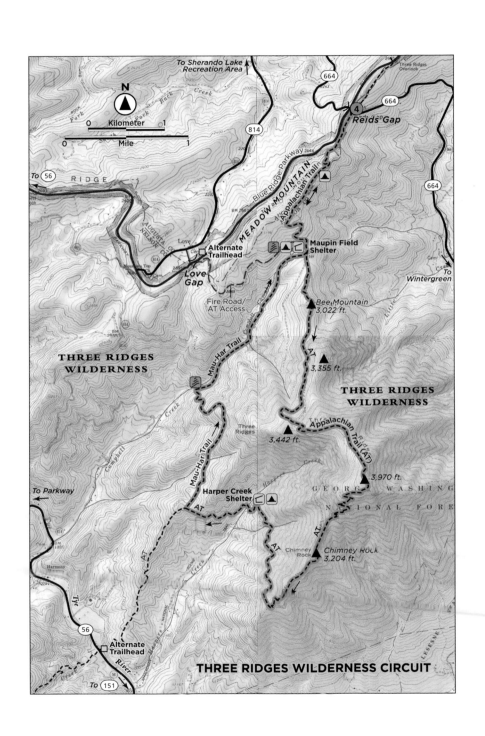

THREE RIDGES WILDERNESS CIRCUIT

Rock at 5.9 miles. Descending the ridgeline to a nice view at 6.3 miles, the trail turns north and descends again on an old road. A side road leads off to the right at 7.9 miles to Harper Creek Shelter and a privy. The stream in front is the water source.

The AT crosses Harper Creek and climbs to a junction on the right with the Mau-Har Trail at 8.8 miles (VA 56 is 1.7 miles to the left on the AT). Turn right and follow the blue-blazed trail along Campbell Creek. Mau-Har slabs the flank of Hanging Rock as it slides into the stream drainage. It rises and falls repeatedly until reaching Campbell Creek near a nice waterfall at 10.3 miles (3.2 miles from VA 56, for a 6.4-mile out-and-back day hike from there). A more gradual ascent along the upper trail brings you to Maupin Field Shelter at 11.8 miles. A left to your car at Love Gap creates a 13.1-mile circuit. Continuing another 1.7 miles on the AT to Reids Gap—with a much more gradual uphill than on the way in—creates a circuit of 13.5 miles.

Key Points

- **1.7** Road grade right to Parkway and Love Gap; side trail to Maupin Field Shelter and Mau-Har Trail.
- **3.7** Viewpoint atop Hanging Rock.
- **4.2** High point of the hike at Three Ridges summit.
- **5.9** Chimney Rocks view.
- **7.9** Harper Creek Shelter.
- **8.8** Right turn onto Mau-Har Trail.
- **10.3** Waterfall on Campbell Creek.
- **11.8** Arrive back at Maupin Field Shelter.

Where the White Rock Falls Trail reaches the Parkway at White Rock Gap, yellow blazes meet the road's yellow lines.

5 White Rock Falls Circuit and Sherando Lake Recreation Area Hikes

Milepost 19.9

This strenuous but worthwhile circuit adjacent to the Parkway can be expanded to start at Sherando Lake Recreation Area, a recommended national forest campground convenient to the first section of the high road. The campground itself has a few nice, easy hikes.

Parkway mile: 19.9
Distance: Shorter hikes include a 2.6-mile out-and-back moderate hike to White Rock Falls and 1.0- and 1.2-mile easy loops around Sherando Lake. Longer, strenuous hikes include a 4.9-mile White Rock Falls circuit from Slacks

Overlook and circuits from Sherando Lake of 8.2 and 9.5 miles.
Difficulty: Easy to strenuous
Elevation gain: 860 feet for the entire circuit from Slacks Overlook
Maps: *USGS Big Levels*; USFS Saint Mary's Wilderness map (best)

Finding the trailheads: From Slacks Overlook (GPS: 37.907968 / -79.051004) enter the woods on the east end of the parking area past a picnic table to a signed junction (blue plastic diamonds) with the Slacks Trail.

To start the White Rock Falls Trail from Slacks Overlook, exit the overlook on foot. Cross the Parkway, turn left, and walk north along the road 200 feet to a right turn into the woods on the signed, yellow-blazed trail.

The lower end of the White Rock Falls Trail and access to the Slacks Trail is available from a recently signed, graveled parking area (expected to be paved when the road next gets new asphalt) on the north side of the Parkway in White Rock Gap (Milepost 18.5; GPS: 37.896234 / -79.045112). From there the White Rock Falls Trail enters the woods across the Parkway at a yellow blaze and a trailhead sign. The orange-blazed White Rock Gap Trail (to the Slacks Trail and Sherando Lake Recreation Area) leaves the north side of the gap to the right on an old road grade.

To start at the lower end of the White Rock Gap Trail—or hike the lakeshore loops—make the quick trip to Sherando Lake by turning north off the Parkway on VA 004 from Reids Gap (Milepost 13.7). Turn right at 2 miles past VA 814 to the left, and at 2.6 miles turn left onto FSR 91 to the campground. The first right on FSR 91B at 3.6 miles leads to the fishermen's parking trailhead for the lakeshore hikes (GPS: 37.926002 / -79.003079). Sherando's main trailhead for the lakeshore and larger loops is located 0.9 mile past FSR 91B, past the bathhouse on the right, just across the bridge by the picnic area (GPS: 37.920240 / -79.006205). To reach the trailhead beside Upper Sherando Lake, pass the main trailhead, various campsites, and a small parking area at the base of the dam to where the trail starts through a gate on the left at 0.7 mile. Park just uphill of the gate in the lot on the left (GPS: 37.918631 / -79.018631).

Option 1: White Rock Falls Circuit

The best short waterfall walk and the best circuit hike start at the same spot—Slacks Overlook.

Cross the Parkway and descend into the woods past a sign honoring the Youth Conservation Corps crew that built the trail in 1979. Another sign prohibits camping, hunter access, and dogs without leashes. The trail meanders down and is soon within earshot of tumbling water. Bearing right across a small side stream at 0.3 mile, the path crosses a bridge at 0.5 mile over White Rock Creek and follows the stream until it plummets into a chasm then bears away right and reaches a crag with great views of the gorge below.

Following clifftops away from the crag, the trail switchbacks left along the base of the cliffs. When the trail reaches the bottom of the first crag encountered above, at 1.2 miles, it switchbacks sharply right—but don't be fooled. The best waterfall view on the entire White Rock Falls Trail continues straight ahead another 0.1 mile on an

White Rock Falls hides in a rocky grotto down a side trail.

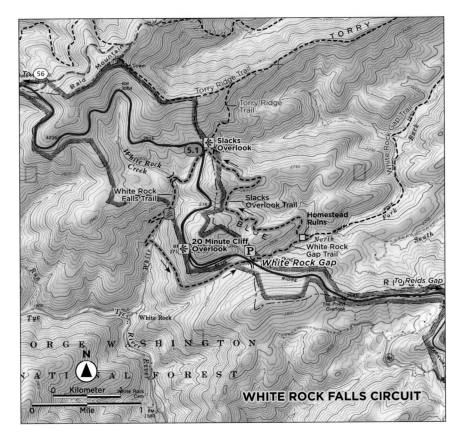

WHITE ROCK FALLS CIRCUIT

obviously used but unsigned and seemingly informal trail below the cliffs. The path dips down to a beautiful cataract and pool amid encircling stone walls. A return to the Slacks Overlook from here makes a moderate and rewarding 2.6-mile hike. ***Caution:*** If you miss this rather obscure side trail to the falls, you could hike the entire White Rock Falls Trail and not see a waterfall!

Back at the switchback, descend steeply on a rocky tread, passing a boulder beautifully striped with quartz intrusions (the falls and nearby gap are named for the prevalence of quartz). Steep, rocky switchbacks continue. The trail approaches the stream again at a deep pool but steeply switchbacks two final times before crossing White Rock Creek below a large pool. Crossing the stream, the trail climbs steeply then rises into a startlingly scenic pine grove. Turn left onto an old wagon road that climbs steeply toward White Rock Gap at 2.2 miles. The old road levels off; a stream and then an old rock wall appear on the right. Three small bridges span seeps, and the Parkway appears high on the left. The trail climbs past roadside signs to the Parkway at 2.5 miles. If you can park a second car here, the hike is mostly downhill. Going from here up to the falls is a strenuous 2.8-mile hike.

Crossing the Parkway, the old grade reappears as the orange-blazed White Rock Gap Trail and descends to the site of an old homestead at 3.1 miles. By the late 1700s, the Blue Ridge was full of hardscrabble farms like this one.

Just beyond the homesite, turn left on the blue-blazed Slacks Overlook Trail. (To the right, Sherando Lake Campground is 2.0 miles down the White Rock Gap Trail.) Climb steeply along another old grade, with evidence of quarrying off to the right. In open scrubby forest at 4.9 miles, turn left into Slacks Overlook.

Key Points

0.5   Cross White Rock Creek.

1.3   Arrive at White Rock Falls.

2.5   White Rock Gap.

3.1   Old homesite and left turn just beyond.

4.9   Arrive back at Slacks Overlook.

Option 2: Sherando Lake Trails

Sherando Lake Recreation Area, where the lengthiest hike and a few very easy ones begin, is a great place to camp on this northernmost portion of the Parkway. The lake has been known as the "jewel of the Blue Ridge" since 1936, when the beautifully rustic facilities built by the Civilian Conservation Corps opened on a twenty-five-acre spring-fed lake. There's a beach; a classic CCC bathhouse (with a small visitor center/gift shop); swimming, boating, and fishing on the big lake; and fishing and boating only on seven-acre Upper Sherando Lake. The campground is open for full service from April 1 to October 31.

To make a long circuit from Sherando with a variety of options, start on White Rock Gap Trail at the Upper Sherando Lake trailhead. This gradual old road grade follows orange-plastic blazes southward along pretty Back Creek to a junction at 2.0 miles with the Slacks Trail near the old pioneer homesite. Go right, pass the access trail to Slacks Overlook at 3.7 miles, and turn right again at 4.4 miles on the Torry Ridge Trail. (Left, it's only 1.2 miles to the sparsely wooded summit of Bald Knob, a nice campsite. You can drive to this trailhead when the gate is open on FSR 162 from Bald Mountain parking area at Milepost 22.1.) Descending with the yellow-plastic blazes of the Torry Ridge Trail, at 6.4 miles turn right onto the first leg of the blue sign–blazed Blue Loop Trail. Just past Lookout Rock, take another right at the junction with the Yellow Trail and descend to site A-6 of the White Oak Campground at 7.3 miles. Go left to the main trailhead by the bathhouse and follow the main road through the campground back to the starting point for a loop hike of 8.2 miles.

For the easiest area hikes, park at the main trailhead by the bathhouse or take FSR 91B to Sherando Lake's fishermen's parking area by the dam. Starting at the main trailhead, the 1.0-mile loop of the Lakeside Trail is very easy in either direction.

There's also a nice circuit east of the lake that pairs one side of the Lakeside Trail with the steeper Cliff Trail, which climbs above the lake. The easy option starts to the

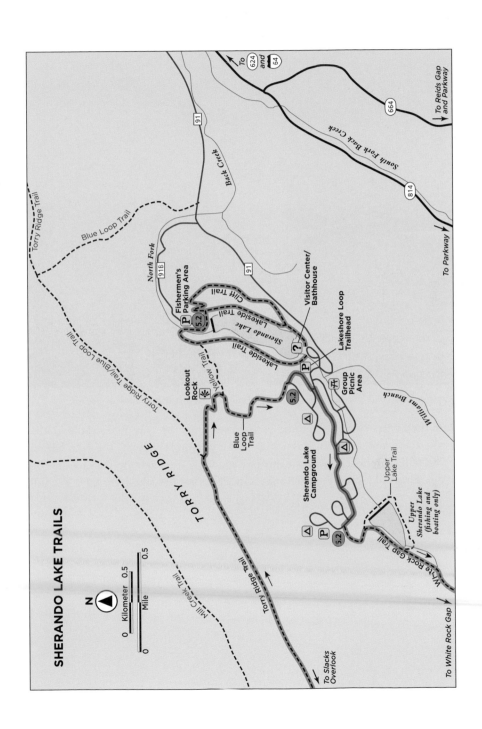

SHERANDO LAKE TRAILS

N

Kilometer 0.5
0
0
Mile 0.5

Torry Ridge Trail

Blue Loop Trail

Mill Creek Trail

Torry Ridge Trail/Blue Loop Trail

TORRY RIDGE

To Slacks Overlook

To White Rock Gap

North Fork

91B

Fishermen's Parking Area

5.2

Lakeside Trail

Cliff Trail

Lakeside Trail

Sherando Lake

Lookout Rock

Yellow Trail

Blue Loop Trail

5.2

Sherando Lake Campground

5.2

Visitor Center/Bathhouse

Lakeshore Loop Trailhead

Group Picnic Area

Williams Branch

Upper Lake Trail

White Rock Gap Trail

Upper Sherando Lake (fishing and boating only)

To Parkway

Back Creek

91

91

South Fork Back Creek

814

664

To 624 and 64

To Reids Gap and Parkway

From Overlook Rock on Sherando Lake's Cliff Trail, there's a peephole look at the lake.

right and then bears right beyond the bathhouse across the grass and up the gradual part of the Cliff Trail. Overlook Rock affords a peephole view of the lake halfway along. The trail switchbacks down its steepest grade to the Lakeside Trail by the fishermen's parking (and a privy) at 0.5 mile. Go left along the lakeshore for a 1.2-mile walk.

6 Saint Mary's Wilderness

Milepost 22.1

This 10,090-acre parcel is the largest of Virginia's federal wilderness areas. The tract lies west of the Blue Ridge Parkway between Milepost 22.1 (Bald Mountain Overlook) and Milepost 27.2 (Tye River Gap).

The Saint Mary's area was never logged. But although the forests may be virgin, rugged slopes and thin soil have not produced towering trees. Many trails in the area were once railroad grades; manganese and other mines operated from the early 1900s to the 1950s. The scenery is nevertheless impressive, and ruins from the mining era are part of the appeal. Oak and hickory forests predominate, and the summits are covered with pitch pine, table mountain pine, bear oak, and mountain laurel. Barren talus fields appear as gray jumbles of rock on otherwise lush, green slopes.

The Saint Mary's Trail starts west of the Parkway in the vicinity of Steele's Tavern and follows the Saint Mary's River. Large pools below waterfalls, some 10 feet deep, attract dippers in the heat of summer. The falls on the Saint Mary's aren't dramatic, but quartzite cliffs and large streambed boulders make the setting a scenic one.

This wilderness is very popular. Regulations prohibit camping around the trailhead parking area, and campfires are banned in the vicinity and within 150 feet of the trail from there to beyond the falls, about 2.0 miles. Groups are limited to ten persons. Weekdays are the best time to visit during the warmer months.

Luckily, that kind of popularity is absent in the upper part of the wilderness. Parkway hikers have easy access to the scenery below—and quick escape to the less-popular area above. The upper Saint Mary's Trail climbs gradually up the valley, where two trails connect to the Parkway.

Deer, turkey, grouse, and a respectable population of black bear call Saint Mary's home. Trout are prevalent in the Saint Mary's River, although increased acidity from acid rain and related phenomena is having a negative impact on at least one species of tiny native fish.

A circuit hike dips from the Blue Ridge Parkway into a lush watershed of the Saint Mary's Wilderness and returns via scenic Green Pond, a natural high-elevation tarn.

Parkway mile: 22.1 or 23.0
Distance: Circuits of 10.3 and 3.8 miles; out-and-back hike of 9.4 miles
Difficulty: Strenuous for the 10.3-mile circuit and 9.4-mile out-and-back; moderate for the 3.8-mile circuit

Elevation gain: 1,280 feet for the longer circuit; 1,400 feet for the out-and-back hike
Maps: USGS *Big Levels, VA*; USFS Saint Mary's Wilderness map

Finding the trailheads: The Mine Bank Trail enters the woods at a roadside parking area reached by a gravel road just south of, and on the opposite side of the Parkway from, Fork Mountain Overlook (Milepost 23.0; GPS: 37.911545 / -79.086798). The Bald Mountain Trail soon branches to the right.

Another trailhead for the Bald Mountain Trail is located on a usually gated gravel road (FSR 162) that leaves the Parkway on the north end of the Bald Mountain parking area (Milepost 22.1; GPS: 37.914118 / -79.073597). The trail branches left from FSR 162 at about 0.7 mile from the Parkway. At certain times of year, this road is ungated and accessible to four-wheel-drive vehicles. The hike uses part of that route. A branch of the road goes right at 0.2 mile beyond the Bald Mountain trailhead and climbs to a trailhead for the Torry Ridge Trail and a nice campsite clearing at the former site of a fire tower atop Bald Mountain (3,587 feet).

The Hikes

This Saint Mary's Wilderness circuit adjacent to the Blue Ridge Parkway offers a combination of streamside and mountaintop scenery and an absence of crowds. Two hike options range from under 5.0 miles to more than 10.0 miles. The longer circuit is a nice overnight trip, with camping on a stream or at Green Pond—a rare, natural pond located on an open ridgetop.

At the parking area across the road from Fork Mountain Overlook, the orange-blazed Mine Bank Trail enters the wilderness. One hundred yards from here, the yellow-blazed Bald Mountain Trail goes right to the other trailhead on FSR 162. Stay on the Mine Bank Trail. The trail quickly descends north to Mine Bank Creek and follows the stream 2.0 miles, dropping nearly 1,100 feet to a junction with the blue-blazed Saint Mary's Trail.

The Saint Mary's Trail runs up and down the stream. Turn right and follow the gradually ascending trail, a railroad grade that once served nearby mines. Cross two creeks to excellent campsites in the vicinity of Bear Branch. The mining that once took place in the area is visible here at Red Mountain Mines. Local mining focused on manganese, coal, and iron. There used to be more than twenty buildings, including residences, in this mining community; foundations are still visible.

The Saint Mary's Wilderness beckons from right beside the Parkway.

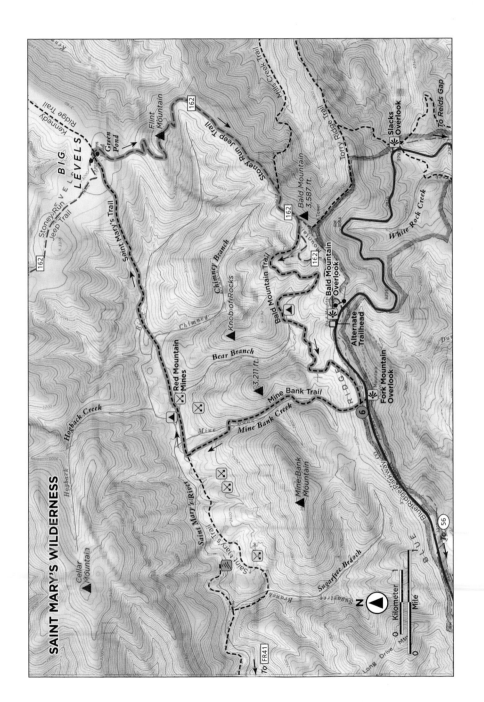

SAINT MARY'S WILDERNESS

BIG LEVELS

Kennedy Ridge Trail

Flint Mountain

162

Stoney Run Jeep Trail

Stoney Run Jeep Trail

Green Pond

162

Saint Mary's Trail

Chimney Branch

Knobs of Rocks

Chimney

Bald Mountain Trail

Bald Mountain 3,587 ft.

Mills Creek Trail

Tory Ridge Trail

162

Slacks Overlook

To Reids Gap

White Rock Creek

162

Bald Mountain Overlook

Alternate Trailhead

Red Mountain Mines

Bear Branch

3,217 ft.

Mine Bank Trail

Mine Bank Creek

Mine

RIDGE

Fork Mountain Overlook

6

Hogback Creek

Hogback

Cellar Mountain

Saint Mary's River

Saint Mary's Trail

Mine-Bank Mountain

Sugarfree Branch

Saint Mary's Trail

Sugartree Branch

Sugartree

Blue Ridge Parkway

56

To 56

BLUE

Long Drive Mtn

To FR41

N

Kilometer

Mile

0

0

The gradual grade of the Saint Mary's Trail continues and then steepens before leveling out on a ridgetop appropriately named Big Levels. The trail exits the wilderness and reaches Green Pond—a tarn surrounded by pines—at about 4.8 miles. Sedges and a colony of cranberry grow in the boggy area. There are excellent campsites by the pond, but camp in a zero-impact manner. The trail continues 0.3 mile farther to reach FSR 162, called the Stoney Run Jeep Trail, at 5.1 miles.

Reaching the jeep trail, turn right and hike the primitive road along a gradually ascending ridge for 3.0 miles. At about 8.1 miles turn right onto the yellow-blazed Bald Mountain Trail. The trail dips into the beautiful headwaters of Bear Branch, where it passes fine campsites before turning out of the stream drainage to ascend and intersect the Mine Bank Trail at about 10.3 miles. A left on the Mine Bank Trail leads to the parking lot. This lengthy hike can be taken in either direction and started from either parking area.

From the Parkway, or the bottom of the Saint Mary's Trail, the Green Pond circuit described above may be the best in Saint Mary's. You can also shorten this hike to a less than 4.0-mile loop of the Bald Mountain Trail. Park at either trailhead, hike to the other trailhead on the 2.2-mile Bald Mountain Trail, then walk between the trailheads on the combination of the Blue Ridge Parkway (0.9 mile) and FSR 162 (0.7 mile) for a 3.8-mile total hike. The FSR 162 section is a pleasant walk in itself. Campers wanting to reach a secluded Saint Mary's backpacking spot quickly can park at either trailhead and take the Bald Mountain Trail to nice campsites in the upper Bear Branch area.

From the Mine Bank Trail's intersection with the Saint Mary's Trail, you could go downhill to the waterfalls, either on a day hike or as a side trip during an overnighter.

Key Points for the Longer Circuit

0.05 Bald Mountain Trail goes right (easy access to good campsites on Bear Branch for Parkway campers wanting a quick overnighter). Continue straight.

2.0 Turn right from Mine Bank Trail onto Saint Mary's Trail.

4.8 Green Pond.

5.1 Turn right onto FSR 162.

8.1 Turn right onto Bald Mountain Trail.

10.3 Go left on Mine Bank Trail to Parkway and your car.

7 Crabtree Falls

Milepost 27.2

One of the South's best waterfall walks also has barrier-free access.

Parkway mile: 27.2
Distance: About 6.0 miles round-trip. The upper falls make a nice turnaround point for a 3.4-mile hike from the bottom trailhead or a 2.6-mile hike from the upper trailhead.
Difficulty: Strenuous from the bottom of the falls; moderate from the top

Elevation gain: 1,500 feet for the entire falls trail from the bottom; 1,000 feet to falls from the bottom; 500 feet to falls from the top
Maps: USGS *Montebello* and *Massies Mill*; Appalachian Trail Conference: Pedlar Ranger District, George Washington National Forest

---

Finding the trailheads: Exit the Parkway at Milepost 27.2 and descend east on VA 56 for 6.6 miles to the large lower trailhead on the right side of the road (GPS: 37.850819 / -79.079371). The upper trailhead for the falls is on VA 826, an unpaved road suitable for use in good weather by higher clearance vehicles (an SUV is the best choice). To reach that trailhead, go east on VA 56 from the Blue Ridge Parkway; in about 3.8 miles turn right onto VA 826. The upper trailhead is on the left in just under 4 miles (GPS: 37.830659 / -79.083115).

The Hike

This Crabtree Falls in the George Washington National Forest isn't the last cataract you'll encounter with that name while driving south on the Blue Ridge Parkway. The second—actually a Blue Ridge Parkway trail—is in North Carolina at Milepost 339.5.

Various publications describe this falls as the "highest in Eastern America," the "highest in Virginia," and the "highest in the Virginia Blue Ridge." Which of those claims to believe probably depends on a long list of qualifiers. Chances are they at least qualify for "highest in the Virginia Blue Ridge" status—and that's being conservative.

Suffice to say that this path follows Crabtree Creek's 1,800 feet of descent to the Tye River. Along the way, five major waterfalls create a truly spectacular cascade.

Starting at VA 56, hikers are in for a climb, but this trail is highly developed and gradual over its entire length. The newest renovation, completed in late 2002, included the construction of a seventy-car parking area, new barrier-free restrooms, and an extensively reworked approach that provides barrier-free access to the first overlook on the falls. The trail's improvements are largely designed to keep hikers away from the cascades, which have claimed more than twenty lives. Stay on the trail, and watch children closely.

Developed observation areas overlook the falls at four places along the trail, the first just above the parking area on the new trail. There's a wood deck overlook at 0.7

CRABTREE FALLS TRAIL AND THE PRIEST

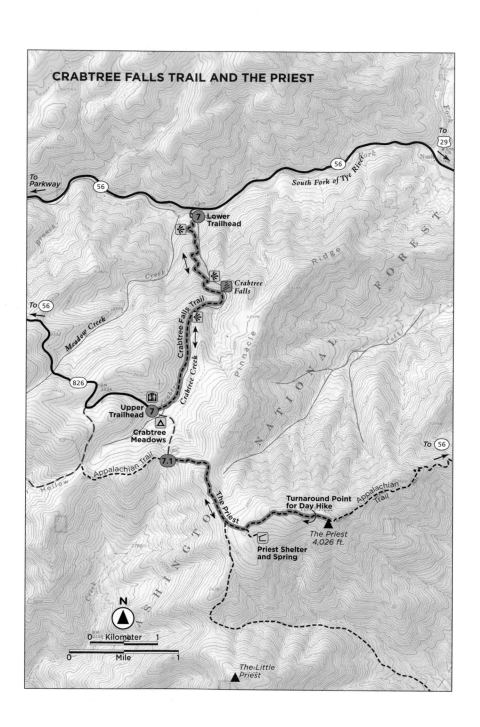

To Parkway

To 29

56

South Fork of Tye River Fork

Nash

56

7 Lower Trailhead

Crabtree Falls

To 56

Meadow Creek

Crabtree Falls Trail

Crabtree Creek

Pinnacle

Ridge

NATIONAL FOREST

826

Upper Trailhead 7

Crabtree Meadows

Appalachian Trail

Hollow

7.1

The Priest

Turnaround Point for Day Hike

Appalachian Trail

To 56

The Priest 4,026 ft.

Priest Shelter and Spring

WASHINGTON

Creek

N

0 Kilometer 1

0 Mile 1

The Little Priest

mile, and at 0.8 mile you can use a small cave to rejoin the trail above. An overlook at 1.4 miles looks up at the upper falls. The last overlook, at about 1.7 miles, surveys the Tye River Valley from above the upper falls. A return from that point makes a nice 3.4-mile hike.

Continuing, the trail follows a gradual old grade and at 3.0 miles reaches an upper trailhead on VA 826. Keep this trailhead in mind for summer and fall weekends, when the lower trailhead may be jammed. Indeed, the upper cascade is actually an easier hike starting from the top. With two cars, a descent of the trail is an easy walk.

VA 826, a bumpy dirt road with a few easy stream fords, is a worthwhile side trip. Camping is not permitted at the Crabtree Falls Trail trailhead or along the trail, but camping is allowed in Crabtree Meadows, an expanse of fields across the split rail fence from the trailhead and privies.

Key Points from below the Falls
- **0.2** First waterfall overlook.
- **0.7** Wooden deck overlook on second cascade.
- **0.8** Cave route.
- **1.7** View of upper falls. This is the turnaround point for a 3.4-mile out-and-back hike.

Option 1: The Priest

This popular AT hike to a shelter and campsites reaches one of the most beautifully shaped summits in the central Blue Ridge.

See map on page 58.
Parkway mile: 27.2
Distance: 2.6 miles out and back; 5.7 miles one-way to Tye River parking area
Difficulty: Strenuous

Elevation gain: 975 feet
Maps: USGS *Montebello* and *Massies Mill*; Appalachian Trail Conference: Pedlar Ranger District, George Washington National Forest

Finding the trailhead: Go east on VA 56 from the Blue Ridge Parkway; in about 3.8 miles turn right onto VA 826, an unpaved road suitable for use in good weather by higher clearance vehicles (an SUV is the best choice). The upper trailhead for Crabtree Falls is on the left in just under 4 miles. The Priest hike starts just 0.5 mile beyond this trailhead.

The Hike

From the west, the massive, dramatically sculpted major summit of the 6,000-acre Priest Wilderness Area is easily accessible. It's a 1.4-mile hike and almost 1,000 feet of rise from an AT parking area just 0.5 mile past the upper parking area for Crabtree Falls. Of course if you truly want to "earn it," more than 3,000 feet and forty switchbacks of ascent are always available from VA 56 via the AT's Tye River trailhead.

The elegantly sculpted ridge of The Priest highlights Virginia's Religious Range.

Not only is this the way to see the summit of The Priest (4,026 feet), but it's also the direction in which to hike this portion of the AT. Leave the trailhead where VA 826 ends at Shoe Creek Hill (3,300 feet). Head left on the AT and pass through a fence, then ascend through a gap at 0.3 mile, going right. After gaining the ridge, the trail to the summit of The Little Priest leads right at 0.7 mile, 1.5 miles away, requiring 500 feet of descent and the same amount of rise back up to reach the peak.

At 0.9 mile a blue-blazed trail goes right to the Priest Shelter, 0.1 mile off the main trail with a spring and tent sites. Heading north, the trail reaches rocky viewpoints at 1.3 miles, a nice turnaround point, with the summit 0.1 mile farther on.

If you're continuing, the trail takes a plunge. A viewpoint at 3.0 miles looks directly down into the cleft of the Tye River where you're going. A bridge crosses Cripple Creek at 4.3 miles, and then a series of road grades carry the trail. The VA 56 trailhead is across the road from the Tye River at 5.7 miles.

Key Points across The Priest on the AT

0.0   Start at the trailhead off VA 826.

0.7   Trail to The Little Priest leaves AT to the right.

0.9   Blue-blazed side trail right to the Priest Shelter.

1.3   Views near summit; turnaround point for day hike.

3.0   View of Tye River Valley.

4.3   Bridge over Cripple Creek.

5.7   Tye River parking area on VA 56.

Option 2: Spy Rock

This spectacular view is the perfect introduction to the central Blue Ridge—the perfect place to take a map and compass to identify the major surrounding summits.

Parkway mile: 27.2
Distance: 3.2 miles out and back
Difficulty: Moderate
Elevation gain: 1,000 feet

Maps: *USGS Montebello* and *Massies Mill*; Appalachian Trail Conference: Pedlar Ranger District, George Washington National Forest

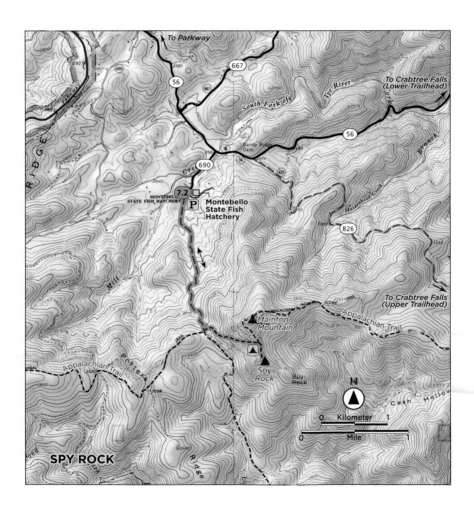

Finding the trailhead: Leave the Parkway to the east, descending on US 56, and in 3.4 miles turn right onto VA 690 at signs for the Montebello State Fish Hatchery. Pass the fish hatchery and turn left at 3.8 miles on an informally signed rough road to trailhead parking on the left at 3.9 miles (GPS: 37.841848 / -79.131213).

The Hike

If you want a truly awesome view, hike to Spy Rock. This is one of the best views in the central Blue Ridge. Much of the hike is on a gradual road grade, and there's a campsite near the viewpoint.

Strike off across the small stream and up gated Spy Rock Road on the right from the trailhead to a junction with the AT at 1.0 mile. Go left; the trail crosses a fence at 1.1 miles. At 1.5 miles the AT bears left at a campsite. Turn right onto the side trail to Spy Rock. The trail emerges on the rocky dome (about 3,900 feet) in just under 0.1 mile.

The all-encompassing summit view includes an excellent vista of the Religious Range—The Priest, The Cardinal, The Little Priest, and The Friar. Retrace your steps from the summit for a 3.2-mile hike.

Key Points

- **1.0** Turn left onto the AT.
- **1.5** Turn right onto the Spy Rock side trail.
- **1.6** Spy Rock summit.

The trail to Crabtree Falls is a highly developed path designed to make access easy and safe.
SARAH HAUSER, VIRGINIA TOURISM CORPORATION

8 Yankee Horse Overlook Trail

Milepost 34.4

This is a quintessential Parkway leg-stretcher trail. Great views of Wigwam Falls combine with an interesting exhibit about the logging railroads that carried off the region's virgin timber.

Parkway mile: 34.4
Distance: 0.1 to 0.2 mile
Difficulty: Easy

Elevation gain: Negligible
Maps: *USGS Montebello*; no Parkway map available

Finding the trailhead: Start on the right side of the overlook, by the interpretive sign (GPS: 37.809238, -79.179800).

The Hike

Blue Ridge Parkway interpretive trails impart amazing insight into how people affected the mountain environment. If you open yourself to the experience, you'll

The Yankee Horse Overlook Trail can teach you how to identify an old railroad grade fading back into the forest.

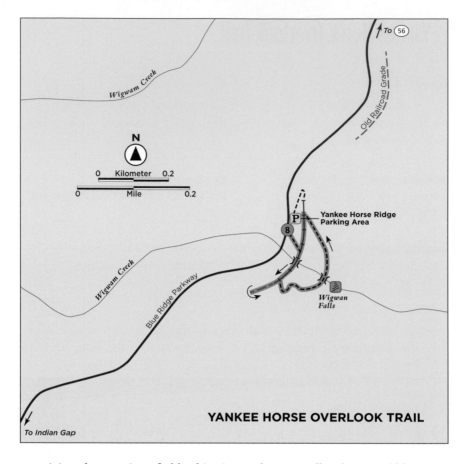

YANKEE HORSE OVERLOOK TRAIL

To Indian Gap

start noticing the remains of old cabin sites and stone walls where you'd least expect them. This trail will change the way you look at trails wherever you hike in the eastern United States.

Remnants of the virgin forests encountered by the colonists are rare in the Appalachians today. The last of that timber was carried away in the early twentieth century on narrow-gauge railroads that climbed into the most impassable places on grades excavated by hand and lifted over precipitous gorges on log trestles. This trail explores a section of railroad reconstructed on the actual grade used by the Irish Creek Railway to transport more than 100 million board feet of lumber. The railway, built in 1919 and 1920, was 50 miles long.

As you climb stone steps, the trail rises and turns right onto railroad tracks across a log-supported bridge that spans gushing Wigwam Creek. The path goes left beyond the bridge, but don't turn yet. Follow the tracks as the rails end and the ties continue. When the ties stop, keep going a short distance and see how the grade softens and the woods encroach.

Many trails use portions of grades like this, and most hikers assume they're old farm or auto roads. Some of the grades you encounter on the Parkway, especially near gaps, may be wagon roads from centuries past. But many are railroad grades, and now you may be better able to recognize them.

Return to where you would have gone left, and turn right (uphill). Go left across two bridges below mossy green Wigwam Falls, most impressive when the small stream has seen recent rain. The trail continues left, levels out above the stream, and then descends on a log-lined treadway to rejoin the tracks. To return to your car, you can go left back toward the bridge then take a right. But go right on the tracks and there's a picnic table where there's a left turn then steps down to your car.

When you finish the hike, drive north a short distance from the overlook. Where the hillside recedes from the road on the right, you can see the trackless, forgotten route of the railroad grade slicing through the woods.

Milepost 469 marks the end of the Parkway at the Great Smokies but 468 other posts line the rest of the route. Be sure to notice these markers and monitor the Mileage Log in the back of the book as you travel for details about facilities and even trails that aren't featured in their own entries.

9 Indian Gap Trail

Milepost 47.5

Parents with children will like the hands-on experience that Indian Rocks gives to young mountain climbers.

Parkway mile: 47.5
Distance: 0.3-mile loop
Difficulty: Easy

Elevation gain: Negligible
Maps: *USGS Buena Vista*; no Parkway map available

Finding the trailhead: The trail leaves the north end of the parking area (GPS: 37.717709 / -79.312946).

The Hike

Take the stone-paved pathway toward the north and pass a picnic table. An old grade comes in from the right, and the trail follows it through a gully. The trail bears right off the grade to a ridgetop with a small peak off in the woods to the left. Amid standing dead timber that's popular with woodpeckers, the trail turns right and wanders through mountain laurel to Indian Rocks.

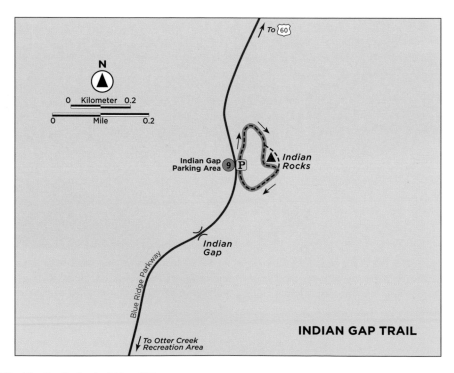

Bootleg trails seem to go everywhere. Stay to the right on the formal trail and you soon realize that a few of these impressive "rocks" are the size of small houses. Descend rocky steps and go left below a huge boulder. The path weaves back and forth below the crags, but you can head left at many points and find yourself at dead ends in rocky fissures. There's even a small cave to crawl into. This is the perfect place for kids to scramble around with adult supervision.

The trail turns right, away from the rocks, and levels off through a corridor in the mountain laurel. The road appears ahead, and the path becomes paved before swinging into the south side of the parking lot.

Peaks of Otter Lodge, at Milepost 85.6, is the single lodging concession on the northernmost part of the Parkway. It provides comfortable accommodations and dining only steps from a brand-new, fully accessible lakeshore path. It's also an educational TRACK Trail, courtesy of the Blue Ridge Parkway Foundation.

10 Otter Creek Recreation Area

Mileposts 60.8–63.6

For almost 10 miles, Otter Creek memorably parallels the Parkway on a descent from 1,100 feet to the James River at 650 feet. Though this is not a lofty portion of the high road, the mixed forest of hardwoods (oaks, sycamores, and beeches) and evergreens (white pines and hemlocks) is reminiscent of higher elevations. All along the 8.5 miles of Otter Creek's dance with the Parkway, broad flats and inviting woods lie beside the meandering stream. Luckily, a wonderful series of overlooks—and the lengthy Otter Creek Trail—permit you to revel in the rich streamside forest. This is a recommended place to pause along the northern part of the Parkway.

This stroll sticks close to the Parkway for its entire 3.4-mile length, so if you hike it one-way, you end up miles from your car. You could enjoyably backtrack for a 6.8-mile round-trip hike—the terrain is so gentle that even that distance would qualify as a moderate hike for honed Parkway hikers.

The best bet may be to start at one or the other end and make Otter Lake your destination. The 1.0-mile loop around this scenic lake is a high point of the trail and divides the Otter Creek Trail into two nice day hikes of different lengths. The longer, 5.8 miles, starts at the Otter Creek Campground trailhead. The shorter, which starts at the James River Visitor Center, is only 2.4 miles. The trail descriptions reflect that organization.

The Otter Creek Trail begins at this major Parkway campground, which had a small pine-paneled restaurant/snack bar and gift shop that was shuttered as this book went to press (check its current status at nps.gov/blri/index.htm).

Option 1: Otter Creek Trail

Enjoy awesome streamside strolling in a memorable mixed forest of hardwoods and evergreens.

Parkway mile: Major starting points at Mileposts 60.8 and 63.6 (other overlook access included in the text and mileage log)
Distance: 6.1-mile lollipop from Otter Creek Campground and 2.4-mile lollipop from James River Visitor Center
Difficulty: Moderate
Elevation gain: 222 feet from the campground; 128 feet from visitor center (including lake loop)

Maps: *USGS Big Island*; Parkway handout map combining the Otter Creek Recreation Area and James River Water Gap, available in season at the visitor center and campground and online at nps.gov/blri/planyourvisit/otter-creek-james-river-trails.htm

Finding the trailhead: Starting at the campground, park at the closed restaurant building (or nearby parking) and head south past the building on the paved then gravel-surfaced trail that dips into the woods along the stream (GPS: 37.576258 / -79.337985). Starting at the James River Visitor Center, park near the trail map sign (GPS: 37.555333 / -79.365428). Descend below the front of the building on the paved path and turn left just beyond the visitor center to follow another paved path above the picnic tables and down into the woods.

The Hikes

From Otter Creek Campground

The Otter Creek Trail leaves the parking area and immediately passes circular concrete stepping-stones that cross the stream left into the campground (you'll see more of these 1950s-looking conveniences all along the trail). Passing campsites, the trail crosses to the east side of the creek at 0.1 mile then slips under Otter Creek Bridge

Below Otter Lake dam in the background, hikers use stepping-stones to follow Otter Creek toward the James or to loop Otter Lake.

#6 at 0.3 mile and wanders west to stone steps that lead left up to Terrapin Hill Overlook at 0.6 mile (Milepost 61.4).

The trail swings south with the stream and goes under two bridges at 0.7 mile, both through the leftmost water tunnels. The Parkway's stone Otter Creek Bridge #7 is followed by the concrete modernity of the VA 130 bridge. Just out of the tunnel, the trail turns right and crosses to the other side of the stream. Along the river rocks on the shore, the stream is deflected hard right by a towering green palisade; turn with it (a side trail across this bend could avoid the streambank in higher water). Paralleling VA 130, the trail again hops to the east side of the stream and rises steeply left to parallel above the Parkway (which has crossed above the other road). The path rises higher and higher along a log-lined treadway through an impressive forest of white oak, hemlock, and white pine to a bench at 1.0 mile. After a dip left into a dry drainage, the trail swings out again and back in to a bridge at 1.3 miles. Swinging into another drainage, then out, the trail is again above Otter Creek, which has come back under the Parkway and is now below. Entering into another drainage, side steps lead to a huge crag with an overhanging shelter spot and a bench. Leaving that rock, the trail swings out and steeply down to Otter Creek at about 1.5 miles.

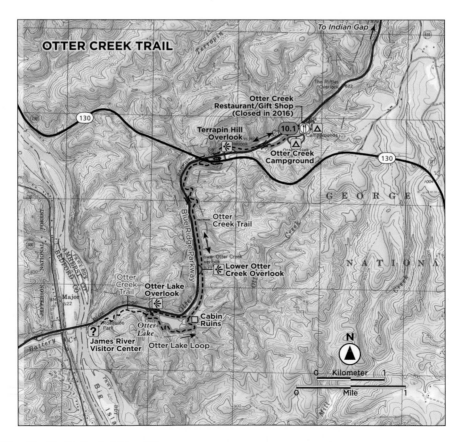

From here to Lower Otter Creek Overlook (Milepost 62.5) at 1.9 miles, the trail stays near the stream, barely undulating with nice views into clear, cold, and at times invitingly deep water. Mountain laurel crops up and you pass another bench. Entering the overlook's picnic table area, take a right across the steel bridge. Walk left along the parking area and immediately go left across the next bridge (the zigzag avoids a cliff face).

Back along the stream, this time on a sandier shore, the Otter Creek Trail enters a more open deciduous forest and at 2.6 miles intersects the Otter Lake Loop. Go right at this junction, crossing two steel bridges. Staying right, emerge from the woods to walk along the Otter Lake Overlook (Milepost 63.1). This is the best way to circle the lake and is the route described under the Otter Lake Loop Trail (see Option 2 of this hike). At the end of that loop, retrace your steps along the Otter Creek Trail for a 6.1-mile day hike.

Key Points on the Longer Lollipop

0.3 Under first bridge.

0.6 Terrapin Hill Overlook.

0.7 Under second and third bridges.

1.9 Lower Otter Creek Overlook.

2.6 Junction with Otter Lake Loop; turn right onto loop.

3.5 Return to Otter Creek Trail.

6.1 Arrive back at campground.

From James River Visitor Center

Heading down to the woods line above the visitor center picnic area, leave the paved path and join Otter Creek. Here it's a quiet stream, backed up into stillness by the lumbering flow of the nearby James River. Soon, though, the stream comes to life as its rise creates a rush of incoming water.

Following the creek beneath the visitor center parking, the path runs atop a stone reinforcement wall at 0.3 mile that protects the road from the curving waters of Otter Creek where nearby hemlocks grapple to stay rooted among mossy-green crags. The trail swings right then left around a bend in the river (where you can see evidence of an old road off to the left) and then crosses more round stepping-stones.

The trail joins an old grade at 0.5 mile and leaves it at 0.6 mile to cross a small stream. This atmospheric evidence of early wagon roads and later logging railroads jibes with the chimneys and other ruins that the alert hiker will notice hereabouts. This was a region of rich soil and impressive forests, and the Kanawha Canal—on the James, just 0.5 mile down Otter Creek—was one of early America's thriving commercial thoroughfares.

Continuing through hemlocks, white pines, and a carpet of running cedar, the river straightens out and the trail dips down railroad-tie steps to cross stepping-stones at 0.7 mile. Just beyond is the stair-stepping cascade of water over the Otter Lake dam.

You could cross the stream and walk up the steps beside the dam to the overlook. Instead go right before the stepping-stones and start the Otter Lake Loop. Hiking the 1.0-mile lake trail (described below) and retracing your steps along Otter Creek to the James River Visitor Center creates a 2.4-mile lollipop hike.

Option 2: Otter Lake Loop Trail

This intensely scenic loop around a man-made lake includes a ruined mountaineer cabin.

Parkway mile: 63.1
Distance: 1.0-mile loop
Difficulty: Moderate
Elevation gain: 108 feet
Maps: USGS *Big Island*; Parkway handout map combining the Otter Creek Recreation Area and

James River Water Gap, available in season at the visitor center, campground, and online at nps.gov/blri/planyourvisit/otter-creek-james -river-trails.htm

Finding the trailhead: Park at the Otter Lake Overlook. The trail starts at the end of the parking lot near the dam (GPS: 37.556858 / -79.358098).

The Hike

Starting at the dam, descend the steps and cross the stream on concrete stepping-stones. Go left and ascend stone steps past crags along the stream and above the dam at 0.1 mile. At lake level, the trail slides around a point and into a drainage to cross a small stream, then switchbacks around the ridge to a bench above the lake at 0.3 mile. A small side trail leads to another view of the lake.

The main trail rises gradually to its high point in the mixed deciduous and evergreen forest. At 0.4 mile another bench amid towering white pines announces the drop down a gully from the ridgetop. Bearing left across a small creek, the trail wanders through sycamores and blond grasses in a wetland fed by inlet brooks. Cross a small bridge at 0.5 mile over Little Otter Creek, and then rise into a white pine grove on a knoll where an old cabin sits in ruins. The huge base of the chimney is nicely intact, but the upper rocks have fallen in much the way the rocks were stacked, directly across the interior of the cabin. A perimeter of rock foundation stones and remnants of large logs may be all you see. A bench is across the trail.

Dipping down into the floodplain below the once artfully sited cabin, turn left at the signed junction and cross two steel bridges at 0.6 mile. At the edge of the Parkway, head left. Rounding a ridge above the wetland, walk into the parking area, past a handicapped-accessible observation deck on the lakeshore to your car for a 1.0-mile loop.

Note: The lake is plentifully signed with fishing regulations (swimming, boating, and ice skating are prohibited).

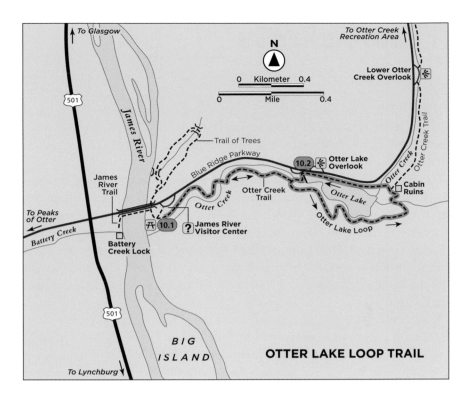

Key Points

0.1 Cross stream and go left to top of dam.

0.3 First bench at side trail to view.

0.4 Second bench.

0.6 Cross bridges to go left.

1.0 Arrive back at dam beside Parkway.

11 James River Water Gap

Milepost 63.6

For all the might of the mountains, the sight of Virginia's biggest river flowing placidly through the breach is sure to impress. Trails on the Blue Ridge Parkway and in the James River Face Wilderness provide an impressive experience of the titanic natural forces at work in this water gap.

The Parkway's two riverside paths are advertised as thirty-minute interpretive walks. Each, in turn, features interpretive signs about the human and natural history of the James River Water Gap. Both begin beside a visitor center that in season offers a variety of other exhibits about the canal and the river. *Travel tip:* Best time to visit for historic insight is during the free mid-July James River Transportation Festival (check the Parkway website for current dates). The Virginia Canals and Navigation Society and others will present exhibits, and a replica of a pre-canal river batteau will be on display.

Be sure to consider the picnic area beside the visitor center. Twelve or so tables and grills dot a split-rail fence–flanked meadow beside the James. You can picnic in the open or just inside the edge of the woods. The Otter Creek Trail starts here near the visitor center, but a lower path also leads along the first part of the stream from a number of picnic sites. It's a wonderful chance to leave the placid silence where Otter Creek merges with the massive James and walk into the woods to see—and hear—the creek come noisily to life as a tumbling mountain stream.

Option 1: Trail of Trees

The geology of the water gap and the diversity of the floodplain forest are the focus for one of the Parkway's best interpretive trails. The path crosses crags with great views of the river.

Parkway mile: 63.6
Distance: 0.4-mile loop
Difficulty: Moderate
Elevation gain: 50 feet
Maps: *USGS Big Island*; Parkway handout map combining the James River Water Gap and Otter Creek Recreation Area, available in season at the visitor center and campground and online at nps.gov/blri/planyourvisit/otter-creek-james-river-trails.htm

Finding the trailhead: Park at the visitor center near the trail map sign and descend on the paved path to the right past the building (GPS: 37.555333 / -79.365428). Continue under the Blue Ridge Parkway's river bridge and go right up the steps. (The pedestrian walkway left across the river leads to the James River Trail.)

The Hike

From the paved patio beneath the bridge, the trail steeply switchbacks right then left up stone steps to where the loop splits just below the level of the Parkway. Heading left, descend a bit to a stone wall–encircled patio and a sign that explains the water gap—a formation typical of the Appalachians (see photo). These gaps played a key role in westward expansion, and the James River Water Gap so dramatically displayed here was particularly important. An early turnpike, railroad, and canal were part of the gap's transportation network. The canal is gone, but a major highway and rail line still course above the river on the opposite bank.

The trail rises away from the view on a soil treadway, passes below some crags, and then climbs again directly above the river. All around are dramatic cliffs and crags that lost the battle with the James. The scenery conjures the romantic early lithographs of canal traffic you see on nearby interpretive signs.

Down more steps and under an overhang, the path dips into a drainage and descends to switchback left along the stream. A bridge spans the stream just before it slips into the James. Rising to a headland, there's another river view and then a second

Start the Trail of Trees with a great view of a major geographic feature, the James River Water Gap.

formal stone viewpoint at the top of more stone steps. The view is of plunging cliffs and nearby islands in the river.

The trail turns away from the river and slabs above the stream you crossed, eventually recrossing it on another bridge. There's a bench in this quiet spot, then more stone steps lift you out of the drainage.

Dozens of signs do a particularly fine job of identifying the trees and explaining the ecosystem of a typical lower-elevation Appalachian forest (at 650 feet, this is the lowest part of the Parkway). A sign here explains that eastern hemlocks "indicate the presence of a stream." Groves of these graceful evergreens (now being decimated by the hemlock woolly adelgid) usually grow in the moist soil along watercourses.

The trail continues a steep climb past another bench, then levels along the edge of the drainage below. You can see directly down on the first bridge you crossed near a sign for the tulip tree, or yellow poplar, the tallest broadleaf tree in North America. Topping out, the path swings right along the height of land past other interpretive signs and scrubby Virginia pine. As you skirt just above the trail you started on, a small fenced graveyard appears off to the left, with headstones—some just rocks—from the early and mid-1800s, when the water gap funneled settlers into the wilderness beyond. A set of steps closes the loop and takes you back down the steeper steps the way you came.

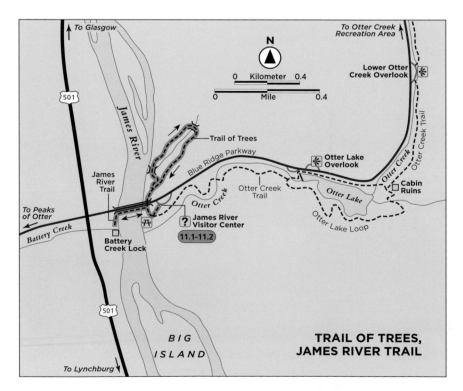

**TRAIL OF TREES,
JAMES RIVER TRAIL**

Key Points

0.1 First viewpoint.

0.2 Cross first bridge.

0.3 Cross second bridge at bench.

Option 2: James River Trail

A pleasant walk across a scenic river bridge leads to a self-guiding interpretive exhibit at a canal lock built in the mid-1800s.

See map on page 76.
Parkway mile: 63.6
Distance: 0.4 mile out and back
Difficulty: Easy
Elevation gain: Negligible

Maps: *USGS Big Island*; Parkway handout map combining the James River Water Gap and Otter Creek Recreation Area, available in season at the visitor center and campground and online at nps.gov/blri/planyourvisit/otter-creek-james-river-trails.htm

Finding the trailhead: Park at the visitor center and descend to the right on the paved path from the trail map sign. Continue under the Blue Ridge Parkway's river bridge and take the pedestrian walkway left across the river.

The James River Trail to Battery Creek Lock explores a key remnant of the James River and Kanawha Canal.

The Hike

The James River Trail crosses the impressive pedestrian span beneath the Blue Ridge Parkway bridge. Descend the steps on the south side of the river and go left across the grassy riverside meadow to Battery Creek Lock. Built in 1848 and used between 1851 and 1880 on the James River and Kanawha Canal, the lock lifted and lowered boats around part of the river's 13 feet of drop from nearby Buchanan, a Shenandoah Valley town and western terminus of the canal.

Signs interpret the lock and the system that used river water to feed the adjoining canal and operate its gates. To vary your route, take the recently mowed route away from the river and along the towpath that creates a little loop before returning to the bridge. Back in the 1960s, visitors could also explore another lock upriver and rangers say that reopening that site is being considered.

Key Points

0.2   Battery Creek Lock.

Times haven't changed that much in the Park Service's first century, celebrated in 2016. Rangers still stand ready to help Parkway motorists.

12 James River Face Wilderness

Mileposts 63.9–71.0

The 9,000-acre James River Face Wilderness is a rugged and scenic area that clings to the cliffs where the mighty James River breaks through the Blue Ridge. Designated in 1975, Virginia's first wilderness area lies north of Petites Gap, a major trail access point at Milepost 71 on the Blue Ridge Parkway. Thunder Ridge, added in 1984, is a 2,450-acre wilderness just south of Petites Gap. That tract is essentially just the sloping western side of the Blue Ridge below the Parkway, though that description doesn't do justice to the unique plants that grow there. Together, the James River Face and Thunder Ridge make up a wilderness tract that rises from the deceptive calm of the James River (about 650 feet) to the lofty altitude of Highcock Knob (3,073 feet) and the Blue Ridge Parkway.

Much of the area was logged early in the last century, and many of the trails follow old grades that were part of the process. Because these old grades provide solid, sustainable footing, horses are permitted in the wilderness on the Balcony Falls, Sulphur Spring, and Piney Ridge Trails. Some precipitous faces above James River escaped early loggers, but thin, rocky soils support scrubby communities of Virginia pine, chestnut oak, and heath-type undergrowth, such as mountain laurel. The deeper coves are home to hemlocks and white pines, but few trails venture there and the area is steep and scrubby enough to discourage bushwhacking. But there are a wealth of hard-to-reach places that offer pristine, primeval scenery and total solitude. As in other Virginia wilderness areas, group size is limited to ten persons.

This is an area of well-signed, radiating ridgetop trails with numerous out-and-back hiking options. Unfortunately, a desire to circuit hike through the James River Face will be largely frustrated. For that reason, this entry offers an overview of the trail network then recommends a few circuit hikes. (Check the accompanying maps while reading this description.)

South of Petites Gap, Milepost 71 on the Parkway, the Appalachian Trail is the single significant trail through the Thunder Ridge tract. From Petites Gap north, the AT runs into the James River Face, over the summit of Highcock Knob, then around the ridgetops, eventually dropping east past Matts Creek Shelter to wander along the James. The trail crosses the James on an impressive 625-foot trail bridge dedicated in 2000 to the late William T. Foot, a Natural Bridge Appalachian Trail Club member who worked to make the bridge a reality.

At the very crest of the wilderness, 2.3-mile sections of the Appalachian and Sulphur Spring Trails undulate along on opposite sides of the main ridge, creating a 5.6-mile circuit with junctions to the north and south. That's a key feature for hikers—a number of basically out-and-back day hikes/overnighters can become circuits by adding that summit loop.

Climbing from the east to meet the above trails are the Matts Creek Trail (part of the AT until the year 2000), which runs from US 501 to the shelter, and the Piney Ridge Trail, part of the original 1930s AT that rises to join the Sulphur Spring Trail on the crest of the wilderness. That trailhead is also very near US 501, on FSR 54. Both trails figure in circuits described here.

Four trails climb to the AT from the west. Northernmost is Balcony Falls, which rises from VA 782 to a junction with the Sulphur Spring Trail and, following that trail, reaches the AT in another 1.4 miles. Gunter Ridge Trail climbs from a trailhead in the vicinity of VA 759 to join the Belfast Trail 0.4 mile from the AT. The Belfast Trail leaves VA 781 and climbs to pass a junction with the Gunter Ridge Trail and then joins the AT. Luckily for hikers, the lower ends of the above two trails are linked by the Glenwood Horse Trail, permitting one of the area's best circuits, also described here.

Option 1: Appalachian Trail Circuit to Matts Creek Shelter

A newer section of Appalachian Trail crosses the James River to a popular trail shelter. This is a perfect riverside hike for anyone who enjoyed the river-related Trail of Trees near the Parkway's nearby James River Visitor Center.

Parkway mile: 63.9
Distance: 2.8 miles out and back to a campsite turnaround on the bank of the James; 4.4 miles out and back to the shelter on the AT; 4.8 miles to the shelter on a circuit with Matts Creek Trail

Difficulty: Easy for the riverside walk; moderate for the Matts Creek hikes
Elevation gain: 650 feet
Maps: *USGS Snowden* and *Glasgow*; Appalachian Trail Conference: Glenwood–New Castle Ranger Districts, Jefferson National Forest

Finding the trailhead: Exit the Parkway at Milepost 63.9. From the stop sign on US 501, go west toward Glasgow, crossing the Snowden Bridge over the James. The trailhead for the Matts Creek Trail, the former AT, is just before the bridge on the left, at about 2.9 miles, beside a historical marker (GPS: 37.589442 / -79.381929). Across the bridge on US 501/VA 130, a major AT parking area is 4 miles from the Parkway (GPS: 37.596747 / -79.391096). Leave the lot and go under a railroad bridge to cross the James River footbridge.

The Hikes

North to south, hikers face a nearly 2,500-foot climb from the James to the crest. But that climb doesn't kick in until you've passed Matts Creek Shelter. That makes this a rare north-to-south AT day hike that's recommended for its ease and a great turnaround point—a trail shelter that makes a nice lunch stop or campsite, especially during the week.

There are a few versions of a Matts Creek hike. The rerouted AT crosses the James on an impressive trail bridge and then follows the river, giving hikers views they never had before because the old AT (now the Matts Creek Trail) was in the woods all the way.

Either one of those routes leads to the shelter and, with two cars, makes a nice circuit hike—especially with the two parking areas so close together.

Head under the railroad bridge and cross the stunning trail span with awesome views of the wilderness area's namesake face dropping into the river. No camping is permitted for the first mile. Turn right and the white-blazed AT follows the riverbank above the watery grave of a nineteenth-century turnpike and the James River and Kanawha Canal.

At 1.4 miles the trail enters the James River Face and goes left at various campsites where Matts Creek tumbles into the James. A turnaround here makes a 2.8-mile day hike or camping trip. Leading away from this memorable meeting of a mountain stream and a major river, the trail ascends gradually into a rich forest. At 2.1 miles the old AT goes left, now called the Matts Creek Trail and marked with blue blazes.

It's another 0.1 mile to the shelter (and picnic table) where the Natural Bridge AT Club has built an impressive bridge across the gorgelike stream. Unlike the various shelters once located higher up at what is now an AT campsite called Marble Spring, the six-person Matts Creek Shelter is likely to stay, despite being located in

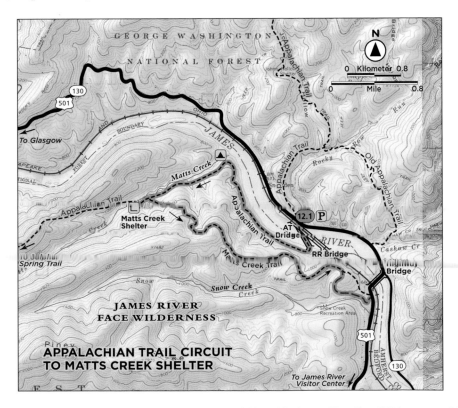

a wilderness area. This is a popular camping spot, so a variety of alternative tent sites have been designated in the area. Midweek and off-season are your best bets for solitude.

A return to your car via the AT is a 4.4-mile hike. To descend Matts Creek Trail, head back on the AT 0.1 mile and go right. That route involves some initial elevation gain before descending along an old road grade for the last mile or so to US 501 at 4.8 miles and a second car.

Key Points for Circuit

1.4 Campsites where Matts Creek meets the James.

2.1 Matts Creek Trail goes left.

2.2 Matts Creek Shelter.

2.3 Return to Matts Creek Trail and go right.

4.8 US 501.

Option 2: Devil's Marbleyard Circuit

This circuit takes in one of the wilderness area's most interesting features—an open slope of bizarre boulders. It also permits a side trip to upper-elevation campsites and views along the Appalachian Trail.

Parkway mile: 71
Distance: 8.1-mile circuit
Difficulty: Strenuous
Elevation gain: 1,700 feet

Maps: USGS *Snowden* and *Glasgow*; Appalachian Trail Conference: Glenwood and New Castle Ranger Districts, Jefferson National Forest

Finding the trailhead: From the Blue Ridge Parkway at Milepost 71, go west on FSR 35 past the Petites Gap AT parking area. Park on the right in the lot at 4.2 miles (GPS: 37.571125 / -79.491570). The trail has limited roadside parking, and the Forest Service asks that you not impede residents of the homes that border the trailhead.

The Hike

The Belfast Trail leads hikers to one of the wilderness area's most interesting natural features, the Devil's Marbleyard. This trail is also the start of the best circuit hike in the James River Face Wilderness.

The blue–blazed trail crosses the East Fork of Elk Creek on a footbridge and passes between the atmospheric entrance pillars to Camp Powhatan, an old Boy Scout camp. The trailhead sign is just beyond, surrounded by the interesting remnants of the camp. The orange plastic–blazed Glenwood Horse Trail comes in from the right (the horse trail does not cross the trail, as it may appear). The two trails climb together along an old road grade before the horse trail goes left (your return route). The Belfast Trail climbs the tightening drainage to the Devil's Marbleyard at 1.4 miles,

Remnants of old Camp Powhatan mark the start of the hike to the Devil's Marbleyard in James River Face Wilderness.

where an open boulder field provides great views of the Arnold Valley and Thunder Ridge Wilderness.

The Marbleyard's local legend is an odd tale. The site was supposedly the secret worship place of a peaceful Native American tribe who lived in the valley. It was lush and grassy and had a stone altar where the people would worship on full-moon nights. One day, two strangers appeared. The man and woman were welcomed, and because they were so strikingly different, the Native Americans wanted to worship these newcomers as spirits. But the man told the Indians that he worshipped a higher power. The Indians eventually were converted, but after a summer of horrendous drought, they blamed the newcomers and their new god. They dragged the missionaries to the altar and burned them alive. As the flames rose, a great storm exploded in the sky. Lightning bolts shattered the altar—scattering its remains all over this once-lush mountainside. Of divine origin or not, the screelike slope of Antietam quartzite is quite a sight. A return from here makes for a 2.8-mile round-trip hike.

After the steep stretch past the Marbleyard, the trail becomes more gradual and passes the Gunter Ridge Trail (about 2,500 feet) on the left at 2.4 miles and reaches the AT at 2.8 miles (with options in either direction for an overnighter). Head left down the blue-blazed Gunter Ridge Trail and run the ridge past a small summit at about 3.8 miles. The trail goes sharply off the ridge and drops down a strenuous series

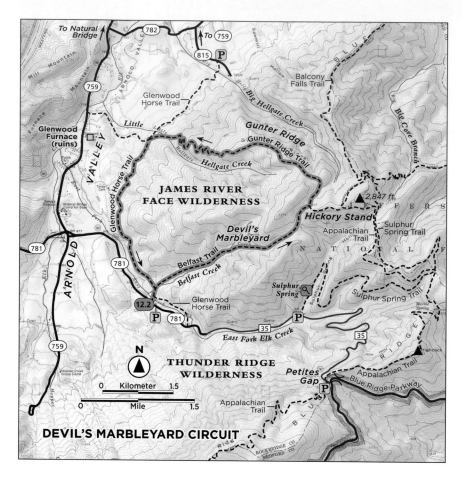

of switchbacks to intersect with the Glenwood Horse Trail at 6.0 miles. Turn left for 1.9 miles on the horse trail and reach the Belfast Trail again at 7.9 miles. Turn right and follow the Belfast Trail back to the parking area for an 8.1-mile circuit.

Key Points

0.2   Bear right on Belfast Trail where horse trail goes left.

1.4   Devil's Marbleyard.

2.4   Go left onto Gunter Ridge Trail.

6.0   Turn left onto Glenwood Horse Trail.

7.9   Go right onto Belfast Trail to parking.

Option 3: AT End-to-Ender and Summit Circuits in the James River Face

This rugged Appalachian Trail traverse of the James River Face Wilderness requires two cars or a ride and a few summit circuits with access from either the Piney Ridge or Sulphur Spring Trails.

Parkway mile: 71
Distance: 9.9 miles end to end; circuits of 11.4 miles via Sulphur Spring Trail and 12.6 miles via Piney Ridge Trail
Difficulty: Strenuous

Elevation gain: 1,647 feet
Maps: USGS *Snowden* and *Glasgow*; Appalachian Trail Conference: Glenwood and New Castle Ranger Districts, Jefferson National Forest

Finding the trailheads: The southern end of this section of the Appalachian Trail begins on FSR 35 just west of the Blue Ridge Parkway at Milepost 71 in Petites Gap (GPS: 37.559333 / -79.458505). The Sulphur Spring Trail starts on the north side of FSR 35, 2.7 miles west of the Petites Gap AT parking area.

To reach the Appalachian Trail parking area to the north, exit the Parkway at Milepost 63.9. From the stop sign on US 501, go west about 4 miles; the parking area is on the left (GPS: 37.596740 / -79.391009).

For the Piney Ridge Trail, exit the Parkway at Milepost 63.9. From the stop sign on US 501, go west toward Glasgow. In 2.0 miles make a left onto FSR 54, about 1 mile before the James River bridge. The small parking area is 0.6 mile on the right.

The Hikes

The white-blazed trail begins its 9.9-mile traverse of the James River Face (8.5 miles in the wilderness area) in Petites Gap. FSR 35 leaves the Parkway there and descends to the Devil's Marbleyard circuit. (See Option 2 of this hike.)

Hike the AT south to north to minimize the nearly 2,500-foot climb from the river. The trail heads north from Petites Gap, climbing the first 1.2 miles steeply to the wooded summit of Highcock Knob (3,073 feet). Plummeting very steeply off the peak, the trail levels off and arrives at the former site of Marble Spring Shelter, now a big campsite, about 1.0 mile from the summit and just over 2.0 miles from the road. There's a spring 150 feet down the side trail to the left.

At about 2.7 miles the Sulphur Spring Trail, an old road grade, crosses the AT. Left, it descends to VA 781/FSR 35 and is part of another circuit hike. To the right, Sulphur Spring Trail soon passes the Piney Ridge Trail, also a circuit-hike option, on its way to meet and cross the AT a second time at the 5.0-mile mark—the 5.6-mile summit circuit mentioned above that figures in two hikes described below.

For the next few miles, the AT undulates southwest of the main ridge, skirting the summits of a crest called Hickory Stand on the way to a junction with the Belfast Trail at about 4.5 miles. This trail to the left and the Gunter Ridge Trail that branches from it make up a portion of the Devil's Marbleyard circuit.

From its route along the southwest side of the main ridge, the AT turns sharply right at the Belfast Trail junction and swings around the north end of the ridge about 5.0 miles from the parking area. The Sulphur Spring Trail crosses here, becoming the Balcony Falls Trail as it heads left 5.7 miles to a valley trailhead. Right, the Sulphur Spring Trail runs back along the north side of the main ridge to rejoin the AT in

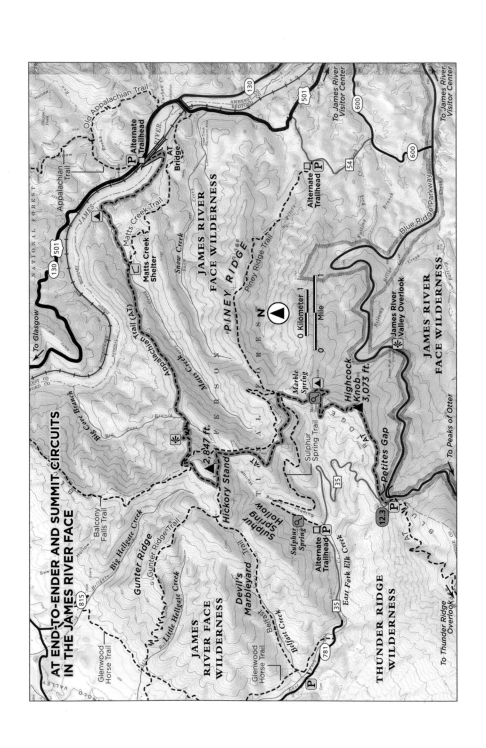

AT END-TO-ENDER AND SUMMIT CIRCUITS IN THE JAMES RIVER FACE

about 2.3 miles—again, part of the summit loop that figures in two inviting circuits covered below.

Swinging northeast, the AT slips across the main ridge of the James River Face and begins a descent of nearly 2,000 feet to the James River—the lowest point on the southern half of the Appalachian Trail. There's a view of the James just beyond the ridgecrest and another in 0.5 mile (winter is the best time for views in this wilderness area). Following a narrowing ridge above Matts Creek, the trail turns right off the ridge and descends to cross a bridge at Matts Creek Shelter (picnic table and a privy) at 7.7 miles. This section of the AT between the ridgetop and Matts Creek Shelter offers great views of the James and glimpses of the area's wildest scenery. Day hikers or overnighters bound for Matts Creek Shelter (see Option 1 of this hike) could climb to these vantage points before turning around.

Just past the shelter, the blue-blazed Matts Creek Trail turns right. The AT continues northeast, following Matts Creek to campsites at 8.5 miles where the mountain stream empties into the James. Swinging along the river (beneath the impounded water lie the remains of a nineteenth-century canal and a turnpike), the path undulates for 1.0 mile before turning left to cross a 625-foot trail bridge to the AT parking area on US 501/VA 130 at 9.9 miles.

The summit minuet between the Appalachian and Sulphur Spring Trails turns a number of otherwise out-and-back routes into circuits.

Sulphur Spring is the southernmost of the westside trails and provides horse and hiker access to the heart of the wilderness area. The trail climbs via a road grade from FSR 35, past Sulphur Spring, to cross the Appalachian Trail at 2.9 miles. The trail then gradually slabs the side of the ridge opposite the AT, passing the Piney Ridge Trail on the way and offering nice views to the river. Out and back on the Sulphur Spring Trail, including the summit circuit with the AT, is 11.4 miles. The Piney Ridge Trail climbs a scenic ridge to the AT from the opposite side of the wilderness and joins the AT at 3.5 miles. Taking the summit circuit from there, the total hike is 12.6 miles. Because they're not the steepest routes to the peaks, both of these side trails see some horse traffic.

Key Points for End-to-Ender

1.2 Summit of Highcock Knob.

2.2 Marble Spring campsite.

2.7 Sulphur Spring Trail crosses AT.

4.5 Belfast Trail goes left.

5.0 Sulphur Spring Trail crosses AT (left to Balcony Falls Trail).

7.7 Matts Creek Shelter, just 0.1 mile before Matts Creek Trail.

8.5 Campsites where Matts Creek empties into James River.

9.9 US 501/VA 130 trailhead.

13 Thunder Ridge Trail and Wilderness

Milepost 74.7

One of the most impressive rock wall–encircled vista spots on the Parkway, this is the perfect place to consider the impact of air pollution on the Southern Appalachians.

Parkway mile: 74.7
Distance: 0.2-mile loop
Difficulty: Easy

Elevation gain: Negligible
Maps: *USGS Snowden*; no Parkway map available

Finding the trailhead: Start on the northeast side of the Thunder Ridge Overlook parking area (GPS: 37.539972 / -79.490200).

The Hike

This short loop overlooks the dramatic Arnold Valley and the upper slopes of the 2,450-acre Thunder Ridge Wilderness. It's an even shorter and easier hike to the

From the Parkway's Thunder Ridge Overlook, this AT hiker peers ahead. The Devil's Marble-yard is visible on the flank of the James River Face Wilderness.

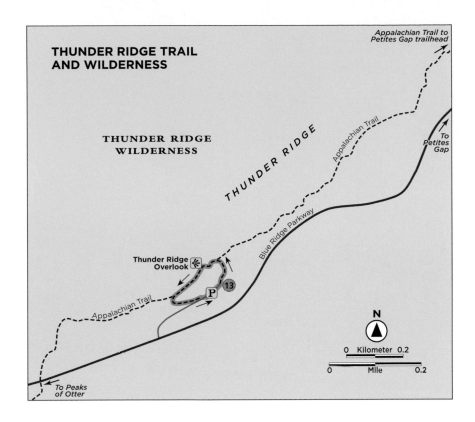

viewpoint if you return the way you came. The Appalachian Trail through the wilderness provides a longer route.

After a few stone steps, the gravel trail leaves the parking area at the farthest corner from the Parkway. The path bears left past a picnic table. The Appalachian Trail comes in on the right to join the Thunder Ridge Trail from an alternative trailhead in Petites Gap (see below). Just beyond the junction, the stone wall–encircled viewpoint offers a commanding vista of Virginia's Great Valley.

An interpretive panel appropriately titled "Seeing is Believing" shows three photos taken from this overlook that alarmingly illustrate how air pollution in the Southern Appalachians has diminished the area's famous views. Farther south on the Parkway, at the Nature Museum on Grandfather Mountain and in Mount Mitchell State Park, similar exhibits illustrate how air pollution has devastated the region's high-elevation spruce/fir forest—not just the view.

The combined Thunder Ridge and Appalachian Trails leave the viewpoint and thread through large boulders along the crest. Eventually the Thunder Ridge Trail turns left where the AT goes straight at a tree with a white blaze. The trail switchbacks left around smaller boulders and parallels the overlook spur road back to the opposite end of the parking area from where the hike started.

All along the northern part of the Parkway, the Appalachian Trail offers aimless out and back wanders and even multi-day backpacking trips.

For a longer hike that follows an original section of the Appalachian Trail, start to the north at the AT trailhead just west of the Parkway at Petites Gap (Milepost 71). The trail climbs past a wet-weather spring on the left at 0.9 mile, traverses the peak of Thunder Ridge at 2.1 miles, and then descends to the overlook viewpoint at 3.3 miles. Retracing your steps creates a 6.6-mile out-and-back hike that passes through Thunder Ridge Wilderness to reach the Parkway viewpoint.

14 Apple Orchard Falls Trail and Cornelius Creek Circuits

Milepost 78.4

The Forest Service is justly proud of this waterfall circuit that features two scenic, well-maintained National Recreation Trails and spectacular Apple Orchard Falls.

Parkway mile: 78.4
Distance: 1.5- or 2.8-mile round-trip day hikes; circuits of 6.1 and 7.6 miles
Difficulty: Moderately strenuous for the easiest falls hikes from the Parkway and FSR 3034; strenuous for the others

Elevation gain: 600 feet for the easiest waterfall hike; 2,000 feet for the lengthier circuit
Maps: *USGS Arnold Valley*; no Parkway map available

Finding the trailhead: From the Parkway, start at the Sunset Field Overlook at Milepost 78.4 (GPS: 37.507774 / -79.524103). For the shortest hike, start on Apple Tree Road (FSR 3034), an easy 4.9-mile drive from the Parkway. Leave north end of Sunset Field Overlook and descend on FSR 812. Turn left in 2.8 miles onto FSR 3034; the trailhead is another 2.1 miles (GPS: 37.520897 / -79.539608).

To hike the circuits from the FSR 59 trailhead, start at the lower trailhead. Take the route to Apple Tree Road, but pass that turnoff and stay on FSR 812. At a T junction go left onto FSR 768. At the next junction turn left again onto FSR 59, which ends at the trailhead.

The Hikes

This figure-eight trail system explores a noteworthy north-facing watershed of old-growth forest below the highest peak in this part of the Blue Ridge. It's a best-kept secret for backpackers and birders. Neotropical songbirds such as the ovenbird, red-eyed vireo, and scarlet tanager can be seen and heard here. (The rare Peaks of Otter salamander is also a resident.) In the early 1990s the Forest Service designated 1,825 acres as a Special Management Area; the trails were upgraded and the focus shifted away from potential timber harvesting to enhancing recreation and wildlife.

From Apple Tree Road

The most direct route to the falls departs from the trailhead sign on Apple Tree Road. Take the 400-foot Apple Orchard Spur across two bridges and go left (southeast) onto the Apple Orchard Falls Trail. The forest here is alive with birdsong and the sound of water. It's a stiff but relatively short climb of 0.75 mile (1.5 miles round-trip) and 600 vertical feet to the falls. The stone steps get really steep as you near a wooden bridge that spans the base of the impressive falls, highest in the Glenwood Ranger District. The USDA Forest Service logo artfully adorns a bench on the bridge.

Apple Orchard Falls is a nice day hike and the heart of a bigger backpacking circuit.

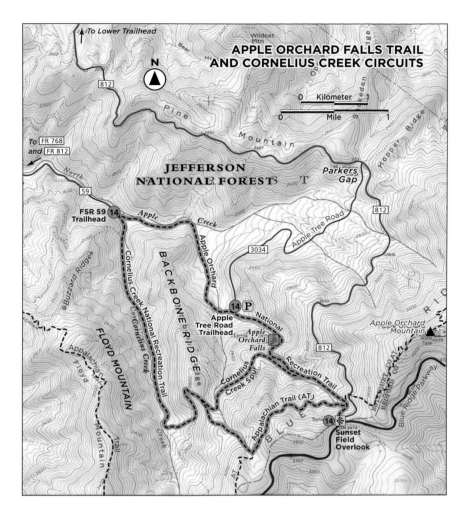

From the Parkway

Pass the "Apple Orchard Falls Trail" sign on the paved path and follow the blue-blazed route.

Cross the Appalachian Trail at 0.2 mile as you head northwest. At 0.8 mile a grassy woods road to the left leads to the Cornelius Creek National Recreation Trail and is part of a few loop hikes. Keep right, there's a sheltering overhang just before the drop to the falls starts at 1.2 miles. Turn around at 1.4 miles, the observation bridge below the falls. Return to the Parkway for a 2.8-mile round-trip with 1,000 feet of rise on the way back.

Key Points from the Parkway

0.2 Cross the Appalachian Trail.

0.8 Grassy woods road of Cornelius Creek Spur leads left to Cornelius Creek Trail.

1.4 Reach views at base of falls.

From FSR 59

A few day-hike or backpack circuits are possible. Starting at the FSR 59 trailhead and going southward, the Cornelius Creek Trail makes a gradual climb. Trails in this area follow old logging roads established before 1917, when the land was owned by the Virginia Lumber and Extract Company. The best day hike is a 6.1-mile waterfall circuit that goes up (south) Cornelius Creek, turns left (easterly) onto the Cornelius Creek Spur (a grassy fire road), then makes another left (northwest) onto the Apple Orchard Falls Trail to pass the falls on the way back to the parking area. This hike gains 1,400 feet.

A longer loop stays right at the grassy Cornelius Creek Spur, climbs to the AT, and goes left (northeasterly). Turn left (northwest) again onto the Apple Orchard Falls Trail. After passing the falls, arrive back at FSR 59 for a 7.6-mile hike (with 2,000 feet of elevation gain).

Campsites are particularly plentiful along this hike. Hikers could start at the Parkway—where it would similarly be best to walk the loop in a counterclockwise direction by descending past the falls northward and going up (south) Cornelius Creek.

Cupped high above surrounding valleys, Abbott Lake and Peaks of Otter Lodge share a stunning setting. CAMERON DAVIDSON

15 Peaks of Otter

Mileposts 83.1–85.9

The Parkway's 4,200-acre Peaks of Otter Recreation Area is one of the most highly recommended places to spend a day or stop for the night. This lofty valley, formed by the stunningly pointed summit of Sharp Top and the bulk of Flat Top, is unique along the Parkway. Its facilities and colorful history are part of the appeal. Its name probably derives from the proximity of the Otter River.

Peaks of Otter Lodge, one of two concessionaire-operated accommodations on the Parkway, is open year-round for lodging and dining, with special buffets on Friday night and Sunday. Facilities operated May through October by the Park Service include a campground, picnic area, gift shop (where Sharp Top bus tickets are available), visitor center, nature center, and restored mountain farm.

Winter access is good because VA 43 is the best route between I-81, west of the Blue Ridge near Buchanan, and Bedford, east of the mountains. That link requires the highway not only to cross the Parkway but actually follow it for 5 miles in a "staggered crossing." Thus the Peaks of Otter stretch of the Parkway is plowed even when the rest of the road is closed due to snowfall.

Archaeological work has established that Native Americans hunted elk thousands of years ago on the fringe of a boggy meadow that is now the site of twenty-four-acre Abbott Lake, the Peaks of Otter's scenic centerpiece and the primary focus for guests at the lodge.

The land was first cleared by European settlers in 1766; by the 1830s an "ordinary" was established that offered lodging and dining to travelers crossing the Blue Ridge. You can still see Polly Woods Ordinary between the Peaks of Otter Picnic Area and Abbott Lake. Early tourist hotels, ancestors of the current Peaks of Otter Lodge, opened as early as 1857.

In 1820 a group of rowdies spent a few days trying to roll one of Sharp Top's summit boulders into the valley. They eventually succeeded with a little dynamite. When the Washington Monument was going up, local officials took a chunk of that boulder in 1852 and embedded it into the obelisk, where its inscription can still be read—"From Otter's

Peaks of Otter claims one of many visitor centers that engage and orient Parkway visitors.

summit, Virginia's Loftiest peak, To crown a monument, To Virginia's noblest son." Of course, Sharp Top is not the state's highest peak—that's Mount Rogers (5,729 feet) in southwest Virginia—but such is the impressive appeal of pyramidal mountains. Nor does the rock actually crown the Washington Monument. It rests in the west wall at the twelfth stairway landing.

By the 1930s a community of more than twenty self-reliant families populated the high valley, including the last of the Johnson family, for whom the Johnson Farm Trail is named. A school and a church stood near the current site of Peaks of Otter Lodge. The families were mostly subsistence farmers, but the tourist traffic up the road to the Sharp Top summit and to the Hotel Mons (the site is visible on the Farm Trail) supplied cash for the locals who had jobs.

The Great Depression ended all that. The Johnson Farm, which got its start in 1852, was sold in 1941, changed hands again, and was then purchased by the National Park Service. It deteriorated until the 1950s, when it was stabilized; it was restored in 1968. The interpretive loop of the Johnson Farm Trail is one of the best places on the Parkway to learn about the lives of the people who wrested subsistence from the rocky Appalachian soil. Warm-weather living-history programs here are among the Parkway's most engaging and extensive. Summer programs also take place at Polly Woods Ordinary. (See the Abbott Lake Trail option for this hike.)

Early settlers generated some income from the primitive tourism economy created by the area's long history of mountain hostelries. Some mountaineers worked in the lodging establishments, and Peaks of Otter farmers grew the produce served in the dining rooms. Built in 1964, Peaks of Otter Lodge continues that long tradition.

When the lodge was built, the boggy mountain meadow was turned into Abbott Lake. This scenic jewel is appropriately named for Stanley W. Abbott, the Parkway's first landscape architect and the man largely responsible for designing what is today considered to be the quintessential scenic road. Ironically, today no one would even propose flooding a high-mountain bog.

Option 1: Fallingwater Cascades Trail

A waterfall loop descends off the Parkway in a region known more for its peaks.

Parkway mile: 83.1
Distance: 1.6-mile loop
Difficulty: Moderate
Elevation gain: 382 feet

Maps: *USGS Peaks of Otter*; Parkway handout map, available at the visitor center, lodge, and online at nps.gov/blri/planyourvisit/peaks-otter-trails.htm

Finding the trailhead: Park in either the Falling Cascades Parking Area (Milepost 83.1; GPS: 37.473119 / -79.580623) or the Flat Top Parking Area (Milepost 83.5; GPS: 37.468392 / -79.580488).

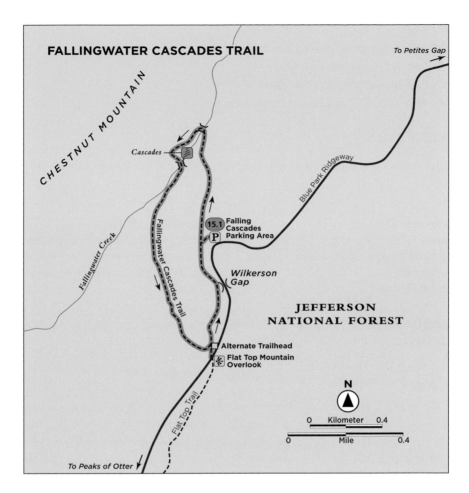

The Hike

From Falling Cascades Parking Area, turn right down the rhododendron-bordered National Recreation Trail. After a steeper stretch and steps, Fallingwater Creek appears, tumbling downward to the cascades. Cross a bridge over the creek at 0.3 mile and go left, descending along the lush streamside through hemlocks, with hardwoods on higher slopes. A few benches offer rest spots on this steeply dropping part of the path, with numerous nice views back uphill to the falls. Pass the base of the cascade and go left back across the creek on another bridge at 0.6 mile. A backtrack return to the car from this point nets a 1.2-mile hike, about 0.4 mile shorter than taking the full loop.

Continuing on the loop, climb above the cleft of the falls past a bench, gradually entering the higher hardwood forest. At 1.0 mile you can go right on a side trail to the Flat Top Parking Area. Continue straight the last 0.6 mile to the Falling Cascades Parking Area.

Key Points

0.3 Cross bridge spanning Fallingwater Creek.

0.6 Recross the creek below the falls.

1.0 Pass side trail to Flat Top Parking Area.

1.6 Arrive back at Falling Cascades Parking Area.

Option 2: Flat Top Trail

A quiet, uncrowded hike takes you to the highest point at the Peaks of Otter—4,001 feet.

Parkway mile: 83.5

Distance: 4.4 miles end to end; 5.8 miles round-trip to the peak from the north, 3.2 miles from the south

Difficulty: Strenuous

Elevation gain: 1,391 feet

Maps: *USGS Peaks of Otter*; Parkway handout map, available at the visitor center, lodge, and online at nps.gov/blri/planyourvisit/peaks-otter-trails.htm

Finding the trailhead: Park in the Flat Top Parking Area at Milepost 83.5 (GPS: 37.468392 / -79.580488).

The Hike

Flat Top (4,001 feet) is the "other" summit of the Peaks of Otter. It's rounded compared with Sharp Top and was once actually called Round Top. Sharp Top's pointed popularity with hikers is due in part to the striking conical countenance it exhibits from a distance. It is stunning views of that pyramidal peak that make Flat Top a highly recommended hike (especially in winter). Flat Top Trail is a quieter, far less frequented path than the one to the summit of Sharp Top. Like the Fallingwater Cascades Trail, the Flat Top hike is a National Recreation Trail.

The crest of the mountain is littered with many crags and outcrops. A few, including the Pinnacle and Cross Rock, are named and accessible on the trail. The Pinnacle and the mountain summit boast the best views.

The easiest hike to the peak rises from the Flat Top Parking Area north of the visitor center/concession area. The Parkway itself is higher in that area—and therefore closer to the summit—although the trail is longer. You could also start at the parking area in the Peaks of Otter Picnic Area (see the Abbott Lake option for how to find the trailhead) if you want a greater elevation gain in a shorter distance.

Leaving the Flat Top Parking Area, the trail skirts along the Parkway boundary before beginning a 2.0-mile switchbacking ascent of the mountain's north side. At about 2.2 miles a side trail goes left to Cross Rock, then you pass the Pinnacle. At 2.9 miles the rocky summit provides panoramic views in all directions. Retrace your steps from here, or keep going another 0.1 mile for another nice view of Sharp Top to the southeast.

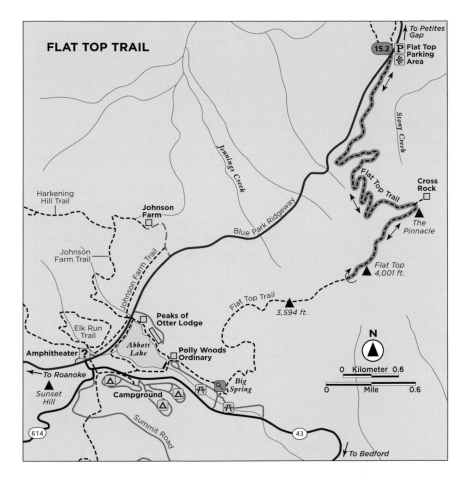

From that last view, 3.0 miles from your trailhead starting point, the trail descends steeply in spots another 1.5 miles down to the picnic area at 4.5 miles. This traverse is a nice hike if you can arrange two cars.

Key Points

2.2 Side trail to Cross Rock.

2.9 Summit views from Flat Top.

3.0 Another nice view of Sharp Top.

Option 3: Abbott Lake Trail

One of the Parkway's best lakeside strolls or cross-country ski tours. The only paved, fully ADA-accessible trail on the Parkway in Virginia. This is also one of the Peaks of Otter's TRACK Trail interpretive paths. Visit kidsinparks.com/peaks-otter.

Parkway mile: 85.6

Distance: 1.6-mile loop from picnic area; 1.7-mile loop from visitor center; 1.0-mile loop around lake

Difficulty: Easy

Elevation gain: Negligible

Maps: *USGS Peaks of Otter*; Parkway handout map available online and at the visitor center, lodge, and online at nps.gov/blri/planyourvisit/peaks-otter-trails.htm

Finding the trailheads: To start at the Peaks of Otter Picnic Area, turn east on VA 43 opposite the visitor center. Take the next left into the picnic area. At the T junction, park across the road at the Flat Top Trail Parking Area, or go left and park beside Polly Woods Ordinary (GPS: 37.444852 / -79.601388).

For a shorter walk, park at Peaks of Otter Lodge; turn into the lodge and take the next right into the small lakeshore parking area by the first building. At busier times of year, you may have to park elsewhere in the lodge lot and take a paved path to the lakeshore. You may also park at the Peaks of Otter Visitor Center on the Parkway. Leave the visitor center on the path north to the Johnson Farm and take the right under the Parkway to Peaks of Otter Lodge (GPS: 37.448447 / -79.605025).

The Hike

Abbott Lake was once a high-elevation mountain bog and a favored Native American hunting area—elk, bison, and other game were attracted to the watery site. Today

There are inspiring views of conical Sharp Top from the Abbott Lake Trail.

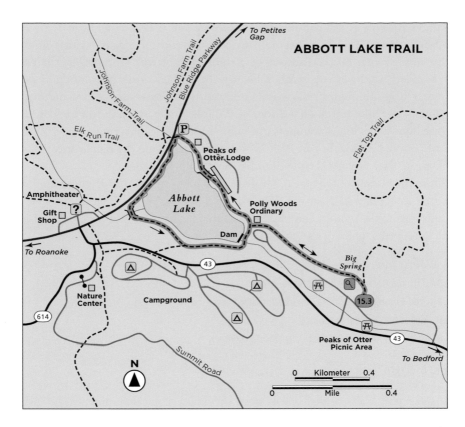

the lake still attracts plentiful wildlife. This is a great place for bird watching—if you can divert your eyes from the knock-your-socks-off view of Sharp Top.

Sharp Top is so close and conical that the view is truly dramatic—especially with autumn color or hoarfrost in winter. It's great for very young, elderly, and even mobility-challenged hikers—not to mention cross-country skiers—because this trail is paved and extremely easy (hence suggested starting points that add to the distance).

The best starting point is the picnic area. The Flat Top Trail takes off from the parking area, so walk up the picnic area road 25 yards and take the trail into the woods by Big Spring, a reliable water source used for centuries by travelers traversing the Blue Ridge. The path passes Polly Woods Ordinary, a modest cabin used as a rustic inn by owner Mary "Polly" Wood between 1830 and 1855. Appropriately, given your destination, the building was originally located up near the lake and served travelers on the Buchanan to Liberty (early name of Bedford, Virginia) Turnpike. Wood's daughter ran the inn for five more years after Polly's death in 1855.

In 0.3 mile you'll turn right onto the paved Abbott Lake Trail and head northwest along the lakeshore. Cross a bridge at 0.4 mile and veer out into the lake on a promontory with benches and great views. Pass the lodge and the small parking area by the last building to reach the main trailhead for the TRACK Trail at 0.7 mile. This is the preferred start for those focusing on the paved path or using the interpretive brochures available at this parking spot. Continue and the lake trail bears left where the Johnson Farm Trail branches right to pass under the Parkway (with a link left to the visitor center on the Parkway or a right to the farm). Continuing, the paved path wanders southwesterly across a boardwalk to a waterside view, then wanders the water's edge through open meadows dotted with dogwoods, cedars, and cattails. You'll cross the inlet brook on a bridge at 0.9 mile and pass a trail to Peaks of Otter Campground at 1.1 miles (campers can come in from this direction). Cross the dam and at 1.3 miles turn right past Polly Woods Ordinary along the picnic area that you came in on. Back at your car, the round-trip is about 1.6 miles.

From the visitor center, hike 0.3 mile toward Johnson Farm and, where the Johnson Farm Trail loops left, take the right toward the lodge and go beneath the road via an underpass to the trailhead brochure kiosk. Turn right at the Abbott Lake Trail. This route is about 1.7 miles.

Key Points from Picnic Area

0.3 Turn right onto Abbott Lake Trail.

0.7 Trail to Johnson Farm Trail and visitor center branches to the right.

0.9 Cross bridge over inlet brook.

1.3 Turn right to trailhead past Polly Woods Ordinary.

Option 4: Sharp Top Trail

This steep trail leads to great views from the rocky, conical summit of 3,875-foot Sharp Top.

Parkway mile: 85.9

Distance: 1.5 miles one-way with bus shuttle; 3.0 miles out and back

Difficulty: Moderate if you ride the bus up and hike down; strenuous from the bottom

Elevation gain: 1,340 feet

Maps: USGS Peaks of Otter; Parkway handout map, available at the visitor center, lodge, and online at nps.gov/blri/planyourvisit/peaks -otter-trails.htm

Finding the trailhead: The trail begins near Milepost 86, on the opposite side of the Parkway from the Peaks of Otter Visitor Center and beside the Nature Center building (GPS: 37.443170 / -79.609312).

The Hike

Sharp Top is one of Virginia's sentinel summits and a major landmark of the Blue Ridge range. Its prominent conical peak, capped by rounded boulders, is visible for miles—from foothills far to the east to the Great Valley on the western side of the mountains. The views from the peak survey that same striking domain, making it possible to look down on springtime from a still-frosty peak or see summer in the valley while immersed in colorful fall foliage.

Sharp Top's summit is intensively developed with stone steps and walkways that lead to unmatched views. SARAH HAUSER, VIRGINIA TOURISM CORPORATION

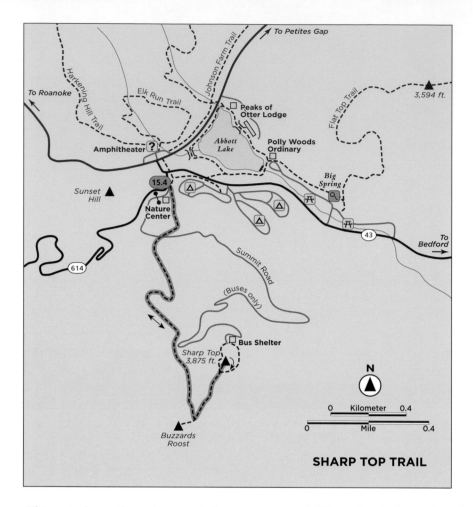

This popular trail can be crowded on summer and fall weekends. Even though this hike is steep, it is often made by families and older persons intent on an adventure. Part of its popularity stems from the fact that a National Park Service shuttle bus ferries riders to the summit of Sharp Top for a small fee, making it easy for people to hike down who might not otherwise make the climb up. Ask about current rates and departure times at the Gift Shop where bus tickets are purchased.

The trail leaves the Nature Center, crosses the summit road used by buses, and switchbacks through a deciduous forest before reaching a junction at 1.2 miles. This 0.4-mile side trail is a half-hour round-trip to Buzzards Roost—a rocky crag that alternates between looking like a large foot or a dragon's head, depending on your vantage point. Here's the place to picnic if the surplus of humanity at the summit isn't for you.

Just above the junction, the trail to the top reaches its steepest section and actually climbs steps cut into solid rock. All of that is just preparation for the summit, a jumble of house-size boulders. Another side path descends to the mountaintop shuttle bus stop, and other highly developed trails lead to viewpoints that take in the entire 360-degree view. A large summit shelter is on hand in case of inclement weather, which can include direct lightning strikes. No camping is permitted in the shelter. Hikers should retrace their steps downhill on the trail or buy a bus ticket from the driver and ride down—walking is not allowed on the road.

Key Points

0.2 Cross summit road.

1.2 Junction; trail on right to Buzzards Roost.

1.5 Summit.

Option 5: Johnson Farm, Harkening Hill, and Elk Run Loop Trails

These scenic, short to moderate-length interpretive trails impart a real sense of how Southern Appalachian mountaineers lived. The outer loop of the Johnson Farm and Harkening Hill Trails roll the human and natural history of the area into one wonderful walk.

Parkway mile: 85.9
Distance: Johnson Farm Trail, 2.1 miles; Harkening Hill Trail, 3.3 to 3.9 miles; Elk Run Trail, about 0.8-mile circuit hike
Difficulty: Easy to moderate for Johnson Farm; strenuous for Harkening Hill; easy for Elk Run Loop Trail

Elevation gain: 814 feet for Harkening Hill
Maps: USGS Peaks of Otter; Parkway handout map, available at the visitor center, lodge, and online at nps.gov/blri/planyourvisit/peaks -otter-trails.htm

Finding the trailhead: All three of these interconnected loops start at the Peaks of Otter Visitor Center (GPS: 37.445629 / -79.609315). An alternative is to park at the lodge and start the Johnson Farm Trail, a designated TRACK Trail interpretive path, from there where brochures are available. (The Johnson Farm Hide 'n Seek and Living in Appalachia brochures seem most pertinent to the farm experience, though nature-oriented pamphlets are available too. This and the Abbott Lake Trail are popular—consider downloading your brochures in advance at kidsinparks.com/.)

The Hike

The Harkening Hill and Johnson Farm Trails are interconnected, which creates an interesting situation: You can be on a section of two different hikes at once. Only the Elk Run Interpretive Loop is a trail unto itself. All hikes are best started from the Peaks of Otter Visitor Center. Together or separately, they offer real insight into the lifestyle of Southern Appalachian mountaineers.

The easy-to-moderate Johnson Farm hike starts at the northern end of the visitor center parking lot (except for TRACK Trail hikers starting by the lodge). Take the scenic roadside path toward Peaks of Otter Lodge and reach a trail junction in about 0.3 mile.

Flowers bloom beside the Harkening Hill Trail as it climbs above Johnson Farm.

The first trail heading uphill to the left is best as the return of the Johnson Farm Loop. Take a left at the second sign—the trail to the farm is flatter that way—and head out into the grassy meadow. (The trail that goes right leads under the Parkway to the lodge and Abbott Lake—head the short distance that way to grab some TRACK Trail brochures.)

Bear right in the meadow along the trees past a sign about the Hotel Mons, the post–Polly Woods Ordinary/pre–Peaks of Otter Lodge summer resort that operated here from 1857 to the late 1930s. Pass a trail sign farther down the meadow and enter the woods at a small bridge. The trail rises and goes left on a road grade into the farm at just under 1.0 mile from the parking area. If the farmhouse is closed, a sign outside has pictures, an interior layout of the building, and a map of the grounds. If the farmhouse is open—this is how the Waltons would have lived in the 1920s.

Leave the old Johnson place one of two ways. The easiest walk is to retrace your steps for the more gradual route. Or leave the house past the front porch and crop plantings and head uphill and left into the meadow beyond to the Johnson Farm return trail. At 1.3 miles the return trail goes straight at a junction where the Harkening Hill Trail turns right. (Go right for the 3.9-mile perimeter circuit formed by the Johnson Farm and Harkening Hill Trails.)

Stay on the Johnson Farm Trail and descend to the first junction you passed at the start of the hike. A right at the junction returns to the visitor center in about the same distance as the other route—around 2.0 miles.

The longest walk is the Harkening Hill Trail—you may choose to walk 3.4 miles (going left at the first sign from the visitor center on the Johnson Farm Trail) or about 3.9 miles (via the longer outer loop of Johnson Farm). This trail explores the now-wooded, wildflower-filled forest that in the 1930s was cultivated fields and road grades between the Johnson Farm and the peak directly above it—Harkening Hill (3,372 feet). The hike is rated strenuous, but it's only moderately so—800 feet of elevation gain from either direction.

The Johnson Farm Loop affords the best start for this hike by adding human context to a setting returning to nature. Whichever side of the farm loop you start on, branch off onto the Harkening Hill Trail. You'll pass through two small meadows at 0.5 mile. A side trail to Balance Rock—a boulder perched on a natural pedestal— heads left at about 0.7 mile. At 0.8 mile above your turnoff from Johnson Farm, you've slipped onto national forest land to the limited rocky viewpoint of Harkening Hill (2.1 miles via the eastern side of the Johnson Farm Loop, 1.6 miles on the west)

The trail undulates down the broad, boulder-strewn summit ridge through scenic open woods with a number of descents, some of them steep. There's a sharp ridgeline and grass-fringed uphill a mile below the peak (3.1 miles from the visitor center via the east leg of the farm trail, 2.6 miles via the west). The trail descends by switchbacks then turns right between the rows of amphitheater seats through the visitor center breezeway at 3.9 miles (3.4 miles using the west leg).

The shortest hike in the three-trail network near the Peaks of Otter Visitor Center is the easy 0.8-mile Elk Run Loop Trail, which starts in the breezeway at the end

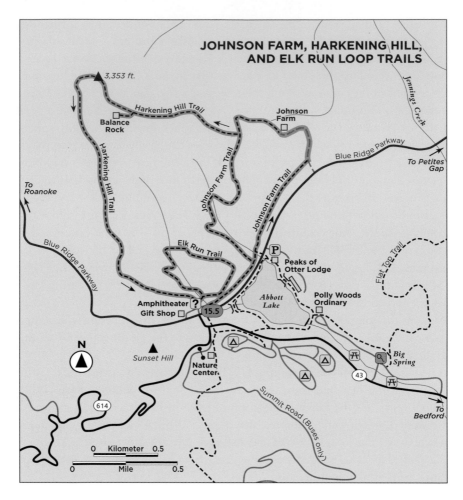

JOHNSON FARM, HARKENING HILL,
AND ELK RUN LOOP TRAILS

of the Harkening Hill Loop. The interpretive signs of this educational nature trail tell of the ecological interaction between plants and animals. Follow the signs through the gap in the visitor center and bear right, coming to the first of many benches in 0.1 mile. An old grade becomes the path on its rise to a cemetery, at 0.7 mile, before dipping back to the visitor center.

Key Points for Harkening Hill Circuit Hike

0.3 Take the second left on the Johnson Farm Trail.

1.0 Johnson Farm.

1.3 Turn right on the Harkening Hill Trail.

2.0 Trail to Balance Rock.

2.1 Summit of Harkening Hill.

3.1 Sharp ridgeline before switchbacks.

3.9 Peaks of Otter Visitor Center.

16 Roanoke Area Trails

Mileposts 110.6–120.4

There are two truly urban areas on the Parkway—Roanoke, Virginia, and Asheville, North Carolina. Purists may be tempted to see them as interruptions in the natural experience of the Parkway, but these are worthwhile Appalachian cities.

Heading south, Roanoke is the first and larger of the two. Unlike the more southerly Asheville, where the Parkway plummets 3,000 feet down to pass the city then gains it all back on the climb beyond, Roanoke embraces the Parkway's glide through town, albeit with increasing suburban development. And in a situation very unlike Asheville, where Parkway facilities are located at high elevation well outside the city, until recently Roanoke had a bona fide Parkway campground where you could camp very close to town. Alas, Roanoke Mountain Campground and the city itself are low enough in elevation that neither basks in the cool climate of higher parts of the Parkway. The former Roanoke Mountain Campground has been turned into a picnic area.

Nevertheless, the spur road from the Parkway to the picnic area leads quickly and directly into downtown and also passes Mill Mountain Park—a Roanoke city park

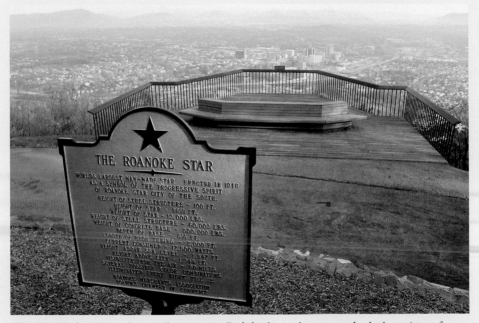

The Star Trail in Roanoke's Mill Mountain Park leads to what are surely the best views of a large urban area along the Parkway.

with a nature center, a great summit view of the city from two overlooks, and a small zoo. There's even a trail that makes the overlooks a nice stroll. This is the best view of the city, not to mention the famous illuminated star that shines from the mountaintop. (The road is open to the star each night till 11 p.m.)

You can stroll the paths around the star to see worthwhile city vistas, but be aware that like many urban areas, Roanoke is expanding its urban trail and greenway system. There are 10 miles of trails and a variety of hikes and mountain biking tours in Mill Mountain Park in addition to the walks featured here, so explore online or get up to date at the Discovery Center. And there are also 18 miles of greenways that link Mill Mountain to downtown and other parts of the city. Two sections of the volunteer-built Roanoke Valley Horse Trail also follow the Parkway for those who want a short stroll and don't mind reminders of equine passage.

The best part: Via the Mill Mountain Spur Road, head down the hill and you can be eating sushi ten minutes from Roanoke Mountain Picnic Area. The Historic Farmers' Market District contains a long list of attractions, including Center in the Square—a concentrated culture fix that combines the Art Museum of Western Virginia, the History Museum of Western Virginia, and the Mill Mountain Theatre. There's a wealth of shops and dining spots in the City Market Building, the heart of this compact, accessible city center. The outstanding Roanoke Transportation Museum is nearby, as is an urban interpretive walk along the railroad tracks that have made the city a hub.

That status may be why Virginia's earliest continuously operating farmers' market (1886)—and still one of the state's best (closed Sunday)—is a lively street scene in the heart of downtown. You will have no better meal in a Parkway campground than one based on produce fresh from Roanoke's Farmers' Market. Crafts and mountain music are often part of special events.

Roanoke has plenty of motels and B&Bs, and the city's resurgent landmark hotel is a special experience. The Hotel Roanoke, built in 1882, like Asheville's Grove Park Inn, is the quintessential mountain city hotel—that sits at the center of two greenways with easy walks and bike rides that include the shoreline Roanoke River Greenway. The hotel almost died in the late 1980s, but a public/private partnership between Roanoke civic leaders and Virginia Polytechnic Institute (VPI) has kept this grande dame of the Blue Ridge alive. It regularly earns accolades for some of Roanoke's finest. A pedestrian bridge takes you from the hotel across the tracks to the heart of downtown in a five-minute stroll.

Option 1: Stewarts Knob Trail

A stroll away from the north edge of the Stewart's Knob overlook leads to a broadened horizon over Roanoke.

Parkway mile: 110.6
Distance: 0.15 mile out and back
Difficulty: Easy
Elevation gain: Negligible

Maps: *USGS Stewartsville*; Parkway's Roanoke Valley Trails overview map available online at nps.gov/blri/planyourvisit/roanoke-valley-trails.htm

Finding the trailhead: The trail leaves the Stewarts Knob Overlook parking area in the turn between the upper and lower lots (GPS: 37.297488 / -79.872083).

The Hike

The Roanoke Valley Horse Trail connects to this path so be sure not to get siphoned away from this short leg-stretcher. Leave the overlook slightly uphill through a lush forest understory. Stay to the right where the prominent Roanoke Valley Horse Trail goes left. The trail switchbacks right then left to a bench at a split-rail fence overlook perched above the spur road that leads to the overlook. Roanoke lies in the distance. The buildings are more impressive in morning light before you set off into the Parkway's green corridor. (For a more imposing city view, see the Mill Mountain Park option.)

Option 2: Roanoke River Self-Guiding Trail

This trail is actually two—a steep fishing trail to the riverside and a loop that offers a view of the river and a hemlock-dotted forest.

Parkway mile: 114.9
Distance: 0.4 mile out and back for the fishing trail; 0.6 mile out and back for a view trail; 0.9-mile loop that includes the view
Difficulty: Moderate

Elevation gain: About 100 feet from the river
Maps: *USGS Stewartsville* and *Hardy*; Parkway's Roanoke Valley Trails overview map available online at nps.gov/blri/planyourvisit/roanoke-valley-trails.htm

Finding the trailhead: Park at the Roanoke River Parking Area and take the paved path from the middle of the lot (GPS: 37.252543 / -79.872106).

The Hike

Leave the lot on the gradual paved descent. A sign warns hikers that the river's boulders are treacherously slick and that strong currents can batter a person to death against the rocks. The now-earthen trail becomes nicely benched through scenic pines to a junction. Left, the blue-blazed fishing trail descends to the riverside. The white-blazed loop goes right.

Consider a short detour left on the nicely maintained upper portion of the fishing trail to an easel that shows early photos of the Niagara Power Plant, visible across the river. The dam and plant were built in 1906, and today, the sign says, it's the smallest hydroelectric plant in the country's electric power system. The plant brought the first electricity to Roanoke. Below the easel, the steeper, rockier trail terminates at the river.

Going right on the loop trail, pass under the Parkway bridge to a trail junction where steps descend left to a fern-flanked observation point overlooking a quiet, rocky spot in the river.

Back on the main trail, continue into a mixed evergreen and deciduous forest where you'll find black locust, white pine, tulip tree, eastern hemlock, and others. The wide, nicely graded, and scenic trail bends to the right high above the river to pass a bench then cross a small bridge and go left, past another bench within earshot of the rapids below.

The trail crosses another little bridge and switchbacks right on the return route to cross a third bridge (on the same stream you crossed on the last bridge, just higher up). A plaque calls humus—decayed trees and other vegetation—the most valuable ingredient of soil. Ferns line the green forest trail; a bench appears and you're back at the junction. Take a left and return to the parking area.

A walk to the river on the fishing trail is about 0.4 mile; it's about 0.6 mile to the viewpoint at the start of the loop. The entire loop is about 0.9 mile.

Key Points

0.1 Junction—fishing trail to the left; loop to the right.

0.2 Side trail to view above river on loop.

0.4 Rejoin loop and go left.

Option 3: Roanoke Mountain Summit Trail

A short loop hike traverses a craggy summit.

Parkway mile: 120.3
Distance: 0.3-mile loop
Difficulty: Moderate
Elevation gain: 60 feet

Maps: *USGS Garden City*; Parkway's Roanoke Valley Trails overview map available online at nps.gov/blri/planyourvisit/roanoke-valley-trails .htm

Finding the trailhead: Take the Roanoke Mountain Loop Road to the top and start at either of the summit parking lots (GPS: 37.211223 / -79.935721).

The Hike

Take one of only two mountain-climbing motor roads on the Parkway to reach this trail. At the other, Sharp Top at Peaks of Otter, only Parkway buses are permitted to drive to the summit.

At Roanoke Mountain, a 4.0-mile, mostly one-way loop road leads to a rewarding path across the summit at 2,193 feet. On the way up, a variety of overlooks are worth a look.

For a more adventurous hike, enter the woods from the upper lot by the sign to walk the loop clockwise. Descend through a boulder garden on a switchbacking

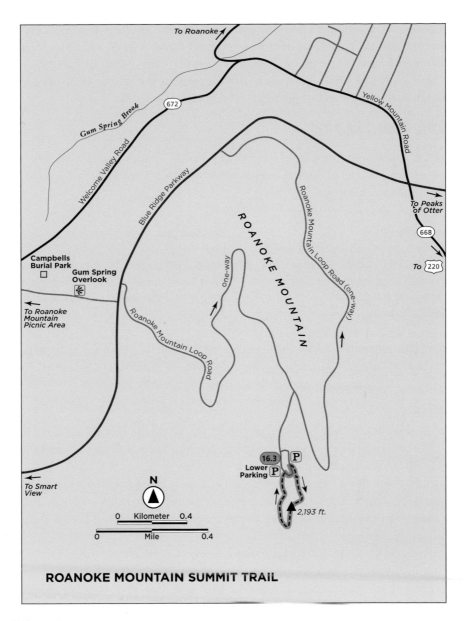

ROANOKE MOUNTAIN SUMMIT TRAIL

flight of stone steps with a handrail. The trail dips through a dramatic little gap, goes left of crags up more flights of stone steps, and then weaves back and forth on more stone stairs to artfully ascend through the summit crags.

Descending across the rounded crest of the mountain, the loop trail returns back into the gap on an easy, pine needle–covered tread opposite the rocks you climbed up earlier. From here, the gap actually appears to be one of those craterlike quarry pits you'll also see at Roanoke Mountain Picnic Area on the Chestnut Ridge Trail and the nature trail. Your path rises gently to the lower of the summit parking areas.

For an easier walk, start from the lower parking lot (the first you enter, on the right) and take the paved trail into the woods. The rise is gentler in that direction (counterclockwise), and most of the flights of stone steps—all with handrails—are downhill. Only one flight leads back up to the upper lot. For an easy walk, just go out and back on this right side of the loop and avoid the stone steps.

Option 4: Chestnut Ridge Trail

A variety of different loops travel on generally gradual grades through oak and pine forests. A few hikes reveal bizarre topography, now nicely reforested, that was created by early mining operations.

Parkway mile: 120.4
Distance: 5.4-mile loop, which can become loops of 2.5 and 3.4 miles. The picnic area has a small, paved, ridgetop trail that offers a barrier-free stroll of 0.2 mile.
Difficulty: Moderate

Elevation gain: About 320 feet for the entire loop
Maps: USGS *Garden City*; Parkway's Roanoke Valley Trails overview map available online at nps.gov/blri/planyourvisit/roanoke-valley-trails.htm

Finding the trailhead: Leave the Parkway on the Mill Mountain Spur Road and go 1.1 miles to the trailhead at Chestnut Ridge Overlook. (GPS: 37.228443 / -79.950713)

The Hikes

The Chestnut Ridge Trail is the single part of the 12.0-mile Roanoke Valley Horse Trail that will most interest hikers (hence most of the horse trail isn't covered in this book). This red-blazed, 5.4-mile trail makes an elongated loop around the Roanoke Mountain Picnic Area (once a campground). Its most interesting feature is evidence of quarrying. This trail system is complex—and both the Parkway's trail map and the sign map at the overlook leave much to the imagination. Keep your eye on the map in this guide.

Starting at the Chestnut Ridge Overlook, a trail goes left and right just off the left side of the parking area at a trail map sign. Right (southeast), it connects down to the loop trail; left (northwest), it crosses the Mill Mountain Spur Road to the picnic area and connects to the loop as well as the network of paved "transportation trails" in this one-time campground. That connection permits you to turn the large loop into at least two smaller ones.

Go right (south) from the overlook, then turn immediately left (east) at a signed junction. The nicely benched trail rises gradually with brief steeper sections and rocky treadway that reflects use by horses.

The trail swings out southeast around a long ridge above a reservoir and then turns northwest around the ridge, following contours. It turns northeast along the Mill Mountain Spur Road before switchbacking lower at about 0.7 mile. The trail rounds a knob before swinging left into the gap where Yellow Mountain Road crosses the ridge. As the trail approaches the road at 1.6 miles, there's a junction. Avoid the right down to Yellow Mountain Road. Go up and left to cross the spur road at small posts with hiker symbols. You'll reenter the woods and go left again on the main trail. Here again a trail comes in from the roadside. Don't be confused. The paths permit riders to walk under the bridge and avoid crossing the spur.

Swinging in and out of the drainages below the spur road, the trail pulls away and rises. Again side trails crop up—left to former campsites; right to residences largely out of sight. Bearing left (west) to miss the Parkway boundary, the trail crosses the ridge at a trail sign at 2.3 miles. A left here goes to the picnic area through pleasant piney woods. Across that road it becomes a paved "transportation trail" and passes a comfort station (and can connect back to the Chestnut Ridge Overlook—see the map).

Pass the sign; other trails go left and right as the path swings in and out along the contours below the south side of the picnic area. Atop the long ridge above, a paved path splits into a tiny end loop that would be suitable as a barrier-free stroll. (Park by the comfort station on the right—see the map.)

The trail swings deeply into drainages. At the second one, a sign points left to an amphitheater at 2.9 miles.

Passing the amphitheater, the trail swings out around another ridge to a trail sign in another turn at 3.1 miles. To return to the overlook, go left here on the obvious road-grade trail. At the next trail sign, the paved path from the amphitheater area crosses the trail (left to the amphitheater, right to a picnic area road). Go straight on the old grade trail—it crosses the road, then the spur road, to the overlook for a 3.4-mile loop hike. (Coming that way from the overlook and going left on the route described below gives you a 2.5-mile loop.)

Continuing on the loop trail, the path rises, and parallels the loop before turning away from the picnic area among azaleas along an old railroad grade.

By now you've noticed the bizarrely disrupted topography of craters and hummocks—remnants of extensive quarrying that occurred in many places in the area. Roanoke is rich with quarries. A particularly odd jumble of these pits—which almost seem like wartime earthworks or the result of heavy shelling—is visible on the paved path through the picnic area (more below).

Not far from the campground, at 3.6 miles, a trail sign marks a path to the left that leads back to the picnic area (see below for a short circuit there).

Continue on the Chestnut Ridge Trail, around Chestnut Ridge, with views of Rockydale Quarry at 3.8 miles. Slabbing below Mill Mountain Spur Road along power lines, reach the grassy roadside of VA 672 at 4.5 miles. Across the road, the horse trail leads onward. Your trail goes left along the shoulder under the bridge, then left into the woods. The trail rises steeply then gradually along the spur road, arriving below Chestnut Ridge Overlook at the junction for a 5.4-mile loop.

Either side of this loop makes a good day hike.

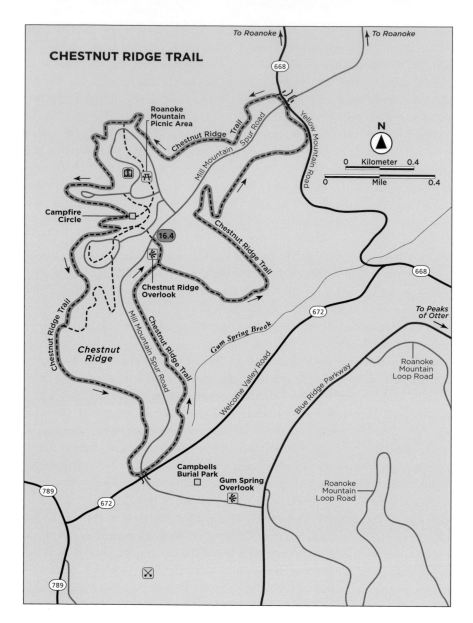

CHESTNUT RIDGE TRAIL

Key Points

1.6 Pass VA 668.

2.3 Trail sign at apex of picnic loop.

3.1 Easy left to trailhead overlook for half-loop hike of 3.4 miles.

3.6 Trail goes left to picnic area.

4.5 Pass VA 672.

5.4 Arrive back at trailhead.

Option 5: Mill Mountain Park and Star Trail

This is the best Parkway-adjacent view of Roanoke—bar none.

Parkway mile: 120.4
Distance: 0.4 mile out and back to Discovery Center from summit parking area; 3.0 miles out and back to summit and star from Riverland Road parking area
Difficulty: Moderate

Elevation gain: Negligible for shorter hike; about 900 feet for longer hike
Maps: USGS *Garden City*; search the Internet for "Mill Mountain Park Trails" (a few maps available online)

Finding the trailhead: From Roanoke Mountain Picnic Area, drive toward Roanoke on the Mill Mountain Spur Road. Turn left into Mill Mountain Park, 1.2 miles beyond the picnic area (2.5 miles from the Parkway). Start at either the Discovery Center (first left; GPS: 37.228443 / -79.950713) or mountaintop trailheads.

To start at a lower trailhead below the park, go to the parking area on Riverland Road beside the Roanoke River (GPS: 37.249335 / -79.921865). There's also a parking slip for a few cars on the right 1 mile north of the entrance to Mill Mountain Park on Fishburn Parkway where the trail crosses the road (GPS: 37.249921 / -79.926544).

The Hike

The Star Trail provides a great view of the city—and that huge star. The historical marker above the view claims that the massive star is the world's biggest. Perched at 1,847 feet—1,045 feet above the city—the star is 88 feet tall and can be seen for 60 miles. It was devised in 1949 by civic leaders as a Christmas decoration and has since taken on a life of its own.

Starting near Riverland Road, you'll reach the Star Trail in 0.2 mile on the Star/Woodthrush Connector Trail, or you could also take the Lower Woodthrush Trail to the Star Trail junction, an easy hiking and mountain biking path.

This yellow-blazed, meandering and gradual Star Trail explores a forest of mostly pines, oaks, redbuds, locusts, and maples. When you reach Fishburn Parkway, cross the street, climb the steps, and bear left into the woods to begin half a dozen long and gradual switchbacks that pass a crossing of the hiking and mountain biking Monument Trail. At the summit, about 1.6 miles, the trail comes to a T junction at a gravel road where a sign containing the trail's interpretive brochure points back down the trail. Head left; the gravel road goes 30 feet to the paved mountaintop parking area, where a right turn onto a paved path reaches the formal viewpoint below the star. Or turn right at the sign on the gravel road and follow it around the peak to the paved path at the viewpoint.

On the paved view path from the parking area, an asphalt trail descends left (west) off the summit, passing right of a picnic shelter to a lower viewpoint on the way to the main parking area at the Discovery Center and zoo in 0.2 mile.

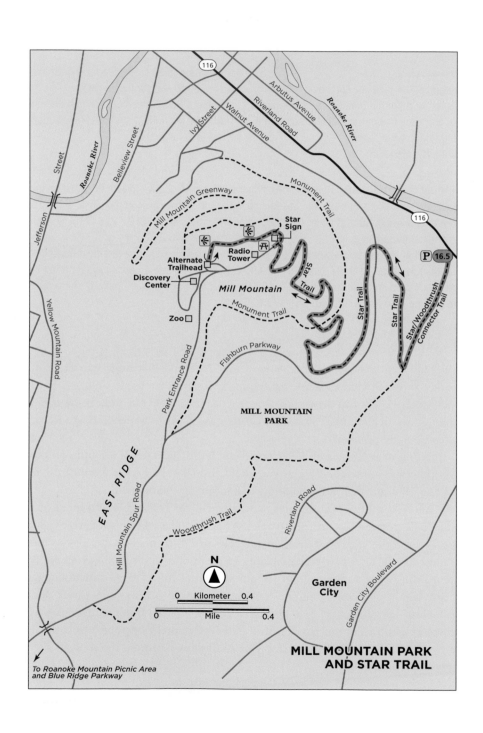

MILL MOUNTAIN PARK
AND STAR TRAIL

The shortest and easiest way to reach the summit viewpoints is to take the first left into the Discovery Center. Park and take the trail across from the building; hike past the lower viewpoint to the higher one and return.

Key Points

1.5 Reach summit junction near star.

Stretching from New York to Alabama, the Great Valley is one of the Appalachians' major geographic features. The overlook at Milepost 99.6 enables expansive appreciation of why the valley was a major migration route in the mid-1700s.

The Blue Ridge Plateau

Mileposts 121.4 (US 220 at Roanoke, VA) to 276.4 (US 421 at Deep Gap, NC)
The 155-mile portion of the Parkway from US 220 at Roanoke (Milepost 121.4) to
Deep Gap at US 421 (Milepost 276.4) could be considered two sections if you split

*Flame azalea and rhododendron bloom on this stretch of Parkway near Tompkins Knob as the
Blue Ridge Plateau climbs into North Carolina.*

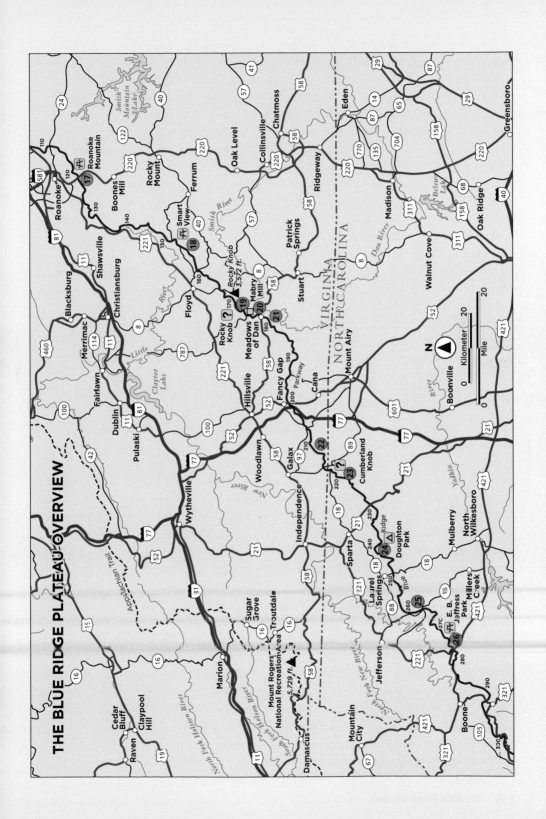

THE BLUE RIDGE PLATEAU—OVERVIEW

it at the Virginia–North Carolina state line—which some people do. I-77 is a nice central access point near the middle.

Both of these subsections share a common flavor. This is where the Appalachian Front undulates south from Roanoke at generally lower elevations to the Virginia line, then rises again in North Carolina. To the east, the Piedmont still lies below— just not as far below—and western views don't generally plummet to deep valleys. This is the Blue Ridge Plateau of rolling uplands, farms, and rural communities—a bucolic side of the Southern Appalachians.

Unlike other parts of the Parkway, here public lands don't lie beyond the National Park boundary. Residential and, increasingly, resort developments are more visible. Groups such as the Blue Ridge Parkway Foundation and Friends of the Blue Ridge Parkway (see appendix B) are working closely with the National Park Service to minimize the impact of what hikers would call "development" but residents of Appalachia often call "economic opportunity." For many of the latter, that opportunity has been a long time coming.

Fittingly, this part of the road is where human habitation of the mountains—and the culture of the mountain people—truly seems to stand out. This part of the road may come closest to fusing the Parkway's interpretation of the past with a sense of the present and future.

You'll see the Parkway's pioneer cabins and structures everywhere (most often on the trails in this book) and even "meet" some of the people who lived in them. Mabry Mill; Cool Spring Baptist Church; and Mathews, Trails, Puckett, Brinegar, Caudill, and Jesse Brown Cabins stand like silent portals to the past. Not all are exhibits. As you motor by, you may not even glimpse Sheets Cabin standing alone below the road at Milepost 252.3—with no nearby parking lot. You'll see fences, too, especially at the Groundhog Mountain exhibit. During the official season, living-history interpreters movingly personify this "land of do without" lifestyle.

You'll see historic structures when you hike into Rock Castle Gorge (Milepost 167) or the backcountry of Doughton Park (Milepost 239), but there's more. You'll notice fields becoming forests again. You'll see nature reclaiming a hardscrabble landscape where people struggled for generations attempting to make a living. Rock walls and stone chimneys are their monuments.

The people who once lived here are gone, but their progeny work or own businesses in the tourism and other industries, including Christmas tree farms, that you'll see all around you. They display their crafts at the Northwest Trading Post (Milepost 258.7), and the traditional mountain music so recently resurgent as a part of the country music scene is featured stunningly in one of the Parkway's newest facilities, the Blue Ridge Music Center (Milepost 213). Extensive exhibits complement the music center's in-season schedule of popular outdoor concerts. Not far off the road, nationally known musical festivals are a major draw. There's MerleFest in Wilkesboro, the last weekend of April (http://merlefest.org/). Floydfest is a landmark week-long music festival held late in July (http://floydfest.com/). The Old Fiddler's Convention comes

On some parts of the Parkway, autumn equals the explosive color of New England.

to Galax, the second weekend in August (http://oldfiddlersconvention.com/). All are real music events that still do what they've always done—tempt people, including Parkway tourists, out of the hollows.

The long list of major Parkway service sites on this 155-mile stretch includes Smart View Picnic Area (Milepost 154.5), Rocky Knob Campground (Milepost 167.1) and Picnic Area (Milepost 169), Mabry Mill (Milepost 176.2), and Groundhog Mountain Picnic Area (Milepost 188.8)—and those are just to the Virginia–North Carolina state line at Milepost 216.9.

In North Carolina, Cumberland Knob Picnic Area (Milepost 217.5) is where Parkway construction started in 1935—80 years ago in 2015. Doughton Park is next, with a campground (Milepost 239.2), a picnic area, and now closed concession facilities that include one-time accommodations at Bluffs Lodge and a restaurant (Milepost 241.1). Check the Parkway website in hopes they'll be open again soon.

With so much private land along the road, this section has a wealth of smaller roads that come and go. Take a chance and explore a few of the public ones. There are surprises. The mountain town of Floyd, Virginia (Mileposts 158.9 and 159.3), is a destination on "The Crooked Road, Virginia Music Heritage Trail"—a 250-mile drive that crosses the Parkway and includes the Blue Ridge Music Center. There's great atmosphere and live music at Floyd Country Store. Nearby Chateau Morrissette's tours and tastings (Milepost 171.5) give a nod to the growing Blue Ridge region wine industry—with a reliably gourmet restaurant and vintages produced on premises. The Mayberry Trading Post (Milepost 180.5) and the cluster of services at Fancy Gap (Milepost 199.4) are enjoyably oriented to tourism.

Check appendix B for a wealth of relevant websites and contact information.

17 Buck Mountain Trail

Milepost 123.2

A scenic trail with views of nearby summits and quarry.

Parkway mile: 123.2
Distance: 1.0-mile lollipop
Difficulty: Moderate to strenuous
Elevation gain: 300 feet

Maps: *USGS Garden City*; Parkway's Roanoke Valley Trails overview map, available online and in season at Roanoke Mountain Picnic Area

Finding the trailhead: Park at Buck Mountain Overlook (GPS: 37.196702 / -79.982475).

The Hike

The paved trail rises out of the parking area and arcs up and left (eastward) over concrete water bars. The bluish-gray–blazed path stays to the left of the ridgeline, and

You can't guarantee clear weather on the Parkway, so pick up Tim Barnwell's excellent book Blue Ridge Parkway Vistas. *His stunning overlook images will let you see what you're missing and identify distant landmarks if you have to drive by in the rain.*

the telltale red-tree blazes of a Forest Service property line appear just to the right of the trail.

At 0.3 mile there's a bench on the left with a partial view. Higher, the trail slides off to the right of the ridge. There's a major split in the trail at 0.4 mile where a well-used path goes right and may look like the start of a loop. It's not. This side trail dips off to the nearby gap then steeply climbs past No Trespassing signs to the summit of Buck Mountain.

Go left on the Parkway trail with the faint bluish-gray blazes. Just above the junction, an obvious concrete National Park Service boundary post sits to the right of the trail. Bearing left, then right, the path again splits, this time into a tiny summit loop that encircles the rounded little mountaintop. Though the view is limited, it's a pleasant spot. There's a bench on the left branch of the loop.

In late 2001 a substantial fire burned this part of the Parkway and adjoining lands and the observant may still see evidence of the fire or the firefighting effort.

Key Points

0.3 Bench to left of trail.

0.4 Stay left at major trail split—trail to right trespasses to summit of ridgeline.

0.5 Circle the tiny summit loop.

18 Smart View Loop Trail

Milepost 154.5

A picnic area loop that offers more, this trail mixes meadows with a deep stream drainage, a visit to a century-old cabin, and a wander through scenic forests.

Parkway mile: 154.5
Distance: Loops of 3.0, 2.1, and 1.6 miles
Difficulty: Moderate

Elevation gain: About 160 feet
Maps: *USGS Endicott*; no Parkway map available

Finding the trailhead: Park immediately off the Parkway in the lot at the gate that closes the picnic area in winter (GPS: 36.927918 / -80.189710). You can also park at the Smart View Overlook for a longer hike and the Trails Cabin Parking Area for a shorter walk.

The Hike

Start the hike through a fat-man squeeze by the trail map sign. Strike off across the meadow to the northeast and pass a trail post and a bench. The trail rises into the woods to a signed trail junction on the right at 0.2 mile where a right leads to the picnic area and a restroom visible in the distance. Continue along a split-rail fence, then barbed wire. The trail continues away from the Parkway, dipping along a now-grassy path to a trail junction and a bench on the right at 0.4 mile. Straight ahead, the trail passes more trail posts and dips below then swings left into the Smart View Overlook. (Starting there adds 0.2 mile to the longest and shortest hikes described.)

Avoid the overlook and turn right at the trail junction to pass through a fat-man squeeze in the split-rail fence. The path dips down and bears right below the picnic area above a stream drainage that plummets left. The trail veers right into a side tributary, goes under a power line, then switchbacks left to cross a split-log bridge at 0.6 mile. Descending past the junction of two streams, the trail steepens and emerges from the stream valley to switchback twice and turn right along the Blue Ridge front. The trail then levels off along the east side of the picnic area where grills and distinctive rock-pedestal picnic tables appear on the right. A large quartz rock announces the crest.

At 1.0 mile the trail swings past a paved and signed access to the easternmost bulge of the picnic loop beside a roofed picnic shelter and across from a restroom. Veering left, the trail swings above what in leafless times is a dramatic drop. Turning back toward the picnic area past old fence posts and a meadow, a side trail goes right to the picnic loop; just beyond, the main path reaches Trails Cabin at 1.2 miles. The unchinked cabin, built in the 1890s by the appropriately named Trail family, perches

Raw, chilly winter days convey a stark appreciation for what life must have been like for the folks who called the Parkway's primitive cabins home.

atop a wonderful view—"a right smart view" in the namesake vernacular of the region. From the cabin, a trail rises a short way along a split-rail fence to a parking area that permits quick access.

Continue past a bench in front of the cabin to dip down around the ridge across a stream spanned by a stone bridge at 1.3 miles. The trail continues right toward a little meadow beside the picnic loop road and then switchbacks left back into the woods. At the switchback near the roadside, a sign points out to a small pond across the road. Walk the road a short distance in that direction back to your car to shorten the hike.

Go left on the switchback away from the stream crossing and around the ridge on a rock-underlain treadway. The trail crests above the pond and its noisy residents. Your parking area can be seen off to the right. Past a bench, the trail flattens in a tall pine forest. At 1.4 miles a signed trail goes right. This trail bisects the last part of the loop through the pines to your parking area (see the end of the entry for this option).

The pinewoods decrease in size as the loop descends away from the picnic area down a broadening ridge. The path rises around a few promontories left of the trail and continues level for some distance through a scenic area of big hardwoods, a fringed understory of pine, and a substantial carpet of running cedar. The trail goes

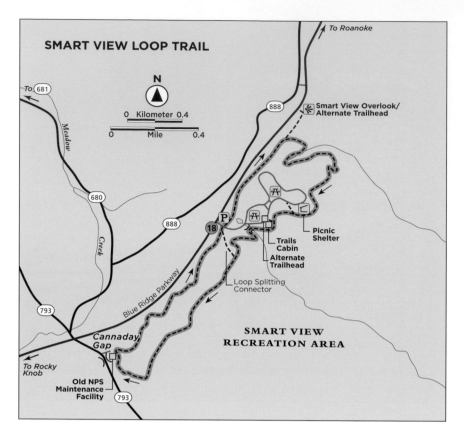

SMART VIEW LOOP TRAIL

To Roanoke

N

0 Kilometer 0.4

0 Mile 0.4

To 681

Meadow

680

888

Creek

Blue Ridge Parkway

793

888

18

P

Smart View Overlook/
Alternate Trailhead

Picnic
Shelter

Trails
Cabin

Alternate
Trailhead

Loop Splitting
Connector

SMART VIEW
RECREATION AREA

Cannaday
Gap

To Rocky
Knob

Old NPS
Maintenance
Facility

793

left, back toward the edge of the Blue Ridge, then swings broadly right at 2.2 miles around and above Cannaday Gap, heading back to the picnic area. The dirt road through the gap appears below.

The Parkway comes in on the left, and the trail slides below a scenic, moss-covered outcrop through a forest dotted with hemlocks and quartz boulders. Past a bench, the path climbs through towering shagbark hickory and white pine. A signed junction on the right at 2.9 miles is the trail you passed earlier that bisects the loop. Go left through a fat-man squeeze and cross the picnic access road to your car.

To shorten this hike to an easier 2.1-mile loop that avoids the drainage and pairs the cabin with the best forest walking, start at the Trails Cabin parking area. Check out the cabin and then go right on the loop in the direction described above. Pass the trail that bisects the loop; when you encounter the trail again, at its second junction, turn right and bisect the loop back to the trail you just hiked. Go left at that junction back to the cabin and your car.

The stream-drainage (north) side of the loop can be a 1.6-mile hike from the original parking area. Take that hike in the above direction, but again use the trail that bisects the loop and return to the parking area beside the Parkway.

Key Points

0.2 Pass stile and side trail to restroom.

0.4 Turn right over stile.

0.6 Split-log bridge.

1.0 Access to picnic area.

1.2 Trails Cabin.

1.3 Stone bridge.

1.4 Trail bisects loop back to parking.

2.2 Trail turns back toward picnic area above Cannaday Gap.

2.9 Left to parking or right back to loop and cabin.

Hikes at Rocky Knob in Virginia and Doughton Park just inside North Carolina showcase still-standing chimneys. See the Rock Castle Gorge Day Hike at Rocky Knob. In Doughton Park, descendants of settlers call this landmark on the Basin Creek Trail "perfect chimney."

19 Rocky Knob Recreation Area

Mileposts 165.3–169.0

Like Doughton Park in North Carolina (Mileposts 238–245), Virginia's 3,589-acre Rocky Knob Recreation Area is a backcountry bulge from the Parkway that contains a trail system extensive enough to permit backpack camping. But unlike Doughton, with its various circuit hiking options, the 10.6-mile Rock Castle Gorge Trail is simply one big loop.

That makes it a strenuous day hike (except in sections). At first glance, backpacking trips seem similarly difficult, largely because the logical place to start, in the valley, is the location of the backcountry campsite where you should be ending up after a day on the trail. On second glance, some backpackers might like this arrangement. Start at the top and arrive at the campsite after a largely downhill hike. That means a significant climb back up the next morning—but your pack should be lighter. Best of all, if a long backpacking trip is not what you want, the backcountry site is so close to the trailhead that it makes a wonderfully accessible place for a quick overnighter.

Rocky Knob boasts a wonderful mix of high-elevation meadows, craggy-summit views, deep coves, scenic streams, and startling reminders that this and many a now-wild Appalachian wilderness were once places where mountain families lived out their lives. You will be startled into head-shaking wonderment at where people chose to establish farms.

Besides a Park Service campground and picnic area, there are also seven rustic cabins that used to be for rent (closed in recent years). These classic Civilian Conservation Corps (CCC) structures are a rich part of the corps' heritage that you find nationwide in state parks, forests, and wherever the corps worked to wrest a legacy of service from the Great Depression. The corps labored to build the Parkway, too, and Rocky Knob's backcountry campsite is their former camp on Rock Castle Creek.

Though most people are likely to tackle the Rock Castle Gorge Trail in sections, a few other trails—the Black Ridge Trail, for instance—coincide with parts of the Rock Castle Gorge Trail, further obviating the need to stick with the path for its full 10.6 miles. The options below treat the Rock Castle Gorge Trail first as a series of shorter day hikes.

Best bets include an out-and-back from the valley up Rock Castle Creek or Little Rock Castle Creek—perhaps as day hikes while spending a few nights at the backcountry campsite. Another good option would be a hike to the summit of Rocky Knob from a nearby overlook or from the vicinity of the backcountry campsite. And if you do hike the entire loop, up Little Rock Castle Creek from the backcountry campsite is the way to do it. It's pretty much all downhill from Rocky Knob.

If you choose to backpack, two overlooks make nice starting points for the backcountry campsite and do not require an overly long hike out the next day. Twelve

O'Clock Knob permits a 5.1-mile hike to the campsite and an uphill return of 5.5 miles. From Rock Castle Gorge Overlook, it's 4.6 miles to the campsite and 6.0 miles back.

Option 1: Rock Castle Gorge Day Hikes

A streamside exploration of a scenic valley imparts a startling sense of what life was like for early-twentieth-century mountaineers.

Parkway mile: 165.3
Distance: 5.4 miles out and back to chimney
Difficulty: Moderate to strenuous
Elevation gain: 1,050 feet

Maps: *USGS Woolwine*; Parkway handout map, available in season at the visitor center and other facilities and online at nps.gov/blri/plan yourvisit/rocky-knob-trails.htm

Finding the trailhead: To start the Rock Castle Gorge Trail near the backcountry campsite, go east on VA 8 from Tuggle Gap (Milepost 165.3) and turn right at the bottom of the hill onto VA 605. Park at the end of this dirt road (GPS: 36.801463 / -80.344530).

The Hikes

A day hike along Rock Castle Creek is one of the area's best. Leaving the parking area on VA 605, cross the gated bridge; the rugged, green-blazed Rock Castle Gorge Trail wanders for nearly 3.0 miles ever higher up the valley. Almost immediately, the higher-elevation side of the loop trail goes right and follows Little Rock Castle Creek. This is the best route if the entire loop hike is your goal (see Option 1a). Staying left in the valley, after a few short climbs, you reach a long streamside stretch that leads into the broad flat of the old CCC camp at 0.3 mile. There's a privy and a variety of campsites—all with grills, many with benches.

The road climbs in steps, with Twelve O'Clock Knob on the high left (2,842 feet). Sycamores and copious quartz outcrops are everywhere. The prevalent six-sided quartz crystals reminded residents of castle towers, hence the name of the gorge. A half mile above the campsite, the road appears less traveled. The first stream crossing (1.2 miles) passes over one of four impressive metal bridges along the trail. The trail climbs steeply then levels with downstream valley views.

At 1.5 miles you enter a private inholding and come upon a barn and an early-twentieth-century white clapboard house with a privy and outbuildings. This is the Austin House, the only home in the gorge today. Built in 1916, it was the finest house in a community of thirty-plus families. The population dwindled when wage-paying industries came to surrounding communities and undermined a lifestyle of subsistence farming focused on growing oats, corn, buckwheat, apples, and the cash crop, chestnuts. The farm is a reminder of human transience—especially with jonquils announcing another spring in a long-untended garden.

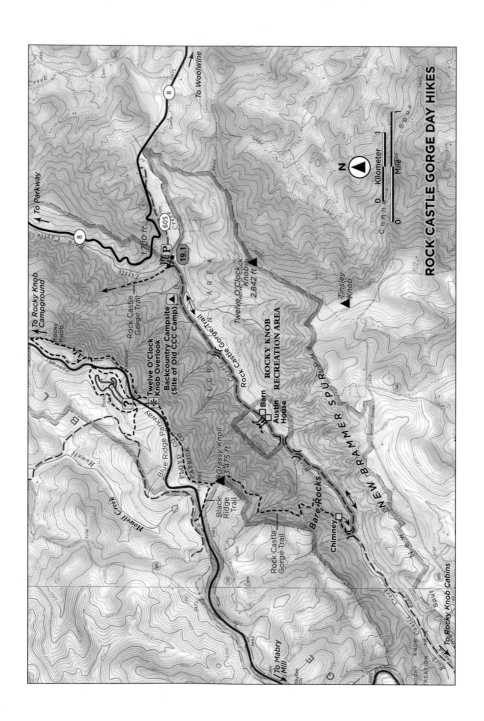

ROCK CASTLE GORGE DAY HIKES

Opposite the house, rough fields lie across the river. In the higher meadow to the left across the bridge, a stone wall enclosure makes a nice focal point for a picnic (but camping is not permitted). A return to your car from here is a moderate 3.0-mile day hike.

Back into the now rhododendron-filled forest, the road narrows with the valley and crosses another bridge back to the right of the stream at 1.7 miles. Soon another bridge crosses back to the left and the old road rises steeply and repeatedly, with great views straight down on the creek. A gorge forms to the right, and the road continues steeply, rising above it with views out the end of the valley.

Just beyond a bench at 2.4 miles, Rock Castle Cascades splash off the cliffs and shower down to the left of the roadside. The trail continues to gain and then crests at a junction and another bench. Left, the grade of the road continues much more gradually along Rock Castle Creek to a gate at the Rocky Knob cabins. Right, the Rock Castle Gorge Trail turns on its way to the Parkway and the high part of the loop. It first descends to another bench and the fourth metal bridge at 2.6 miles.

This makes another nice turnaround point, for a strenuous 5.2-mile day hike. But go just a bit farther. The upcoming 0.8-mile portion of the Rock Castle Gorge Trail used to be called the Hardwood Cove Nature Trail. A brochure, now out of print, used to interpret the uses for the trees along the trail. Just bring your tree book and head up the trail a short way, around at least a few more ridges, where a stout chimney stands alone in the woods. Imagine making a living here. This turnaround spot makes a 5.4-mile day hike. Or stick with it for another 0.1 mile or so to Bare Rocks—a major rib of boulders. From here it's only 1.8 miles farther to the junction with Black Ridge Trail and the crest portion of the Rock Castle Gorge Trail.

Key Points

0.3 CCC backcountry campsite.

1.2 Cross first bridge.

1.5 Arrive at the Austin House.

1.7 Cross second bridge and third bridge, 0.1 mile beyond.

2.4 Rock Castle Cascades shower left side of the trail.

2.6 Final bridge at bench; start of the former Hardwood Cove Nature Trail.

2.7 Chimney at old homesite.

Option 1a:

An option from the same trailhead as the above hike is a walk up (north on) Little Rock Castle Creek (the opposite direction of the hike above, were you to make the entire loop). This is one of the least-used portions of the Rock Castle Gorge Trail and makes a nice uphill streamside hike to the meadows opposite the campground and even to the top of Rocky Knob. (See Option 2: Rocky Knob Day Hikes for more.) This is the direction to go to hike the entire loop. To the campground meadows, a hike up Little Rock Castle Creek is a 6.0-mile round-trip. On the way, you pass many benches for resting and more evidence of farming activity. Add the loop of Rocky Knob described below, and at 8.3 miles this hike becomes one of the area's most diverse longer walks—summit views and streamside hiking that's lacking on the hike up Rock Castle Creek. To the meadows the rise is 1,390 feet. To the summit of Rocky Knob, it's a stiff and strenuous 1,869 feet.

Option 2: Rocky Knob Day Hikes

A few day hikes climb to Rocky Knob's signature summit, one across scenic grassy meadows.

Parkway mile: 168
Distance: 1.1-mile loop from Saddle Overlook; 2.3-mile loop from campground
Difficulty: Easy to moderate
Elevation gain: 190 feet and 480 feet

Maps: *USGS Woolwine*; Parkway handout map, available in season at the visitor center and other facilities and online at nps.gov/blri/plan yourvisit/rocky-knob-trails.htm

Finding the trailhead: The trail leaves the south end of the Saddle Overlook (GPS: 36.822842 / -80.341634). To park at the campground, leave your car near the entrance and walk directly across the Parkway—the fat-man squeeze provides a route through the fence. Turn right; signs direct hikers through the meadows.

To start at the picnic area, park at the visitor center (GPS: 36.811371 / -80.350549). Pull past the building on the right and turn left into the lot before entering the picnic area. Walk across the road you took into the lot behind the visitor center and follow the yellow-blazed Picnic Loop Trail east.

The Hikes

Rocky Knob's namesake summit is known for some of the area's best views, especially of Rock Castle Gorge. Indeed, the entire crest of the Parkway across the Rocky Knob area is a succession of meadow vistas. And there is also a historical oddity—the shelter on the summit of Rocky Knob was an Appalachian Trail shelter before Parkway construction forced the path far to the west. Ironically, when that relocation occurred, even the Blue Ridge Parkway was considered just another road destroying a trail.

Saddle Overlook is the best starting point for the easiest hike over Rocky Knob. Head south out of the overlook; when the green-blazed Rock Castle Gorge Trail goes left to climb the peak, bear right onto the easy, red-blazed side trail that avoids the summit. Another red-blazed side trail links left toward the summit trail—stay right. In 0.5 mile turn left; the trail climbs steeply to the crest of the ridge. Dipping through a swale on the crest, the path runs to the summit (3,572 feet) and the shelter at 0.9 mile. Descending steeply off the peak toward the Saddle Overlook, pass an intersection with the red-blazed linking trail. Rejoin the side trail that bypassed the

The Appalachian Trail had to be moved far to the west when the Parkway destroyed the trail. Nevertheless, one of the AT's earliest shelters still sits atop Rocky Knob.

peak, returning to the Saddle Overlook at 1.1 miles. This hike gains only 190 feet of elevation.

Extend the Saddle Overlook walk by starting farther north at the Rocky Knob Campground. That option adds another 1.2 miles for a 2.3-mile hike that includes summit views but begins and ends with wonderful meadow scenery. The elevation gain is still moderate at 480 feet. Start from the campground entrance, cross the road, and pass through the split-rail fence at a fat-man squeeze to a signed junction. Posts with arrows direct the route in either direction over the grassy areas. Left, the trail descends Little Rock Castle Creek 3.0 miles to the vicinity of the backcountry campsite. (See the end of the Rock Castle Gorge option. Starting there creates one of the best day hikes, at 8.3 miles.)

Turn right; the trail climbs the meadows with expanding views along the way. Cross a fence at the edge of the meadow at 0.3 mile and gain a small knob in another 0.1 mile. From there the trail descends to the north end of the Saddle Overlook at 0.6 mile. Do the loop described above for a 2.3-mile hike.

If you just stay left on the Rock Castle Gorge Trail, hit the shelter and summit, and return, the trek is only 0.8 mile to the top, for a 1.6-mile hike.

You can start farther south; see the Rocky Knob Picnic Loop (Option 4) for that hike.

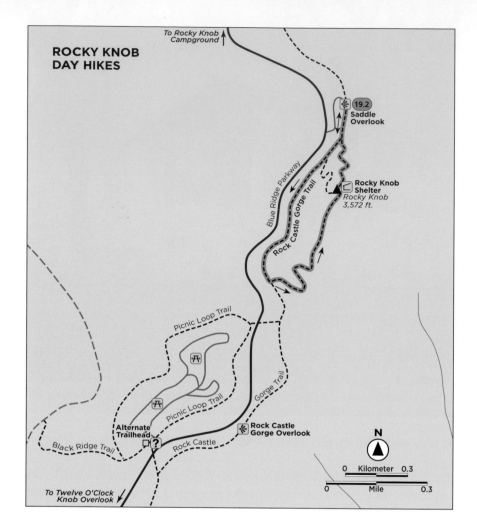

Key Points from Saddle Overlook

0.05 Bear right on the trail bypassing summit.

0.5 Turn left onto Rock Castle Gorge Trail to peak.

0.9 Reach summit of Rocky Knob.

1.1 Return to parking lot.

Option 3: Black Ridge Trail

This loop has a little bit of everything—dense forest, an old homestead, forest roads, and outstanding meadow views.

Parkway mile: 169
Distance: 3.1-mile loop

Difficulty: Moderate
Elevation gain: 486 feet

Maps: *USGS Woolwine*; Parkway handout map, available in season at the visitor center and other facilities and online at nps.gov/blri/plan yourvisit/rocky-knob-trails.htm

Finding the trailhead: Drive past the right side of the visitor center and turn left into the parking lot before entering the picnic area (GPS: 36.811371 / -80.350549). To reach the Black Ridge Trail, walk across the grass from the lot toward the Parkway and to the right of the visitor center. Turn right at the trail signpost with a yellow arrow beside the building (technically the yellow-blazed Picnic Loop) and head into the woods. A blue-blazed trail heads left to and then across the Parkway (your return route for the Black Ridge Trail). Stay right; the trail is now a blue- and yellow-blazed combination trail.

The Hike

It's a bit hard to locate the trailhead for this hike (hence the detailed directions above). Heading away from the visitor center on the now blue- and yellow-blazed combination trail, the path weaves along a power line then descends through open woods. At 0.2 mile veer left on the blue-blazed trail where the yellow-blazed trail goes right into a meadow on its way around the picnic area.

The trail gets rockier on the descent through areas of running cedar then swings into and along a power line right-of-way that's full of beautiful ferns and mossy logs. A quiet brook appears off to the left. On the right, a towering chimney marks a cabin site at 0.4 mile. Here's as good a place as any to wonder about the people who lived here before the Parkway. With warm fertile valleys not so far away, someone chose this high, inhospitable place to scratch out a living on this north-facing slope.

Just past the chimney, the trail reaches a T junction with an old road grade that shows evidence of occasional use. Turning left, the trail hops the stream and follows the steep, at times eroded road through a not-so-scenic area.

Eventually the road levels, becomes grass and moss covered, and parallels a fence-line beside expansive meadows with a high-elevation feel and extensive views to the right. The adjoining meadow has outcrops close to the trail that would make wonderful picnic viewpoints. (Be respectful—portions of this road lie on private property.)

The road continues to rise into hemlocks and rhododendron and turns right to closely parallel the Parkway. Passing a shed and a gate, the road swings right, away from the Parkway, and appears to be more frequently used by vehicles. Just past the start of a white wooden fence on the right at 1.5 miles, the path exits the road at a trail marker post that points left. Following trail posts across the crest of the meadow, the Parkway appears at 1.6 miles. Cross the road, climb the stile over the split-rail fence, and set off up Grassy Knoll.

This is high, scenic country. It can also be very foggy. If you cross the stile in zero visibility, set off straight into the meadow in the direction the steps are pointing but bear just slightly right and you'll see the first blue-arrow trail post.

The posts cross the meadow and rise slowly to join an old grade along a fenceline on the right. Near the crest of the meadow, signs announce that the green-blazed

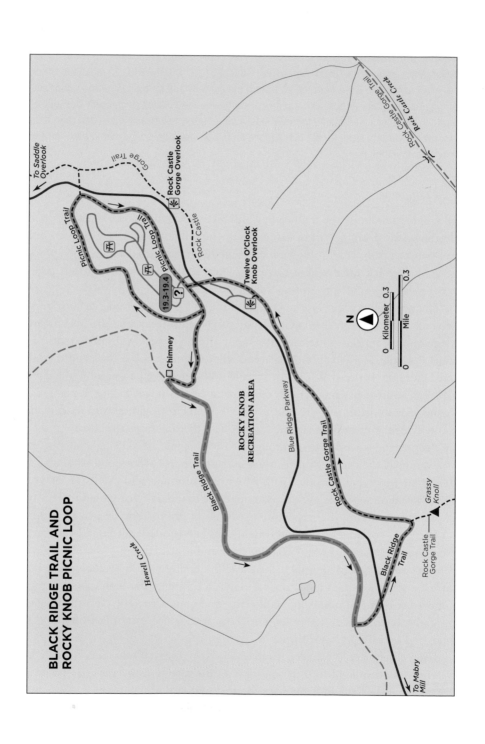

BLACK RIDGE TRAIL AND
ROCKY KNOB PICNIC LOOP

To Saddle
Overlook

Gorge Trail

Picnic Loop Trail

Picnic Loop Trail

19.3-19.4

Rock Castle
Gorge Overlook

Rock Castle

Twelve O'Clock
Knob Overlook

Chimney

Black Ridge Trail

ROCKY KNOB
RECREATION AREA

Blue Ridge Parkway

Howell Creek

Rock Castle Gorge Trail

Black Ridge
Trail

Grassy
Knoll

Rock Castle
Gorge Trail

Rock Castle Gorge Trail

Rock Castle Creek

N

0   Kilometer   0.3

0   Mile   0.3

To Mabry
Mill

Rock Castle Gorge Trail comes in from the right at 1.8 miles. Together the two paths turn left along the fenceline following posts with blue and green arrows. Protruding rocks, a bench—and cow pies—dot the meadow. Following the fenceline near the woods, the trail crosses a stile at 2.2 miles, dips into the forest around a ridge, bears left, and follows a lower meadow. Soon you're just to the right of the Parkway.

A side trail goes left to Twelve O'Clock Knob Overlook. Stay on the main trail past the overlook and the path dips below the lot to a junction at 2.9 miles. The Rock Castle Gorge Trail heads off to the right for Rocky Knob. Go left; the blue-blazed Black Ridge Trail rises into the meadow. The formal trail from Twelve O'Clock Knob Overlook joins from the left as you continue up the grass to the Parkway roadside.

Here you could ascend the obvious trail steps, but just walk to your car at 3.1 miles across the grass to the left of the building.

Key Points

0.2 Bear left when Picnic Loop goes right.

0.4 Old cabin site; left onto dirt road just beyond.

1.5 Turn left from road into meadow.

1.6 Cross Parkway.

1.8 Turn left with Rock Castle Gorge Trail at signed junction near meadow summit.

2.2 Cross fence.

2.9 Turn left to Parkway and parking area when Rock Castle Gorge Trail goes right.

Option 4: Rocky Knob Picnic Loop

This easy loop around the picnic area makes a nice start to a hike up Rocky Knob.

See map on page 138.
Parkway mile: 169
Distance: 1.3-mile loop; 2.7- and 3.2-mile hikes that include the circuit over the summit of Rocky Knob
Difficulty: Easy

Elevation gain: 120 feet
Maps: *USGS Woolwine*; Parkway handout map, available in season at the visitor center and other facilities and online at nps.gov/blri/plan yourvisit/rocky-knob-trails.htm

Finding the trailhead: Drive past the right side of the visitor center and turn left into the parking lot before entering the picnic area. Two access points are possible (GPS: 36.811371 / -80.350549).

To go to the west, walk toward the Parkway, across the grass from the lot to the right of the visitor center. Turn right at the trail signpost with a yellow arrow beside the building. Head into the woods and pass the blue-blazed Black Ridge Trail that goes left, staying right on the now blue- and yellow-blazed combination trail. The Picnic Loop soon turns right off that trail.

To take the Picnic Loop east, which is a nice way to start a hike to Rocky Knob, walk across the road you took into the lot behind the visitor center and follow the yellow-blazed trail.

The Hike

This is your basic picnic area loop through a scenic higher-elevation forest. Heading west, the yellow-blazed trail veers right, away from the Black Ridge Trail at 0.2 mile. (For a nice side trip, an old cabin site is just 0.2 mile left on the Black Ridge Trail.) Going right, the Picnic Loop wanders below and around the picnic area through hemlock and hardwood forest. Cross a small stream and the trail turns right toward the Parkway. After a bit of a climb at 0.9 mile, the red-blazed connector to Rocky Knob goes left, reaching the summit loop in 0.3 mile. Continue right and back to the lot for a 1.3-mile hike. Hiking the loop this way and adding a circuit over the summit of Rocky Knob is a neat option for a 3.2-mile hike.

Going the opposite direction, east from the visitor center, the connector to Rocky Knob peels off at 0.4 mile from the start. That permits a 2.7-mile hike over the summit—one of the best ways to tackle Rocky Knob.

Key Points Going West

0.2 Bear right where blue-blazed trail goes left.

0.9 Red-blazed trail goes left to Rocky Knob.

Parkway historic sites often showcase summertime living-history activities. Here two kids enjoy the blacksmithing demonstration at Mabry Mill's Mountain Industry Trail. JEFFREY GREENBERG

20 Mountain Industry Trail at Mabry Mill

Milepost 176.2

This highly developed and popular paved path (wheelchair accessible) explores a virtual mountain community. Mabry Mill, probably the Parkway's most photographed site, is surrounded by historic structures and informative exhibits about the early Appalachian economy.

Parkway mile: 176.2
Distance: 0.5-mile loop
Difficulty: Easy
Elevation gain: Negligible

Maps: *USGS Meadows of Dan*; Parkway trail map, available in season at the Mabry Mill restaurant/gift shop

Finding the trailhead: Parking is available at the restaurant/gift shop (GPS: 36.750179 / -80.405464). Access to overflow parking lots is signed on the Parkway from both directions. See the accompanying map.

The Hike

How popular is this trail? One indication is that two Parkway trail maps are printed—one oriented from parking at the restaurant/gift shop, the other from overflow parking lots farther away. Signs at those sites mirror the maps.

But don't let tour buses deter you. This trail features what is perhaps the Parkway's most photographed site, Mabry Mill—a scene notoriously claimed by postcards from states other than Virginia. A stop here also impresses with what is surely one of the more complex systems of water flumes ever devised to feed an otherwise primitive water-powered facility. Indeed, Mabry Mill and the blacksmith shop are no relocated historic structures, as some are along the Parkway. This is their original, if landscaped, location. Surrounding structures—including an 1869 cabin—as well as a variety of implements were collected here in the 1940s and 1950s. Together they tell a compelling tale.

Before taking the trail, check out the shop and restaurant. (A few dining alternatives are close by on US 58 at Meadows of Dan, a recommended stop.)

Mabry Mill is among the most active interpretive sites on the Parkway. Signs throughout the area explain the exhibits, and during the warmer months, this is one of the Parkway's principal living-history sites. The gristmill often operates Friday through Sunday, and interpreters offer talks about the process. Blacksmithing demonstrations occur Wednesday through Sunday, and weaving and spinning take place at various times. Mountain music and dancing bring out the locals from 2 to 5 p.m. on Sunday.

Mabry Mill is the heart of a quintessential Parkway interpretive path.

Edwin Mabry, a miner, blacksmith, and chair maker, built the mill in 1910. He and his wife, Mintoria Lizzie Mabry, lived here until 1936, grinding corn for the Meadows of Dan community. In 1945 the National Park Service restored and landscaped the mill.

Significant restoration of the structure took place over winter 2002 through the user fees that Congress allowed the Park Service to charge. Extensive restoration occurred in 2014 when the pond was dredged and the waterwheel and flumes saw significant repair. The Blue Ridge Parkway Foundation is still collecting donations to pay for the work (brpfoundation.org/).

Starting at the mill side of the restaurant/gift shop, pass the No Picnicking sign and pause on the left at the paved patio. This is the quintessential view of Mabry Mill.

Head left at the first junction—the prescribed way to go. A short side trail veers left 100 feet beyond and showcases the action of the overshot wheel. Going uphill, take the boardwalk left along one of the many wooden aqueducts that permit this water-hungry mill to work so well. This is one of the auxiliary water sources that feed the main millrace—a necessity because this mill does not gain sufficient waterpower from its main stream. You'll see the origin of this side source of water, and perhaps gain a better understanding of Mabry's ingenious system, on the way back.

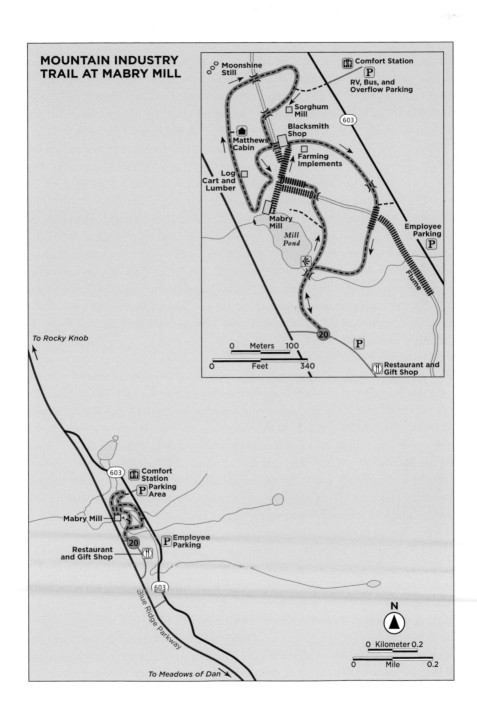

MOUNTAIN INDUSTRY TRAIL AT MABRY MILL

Moonshine Still

Comfort Station

P RV, Bus, and
Overflow Parking

Sorghum Mill

Blacksmith Shop

603

Matthews Cabin

Farming Implements

Log Cart and Lumber

Mabry Mill

Mill Pond

Employee Parking

P

Flume

0 Meters 100

0 Feet 340

20

P

Restaurant and Gift Shop

To Rocky Knob

Comfort Station

603

P Parking Area

Mabry Mill

20

P Employee Parking

Restaurant and Gift Shop

603

Blue Ridge Parkway

To Meadows of Dan

N

0 Kilometer 0.2

0 Mile 0.2

Off the boardwalk, turn left and go through the blacksmith shop and down to the mill. On the way you'll learn that just before the wide availability of flour from roller mills around the country made gristmills obsolete, the Mabrys employed an engine to turn the wheel. Beyond the mill is a display of millstones.

Turn right along the Parkway and you'll next encounter a log cart used to haul timber. Not far beyond is one of the Parkway's neatest cabins—the Matthews Cabin. Built near Galax in 1869, the rustic structure was donated to the Parkway and moved here in 1956 after its metal roofing and outer weatherboarding were removed. In season you can go inside to see cloth being woven on an old loom. The Mabrys built a frame house on this site in 1914—not uncommon at the time due to the prevalence of small sawmills in rural areas. Hikers in the nearby Rocky Knob Recreation Area can see such a home from that same era, the Austin House, just 1.5 miles from the lower trailhead on the Rock Castle Gorge Trail.

Past the cabin is a bark mill, a horse-powered machine that would grind oak and hemlock bark for tannin used to make bark liquor (a tanning treatment for hides). Not far beyond, look over the edge of the bluff and down on the creekside makings of a different kind of liquor—a moonshine still. An illustration depicts how corn was efficiently turned into a portable, and potable, commodity—corn whiskey. Up to twenty gallons of corn whiskey could be produced in a night. Water was a key to the process in these well-watered mountains. If you look beyond the still, you'll see the dam that feeds the second of the mill's two flumes.

Continuing, the trail crosses the stream and then makes a right turn. A left leads to the overflow parking area and comfort station opposite the Parkway side of the mill. Just beyond is a sorghum press, a horse-powered squeezing device used to make the sweet substitute for maple syrup that became popular during the Civil War. Continue right; the evaporator where juice from the squeezing process is cooked sits on the left side of the path (one gallon of syrup is made from ten gallons of extract).

Bearing right, pass a horse-drawn wagon and go left back through the blacksmith shop. The boardwalk you came in on goes right (the fastest way back to your car). Continue past a variety of plows and farm implements, over the not-so-rushing stream that should be the mill's main water source, and into a forest of white pines to the last leg of the loop. A paved left soon leads in a short distance to VA 603, access to overflow parking on the left by the comfort station, and a more remote employee lot to the right.

Just beyond the turnoff is a great view to the left of the impressive wooden aqueduct that feeds the upper end of the flume at the start of the hike. Off to the left, the neighboring stream that would otherwise rush into the millpond is raised up by a wooden aqueduct and carried to where it flows through the flume beneath you and into the mill's main race. An overflow on the wooden aqueduct permits excess water to spill out. To see how this stream is diverted into the aqueduct, take the paved trail behind you to VA 603 and walk right on the road to where the aqueduct starts behind the visitor center.

Returning, the path dips past the leftward view of the aqueduct. As you descend, remnants of the diverted stream flow to the left of the trail and into the pond at the spot where you started your hike. If you walk away with nothing else, an appreciation of Mabry's system aptly illustrates why the Appalachians have long been called the "land of make-do."

Key Points

0.1   Reach Mabry Mill.

0.25 Turn left to walk road to start of flume.

0.35 Return to trail and go left on last leg to lot.

The trails of the Parkway's Blue Ridge Plateau hide evidence of early residents. Not far south of Mabry Mill, this millstone beside Doughton Park's Basin Creek Trail was washed far from its long-gone mill by the flood of 1916.

21 Round Meadow Creek Trail

Milepost 179.2

This short loop hike along a rushing mountain stream is a twenty-minute leg-stretcher that might tempt you to tarry.

Parkway mile: 179.2
Distance: 0.4-mile loop
Difficulty: Easy

Elevation gain: 100 feet
Maps: *USGS Meadows of Dan*; no Parkway map available

Finding the trailhead: Take the right fork of the paved path at Round Meadow Overlook (GPS: 36.716426 / -80.423050).

The Hike

The paved treadway soon becomes gravel as it meanders right and down over water bars and log steps. The forest is immediately interesting. A mix of deciduous

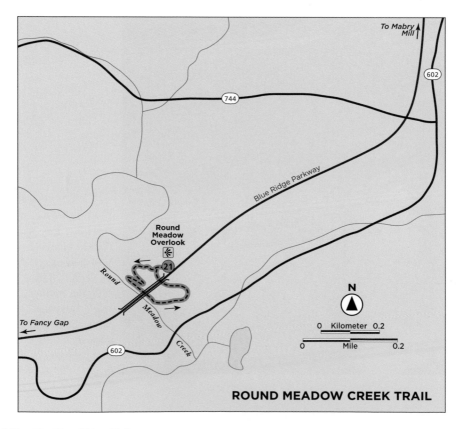

ROUND MEADOW CREEK TRAIL

hardwood trees and evergreen hemlocks, rhododendron, and mountain laurel, it's the quintessential Parkway woodland. Even if the weather hasn't been particularly wet, you'll probably hear the stream rushing below.

Past running cedar, the trail switchbacks to the streambank. Head left on an old road grade along the river. The Parkway span is high above, and the opposite bank is covered in towering hemlocks and dense rhododendron.

Passing far below the bridge, follow a left-pointing arrow off the road grade. The pine needle–covered path strikes off into a white pine and hemlock forest. A state highway is visible off to the right when the leaves are down. The trail arcs up and left, eventually reversing direction back to the Parkway. The bridge you walked far beneath appears ahead. Go under it on a now-paved path; a right turn puts you back in the driver's seat.

Key Points

0.15 Turn left along the river on a road grade.

0.3 Turn left off the road grade.

The Primland Resort's 11,000 acres, landmark lodge, and surrounding trails offer great views of distant North Carolina state parks, Pilot Mountain, on the right, and Hanging Rock, center. See the Mileage Log at 177.7. COURTESY PRIMLAND RESORT

22 Blue Ridge Music Center

Milepost 213.0

One of the Parkway's newest facilities, the Blue Ridge Music Center is dedicated to the stirring fusion of Irish, English, Scots-Irish, and African music and instruments that came together early in US history to create the nation's traditional music. Exhibits trace Appalachia's early ballad-based music from the 1700s through the early twentieth century emergence of "hillbilly music," then bluegrass, and on to commercial country music and the growing popularity of traditional mountain music.

Music erupts on the center's breezeway every day in summer with the Mid-Day Mountain Musicians series. There's a weekend concert series from June into autumn in an impressive outdoor amphitheater (dedicated in October 2001 by Ralph Stanley and the Clinch Mountain Boys). Visit blueridgemusiccenter.org/index.htm for more music information.

After four years of finalization from 2008 to 2011, the Music Center's groundbreaking and interactive Roots of American Music exhibition is complete and ready to wow anyone interested in virtually any branch of our national soundtrack. The center is operated by the National Park Service and the Blue Ridge Parkway Foundation manages programming.

Two red-blazed trails explore the surrounding fields and forests. One offers an out-and-back walk through meadows and wetlands, the other a longer loop hike up to forested Fisher Peak (where there is a view). In 2013, the Piedmont Land Conservancy added an additional 550 acres to the center's existing 1,700-acre natural area.

Parkway mile: 213
Distance: 2.7-mile out and back on High Meadow Trail (a TRACK Trail); 3.3-mile Fisher Peak Loop
Difficulty: Easy to moderate
Elevation gain: 290 feet maximum

Maps: *USGS Lambsurg*; Parkway trail map available online and at the Music Center and online at nps.gov/blri/planyourvisit/misic-center-trails.htm (Despite the misspelling of "music" this link worked at press time.)

Finding the trailhead: Enter the Music Center at Milepost 213. Continue straight at the intersection with VA 612 to the museum and park in the lot beyond; the trail branches near the east side of the building (GPS: 36.574090 / -80.849354).

Be aware the center prefers that hikers park at a second satellite trailhead, located on VA 612. From the museum, go left on VA 612 at the junction you passed on the way in; park at 0.5 mile in the curve at the other trailhead (GPS: 36.567698 / -80.858267). From the Parkway, turn onto VA 612 at Milepost 213.3 and park at the trailhead in the curve at 0.2 mile. *Note:* The gate to the Music Center trailhead is locked at 5 p.m., which further urges starting the hike on VA 612.

The Hikes

The High Meadow Trail is the Blue Ridge Music Center's TRACK Trail and this experience is special indeed. The trail's "Music from the Mountains" guide booklet shows the role specific local trees play in the construction of popular Appalachian instruments, the banjo, mandolin, and dulcimer. Other brochures feature nature topics. See the TRACK Trail map and download brochures here: www.kidsinparks.com/blue-ridge-music-center.

From trailhead to trailhead, the High Meadow Trail runs 1.35 miles under Fisher Peak through fields near the forest edge (a 2.7-mile out-and-back). The elevation gain is only 100 feet. Starting at the VA 612 trailhead, cross the road and enter the woods. The trail has a wonderful mix of meadows and forests. The Fisher Peak Loop branches to the right at 0.4 mile. Continue straight. After a meadow section, you'll cross bridges over a wetland at 0.7 mile, and slab past benches under a rock outcrop in the woods at 0.9 mile. The Fisher Peak Loop rejoins on the right just beyond and two more bridges cross Chestnut Creek as you near the Music Center. Check out the exhibits or listen to a local musician and return to your car.

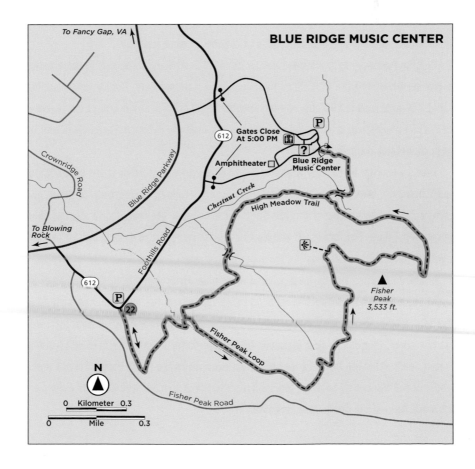

THE BIRTH OF THE BLUE RIDGE PARKWAY—HIGH ROAD TO THE PAST

The earliest parkways—among them New York's Westchester Parkway and the George Washington Memorial Parkway from Washington, DC, to Mount Vernon, Virginia—were built to merge scenery with speed in an early ideal of motoring as both travel and recreation. That ideal got its start not long after the creation of great urban parks by Frederick Law Olmsted, himself an early Parkway proponent.

The original idea for a Blue Ridge Parkway–style road seems to have originated as far back as 1909 with Joseph Hyde Pratt, director of North Carolina's Geological and Economic Survey. He dreamed up a privately funded ridgetop Appalachian toll road, surveyed portions of a proposed route, and by 1912 had even constructed a section near Linville, North Carolina, that would later become part of the Parkway. The turmoil of World War I put an end to this dream.

By 1930 the possibility of actually building a Blue Ridge Parkway had been furthered by a number of developments. Building scenic roads between national parks had become a topic of discussion, and the Great Depression had prompted legislation permitting the Public Works Administration to build and maintain roads to counter unemployment.

But the Parkway can trace what may be its most immediate precedent to the creation of the Skyline Drive atop the Blue Ridge in Shenandoah National Park. Construction had begun on that 100-mile road in 1931 as a Depression-era relief project, and it wasn't long before the idea surfaced to extend the road into a park-to-park highway between Shenandoah and Great Smoky Mountains National Parks.

That's when the battle over where to locate that Parkway started—a struggle detailed in Anne Whisnant's book *Super Scenic Motorway*. The years-long controversy centered on the Parkway's strong suit—scenery. Virginia got the nod because the road had to start at Shenandoah National Park. But Tennessee and North Carolina were left to duke it out for the Smoky Mountain connection, each claiming the superior scenery.

Interior Secretary Harold Ickes wanted more objective information, so in summer 1934 he sent Forestry Director Robert Marshall to weigh the two routes. Marshall had early on challenged the idea of the Parkway on the grounds that it would further chop up what little wilderness remained. (Montana's Bob Marshall Wilderness today honors the man who ultimately devoted much of his life to wilderness preservation, both in the USDA Forest Service and as a founder of the Wilderness Society.) Marshall reported back to Ickes that he could defend either choice but favored the North Carolina route.

The political maneuvering of the route-selection process climaxed at a September 18, 1934, hearing in Washington, DC. The Asheville Chamber of Commerce, motivated by a desire to sustain the city's century-long tourist economy, hired a train to pack the hearing. The group appeared to be winning until Tennesseans revealed the supposed secret that Ickes's selection committee had recommended the Tennessee route. But on November 10, 1934, Ickes overruled his own selection committee and gave North Carolina the Parkway (largely due to his opinion that the route was scenically superior). But controversy continued.

Indeed, the entire project—finessed into existence as a relief project by Roosevelt's Public Works Administration—was still in doubt because Congress had never approved it. Then North Carolina congressman Robert Doughton introduced a bill to formally name the road the Blue Ridge Parkway and transfer control to the National Park Service when completed. On June 20, 1936, by a vote of 145 to 131—with 147 abstaining—the bill barely passed the House.

Parkway construction had already started in North Carolina, heading south from the Virginia state line in September 1935. The first construction in Virginia started south of Roanoke on February 29, 1936. Right-of-way problems and a desire to employ people first in the most economically depressed areas (most workers were unemployed locals) meant that for decades large uncompleted sections of road interrupted the route.

By 1970 the road was complete save for a short section at Grandfather Mountain. This "missing link" had been debated for decades between the National Park Service and the Mac-Rae family who owned Grandfather. By the 1950s, MacRae descendant Hugh Morton had built a tourist road to a "Mile-High Swinging Bridge" on the peak and the stage was set for stalemate. The Parkway wanted a higher route for the road to assure great views on public land. Morton wanted a lower route, ostensibly to preserve the mountainside but also to protect the appeal of his tourist business. Morton and the Park Service battled for decades until North Carolina citizens and the state sided with Morton. A "middle route" was chosen. The gap was closed—and the Parkway debuted—in 1987, two years after the Parkway's fiftieth anniversary. Today the Parkway is a seamless journey, and many motorists would agree that Grandfather Mountain and the famous Linn Cove Viaduct that helped close the gap are scenic highpoints of the high road experience.

The 2.24-mile Fisher Peak Loop branches from and returns to the lower trail not far from either trailhead. Starting from and returning to the VA 612 trailhead, the total loop is 3.3 miles. Leave the trailhead and turn right on the Fisher Peak Loop at about 0.5 mile. You'll walk under power lines at 0.7 mile. As you crest a ridge, head left on a short trail to a bench and nice view of the Music Center. Depending on when you hike, you could hear mountain music echoing up from the hollow below. At 2.2 miles turn left on the High Meadows Trail and soon pass under a cliffy outcrop with a few benches for resting. You're back at your car at 3.3 miles.

If you time it right, you may hear music on the trail while hiking during a summer performance at the Blue Ridge Music Center. COURTESY BLUE RIDGE PARKWAY FOUNDATION

23 Cumberland Knob Recreation Area

Mileposts 217.5–218.6

Just below the Virginia–North Carolina line, a historical marker calls the Parkway "the first rural national parkway." Less than a mile south, at Cumberland Knob, is the spot where construction of the Blue Ridge Parkway started on September 11, 1935. Cumberland Knob's information building and an atmospheric picnic shelter atop the knob are among the Parkway's earliest structures.

At just about 2,860 feet, Cumberland Knob isn't a spectacular peak, but the 1,000-acre watershed makes a great day hike. Cumberland Knob's primary facilities are a large picnic area and an information/comfort station.

A monument on the plaza in front of the information station honors the Parkway's fiftieth anniversary on September 11, 1985, and memorializes the contributions of the landscape architects who've shaped the park experience.

A small cemetery reminds visitors how hard life was less than a century ago in these isolated mountains. A sign tells of a sixteen-year-old mother-to-be who asked the landowner for permission to be buried under an apple tree on this spot. He said OK, thinking that her death was far off. Rebecca Smith Moxley died soon after her baby was born.

Option 1: Gully Creek Trail

One of the most worthwhile trails that dip from the Parkway's heights, the Gully Creek Trail explores a topographically intriguing watershed.

Parkway mile: 217.5
Distance: 2.5-mile loop
Difficulty: Strenuous
Elevation gain: 820 feet

Maps: *USGS Cumberland Knob, Virginia/ North Carolina*; Parkway handout map available online at nps.gov/blri/planyourvisit/ cumberland-knob-trail.htm

Finding the trailhead: Park near the information station in the Cumberland Knob Picnic Area (GPS: 36.553924 / -80.907362).

The Hike

From the vista side of the information station (there's a nice view of Pilot Mountain), head left at the Woodland Trail sign to start the Gully Creek Trail; as you near the picnic loop, turn right downhill on the paved trail.

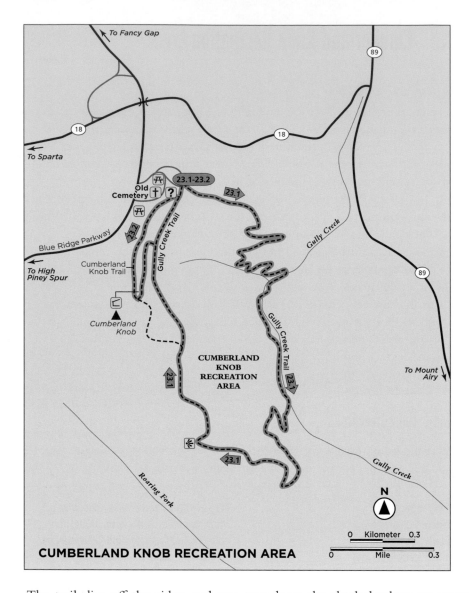

CUMBERLAND KNOB RECREATION AREA

0   Kilometer   0.3

0   Mile   0.3

The trail dips off the ridge, and you soon leave the rhododendron on many switchbacks down the dry ridge to Gully Creek. Beyond, the green fields of farms lie 1,000 feet below.

The trail switchbacks repeatedly on the sunny southeast side of the ridge, a growing stream continually blocking the trail's route. When Gully Creek tumbles in from the left, cross it for the first time at 0.5 mile on rocks. There's a bridge, many waterfalls, and more crossings before you finally rise away from the stream at 1.2 miles. Off to the left, pines cap the portal where Gully Creek escapes into the Piedmont.

The trail rounds the apex of the ridge at 1.4 miles and, bam, the lush and mossy rhododendron and hardwood ecosystem on the wetter, colder, more northerly slope gives way to the dry and sunny southeastern-side forest of mountain laurel and pine. A carpet of needles scents the air.

The trail makes a steepening climb along the ridge then slides off to the right along the top of a drainage under the bulk of Cumberland Knob. At 2.2 miles, the Cumberland Knob Trail goes left 0.2 mile to the historic picnic shelter atop the knob. Stay right; the trail becomes paved near the parking area.

Key Points

0.0 Leave trailhead.

0.5 Cross Gully Creek.

0.9 Small falls at creek crossing.

1.2 Leave Gully Creek.

1.4 Dramatic change in vegetation.

2.2 Left goes to Cumberland Knob; keep right.

2.4 Another left to Cumberland Knob; keep right.

2.5 Arrive back at parking area.

Option 2: Cumberland Knob Trail

An easy amble takes you to a classic stone picnic shelter atop Cumberland Knob.

See map on page 154.
Parkway mile: 217.5
Distance: 0.5-mile loop
Difficulty: Easy
Elevation gain: 100 feet

Maps: *USGS Cumberland Knob, Virginia/ North Carolina*; Parkway handout map available online at nps.gov/blri/planyourvisit/ cumberland-knob-trail.htm

Finding the trailhead: Park near the information/comfort station in the Cumberland Knob Picnic Area (GPS: 36.553924 / -80.907362). Walk to the right of the building and through the porch to the sign that reads "Woodland Trail."

The Hike

Two paved trails go right from the "Woodland Trail" sign. The shortest, easiest loop hike to Cumberland Knob goes hard right past the cemetery and up the paved path along the picnic tables near the parking lot. (The paved path on the left through the meadow is your return route.) As the path leaves the picnic tables, it rises over rougher treadway at the summit to the right of an old stone-and-log shelter with a shake roof and a fireplace at about 0.3 mile.

Turn left across the front of the shelter—there's not much of a view—and gradually descend into the woods, then swing right to intersect Gully Creek Trail (this is the second path that branches left near the end of the Gully Creek walk). Go left;

the path is paved as it crosses the meadow to the information station for a loop of 0.5 mile.

Key Points

0.3 Summit shelter.

Option 3: High Piney Spur

A level paved path leads to a striking viewpoint.

Parkway mile: 218.6
Distance: 100 yards
Difficulty: Easy, handicapped accessible

Elevation gain: Negligible
Maps: *USGS Cumberland Knob, Virginia/North Carolina*; no Parkway map available

Finding the trailhead: Take the spur road from Fox Hunter's Paradise Overlook to a lot at High Piney Spur (GPS: 36.541550 / -80.918864).

The Hike

This flat, paved trail is so short that the sign just says "Pedestrian Walkway." The path departs from a shady bluff that projects away from the Parkway at 2,830 feet. It terminates at a stone observation deck on the very prow of the ridge. This is High Piney Spur, a dramatically airy perch with a great view into the Piedmont.

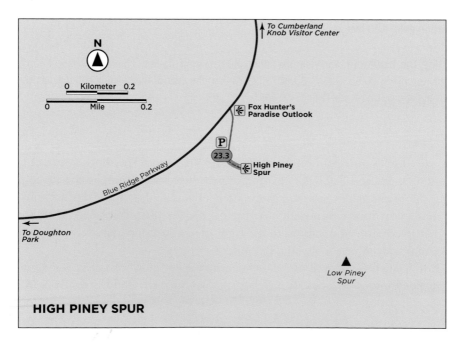

MOUNTAINS-TO-SEA TRAIL

The Mountains-to-Sea Trail (MST), which leaves the Blue Ridge Parkway south of High Piney Spur at Devil's Garden Overlook (Milepost 235.7) on its way to the coast, got its start in the 1970s with the dream of a statewide trail from the Great Smokies to the Outer Banks.

The trail through the mountains of North Carolina is quickly nearing completion, with much of that route skirting its way along the Blue Ridge Parkway. From northerly Devil's Garden Overlook, the trail turns east and drops precipitously down the Blue Ridge to Stone Mountain State Park. To the south, there are two competing routes into the Smokies from the Parkway's Waterrock Knob (see the Mileage Log at Mileposts 451.2 and 458.2). One path enters the park's backcountry from Heintooga Spur Road, and another route dips from Waterrock Knob area into the valley towns of Sylva and Bryson City before entering the park's Deep Creek Area.

Between the two areas much of the trail is in place, including stretches that flank the Parkway that could be considered by Parkway visitors.

The great plus for Parkway motorists is that at any crossing of the MST, and there are many, you can stride off into the woods for a leg-stretcher. (Check the Mileage Log in the back of this guide for the latest crossings.) The less-ideal side of the situation is that most walks on the MST will be out-and-back hikes (unless you use two cars), and relatively few circuit opportunities exist, especially on the Parkway. In addition, camping is prohibited on the Parkway except at formal sites. That complicates an end-to-end trek. But times are changing. At publication, there are three formal backcountry campsites on the Parkway (Rocky Knob in Virginia, and Doughton Park and Price Park in North Carolina). But more campsites along the Parkway are now being formalized on the MST (a permit will be required), and camping is easy along the MST in national forests.

For all the above reasons, this book doesn't detail all the MST's roadside strolls, but a selection of awesome Mountains-to-Sea Trail hikes is featured below. Best of all, the increasingly vibrant Friends of the Mountains-to-Sea Trail organization now offers free online and inexpensive printed guides to the trail that are the preferred resource if you really want to hike big stretches of the MST, which more and more people are doing. This trail is changing frequently and evolving, and the Friends' guides are updated often. Visit ncmst.org/.

A great burst of enthusiasm launched the MST effort in the 1980s, followed by a lull in the early 1990s. Enthusiasm was reignited when the route gained state park status and more funding. Growing participation in the Friends of the Mountains-to-Sea Trail's regional task forces has since sparked faster trail construction and consolidated funding. The trail

(continued)

is rapidly finding its way across the state, with an expected completion date of 2020. Where a path isn't practical, bikeable sections of road and paddleable sections of river are the choice.

Besides referring to the hikes in the body of this book, check the Mileage Log for additional access points.

MP 235.7: Devil's Garden Overlook

From Devil's Garden Overlook, it's a 3.3-mile descent to a scenic waterfall and streamside camping on the Widow's Creek Trail at Stone Mountain State Park's backcountry campsites. Backcountry permits are required and need to be picked up at the registration sign on the Widow's Creek Trail in the state park. If you hike down, you'll need to register while dropping a car. Your best bet is to start at the state park and hike up Widow's Creek Trail. (See Mileage Log, MP 229.7. Take US 21 east to a well-signed right turn onto NC 1100 for Stone Mountain State Park and access to Widow's Creek Trail.)

MP 242.4: Doughton Park

Doughton Park's Bluff Mountain Trail is a stunning meadow-covered section of the MST. (See Hike 24, Option 2.)

MP 272.5: E. B. Jeffress Park

Two separate paths at two overlooks are portions of the MST. Link them to create a great easy waterfall walk that's a partial loop (Hike 26).

MP 291.8–294.6: Moses H. Cone Memorial Park

The MST snakes through Cone Park on an intricate assortment of moderate "carriage roads" that permit long loop hikes. (For MST circuits, check out Hike 27, Options 6, 7, and 8.)

MP 295.9–297.2: Julian Price Memorial Park

The northern terminus of the Tanawha Trail is in Price Park Campground, and the path is designated as the MST all the way to its southern terminus at Beacon Heights on Grandfather Mountain (Hike 31). This meadow-dotted area includes many particularly nice out-and-back walks, one new stellar circuit called the Holloway Meadow Loop, and a few overnighters that feature Price Park's backcountry campsite (Hike 29, Options 1 and 2).

MP 299.1–305.1: Grandfather Mountain

This trail offers some of the most scenic sections of the MST. By starting south of Grandfather Mountain at Beacon Heights and ending up at Moses Cone Park, you could camp midway in

Grandfather Mountain State Park, and end up at Price Park Campground or the park's back-country campsite for a two-night backpack. Hike out to Shull's Mill Road the third day (or start there and do it in reverse). A new bridge across Boone Fork makes this stretch a seamless and attractive backpack trip. (See Hike 28 Option 2, Hike 29, Option 1 and 2, Hike 30 Option 1, and Hike 31).

MP 344.1: Mount Mitchell

The MST climbs from Black Mountain Campground to the top of the East's highest peak for those who want to take the full measure of the mountain (Hike 38, Option 1).

MP 359.8–355.3: Walker Knob Overlook (formerly Balsam Gap Parking Area) to NC 128

One of the most scenic sections of the MST runs for 4.6 miles from Walker Knob Overlook to NC 128 along the junction between the Great Craggy and Black Mountains in an area that some say resembles the Pacific Northwest. Hike north or south from either trailhead to spectacular viewpoints on Blackstock Knob and return for ideal day hikes. (See the Mileage Log, MP 359.8.)

MP 363.4: Craggy Mountains

Leave Graybeard Mountain Overlook (Milepost 363.4) and hike south for out-and-back hikes through the dramatic summit scenery of the Great Craggies' wind-stunted high-altitude vegetation, perhaps turning around at the summit above Craggy Flats Picnic Shelter for a 6.2-mile round-trip (Hike 39).

MP 396.4–407.6: Shut-In Trail

The Shut-In Trail section of the Mountains-to-Sea Trail follows the route of George Vanderbilt's access trail to his Buck Spring Hunting Lodge (Hike 40, Option 3, and many access points in the Mileage Log).

MP 418.8: Graveyard Fields and Shining Rock Wilderness

The Graveyard Fields Overlook accesses the Mountains-to-Sea Trail for a few nice loops. One explores the waterfalls of Yellowstone Prong. Another crosses meadow-covered Black Balsam Knob (Hikes 41 and 42, Option 2).

MP 422.4: Devil's Courthouse

Take in Devil's Courthouse, then cross over a Parkway tunnel to the MST for a great view of the Shining Rock Wilderness (Hike 43).

24 Doughton Park

Mileposts 241.1–248.1

After the Parkway's journey south over pastoral rolling scenery to the Virginia state line, North Carolina's Doughton Park signals the road's return to loftier country.

Doughton Park rears to an abrupt escarpment of rocky cliffs and plunging coves. Across this crest—where the Parkway winds along the edge of prominent headlands—dramatic bluffs afford great views, hence the area's originally being called the Bluffs.

Doughton—roughly Mileposts 238.0 to 246.0—includes a dramatic drop into Basin Cove, a watershed more than 2,000 feet deep that plummets southeast from the roadside. This 6,000-acre area is one of only three places on the Parkway where overnight backpacking is permitted.

At Parkway Milepost 238.5, rustic Brinegar Cabin is the only Parkway log cabin listed on the National Register of Historic Sites. This and adjoining structures are the real thing: an original cabin built circa 1880 by Martin Brinegar at a lofty 3,500 feet. In summer, interpreters plant a garden behind the structure and demonstrate Carolyn Brinegar's original loom that sits inside.

At the easy-to-reach viewpoint of Wildcat Rocks, glimpse over the edge at Caudill Cabin, built in 1894. It sits as far back in a hollow as Martin Caudill could get without climbing up the mountainside. Here he raised fourteen children—six fewer than his father, James Harrison Caudill, the area's first settler.

The isolated valley was once a thriving community with a school, store, church, and post office. The last residents moved out after the horrific flood of 1916. Most Parkway motorists just peer off the road at the cabin and drive on but the bulk of Doughton's 30-mile trail system explores the old Basin Cove community. The cabin may be the best-preserved relic (it was last restored in summer 2001), but hikers will also encounter old chimneys, foundations, fences, and fields being reclaimed by forest. Backpackers require a free camping permit to use the designated backcountry campsite. The best place to acquire permits in season is the Doughton Park Campground kiosk, Milepost 239.2. If you have a few weeks before your trip, call (336) 372-8877 and request a permit by mail. In winter you can also call the Bluffs District office at Doughton, Milepost 245.5 (828-348-3487).

You can reserve sites at Doughton Park Campground in advance by using the recreation.gov website or calling (877) 444-6777. Doughton also has a picnic area, but sadly, the park's concession-operated coffee and gift shop and twenty-four-room Bluffs Lodge have been shuttered in recent years. Being optimistic, I put them on the map. Check the Parkway website for the latest.

The Caudill family still visits their ancestral cabin in Doughton Park. Brothers Larry (bottom) and Lenny (top) return from doing a little volunteer maintenance with Lenny's son Alex.

Option 1: Wildcat Rocks and Fodder Stack

An easy paved trail to a view of Caudill Cabin and a rugged but short scramble to a spectacular crag—both head out from the same trailhead.

Parkway mile: 241.1
Distance: 0.3 mile out and back for Wildcat Rocks; 2.0 miles out and back for Fodder Stack
Difficulty: Easy for Wildcat Rocks; moderately strenuous for Fodder Stack

Elevation gain: Negligible for Wildcat Rocks
Maps: *USGS Whitehead*; Parkway handout map, available at the ranger station (Milepost 245.5), campground kiosk in season (Milepost 239.2), and online at nps.gov/blri/planyour visit/doughton-park-trails.htm

Finding the trailhead: Leave the Blue Ridge Parkway at Milepost 241.1. Bear left at the turn to the lodge. Park in the farther lot (GPS: 36.430291 / -81.175220).

The Hike

If you don't have much time for a hike here, this single location serves as a nice introduction to the scenic grandeur of Doughton Park. Both walks start beyond the now closed lodge on the broad bluff that juts out into the void over Basin Cove. In the parking area, a bas-relief bust honors Robert Doughton, a member of the U.S. House of Representatives who played a key role in the creation of the Blue Ridge Parkway. He purchased this tract in 1930 and became its namesake.

Even if you decide not to hike to Caudill Cabin, a glance down from Wildcat Rocks at the tiny structure is a moving experience.

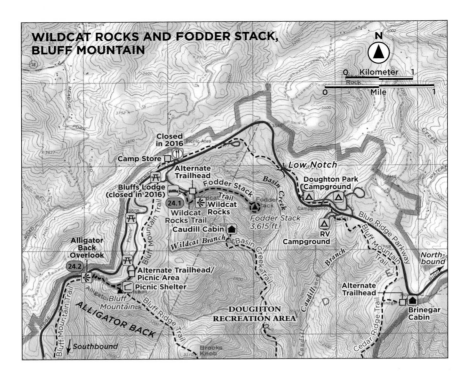

Wildcat Rocks is just above the lot where a rocky outcrop and stone wall survey the entire watershed. Take the ascending paved path up to the right. Some people picnic on the sunny rocks. Peer over to the southeast, past the summer wildflowers, and Caudill Cabin sits far below.

Nearby Fodder Stack is aptly named—it's a bumpy lump that juts out from the main ridge and stands on its own above steeply dropping terrain. The trail veers left off the back of the parking lot and descends steeply down switchbacks to a bench amid great views into Basin Cove. The trail passes a few more benches, ascends craggy outcrops, and breaks into an end loop that circles the summit to a final bench at 0.5 mile. In leafless seasons, there's a feeling of being out in the middle of it all.

Key Points for Fodder Stack

0.1   Bench with a view of Caudill Cabin.

1.0   Bench at summit view.

2.0   Arrive back at parking lot.

Option 2: Bluff Mountain Trail to Bluff Mountain

Any stretch of this yellow-blazed, 7.5-mile roadside path through meadows and forests is worth a wander (now part of the Mountains-to-Sea Trail). Two hikes feature a view from the trail shelter atop the crest of Bluff Mountain at 3,796 feet.

See map on page 163.

Parkway mile: 242.4

Distance: 1.6 miles out and back from Alligator Back Overlook; 0.6 mile out and back from the Doughton Park Picnic Area

Difficulty: Moderate to Bluff Mountain from Alligator Back Overlook; easy from the picnic area; other stretches easy to moderate

Elevation gain: 320 feet from Alligator Back Overlook; 50 feet from picnic area

Maps: *USGS Whitehead*; Parkway handout map, available at the ranger station (Milepost 245.5), campground kiosk in season (Milepost 239.2), and online at nps.gov/blri/planyourvisit/doughton-park-trails.htm

Finding the trailhead: Alligator Back Overlook is at Milepost 242.4 (GPS: 36.421039 / -81.190113); Doughton Park Picnic Area is at Milepost 241.1 (GPS: 36.421575 / -81.183319).

The Hike

The arching "alligator back" is one of Doughton Park's most inspiring roadside sights. The cliffs and crags promise great views. Reaching the peak is worth the walk.

From Alligator Back Overlook, descend and go left onto the Bluff Mountain Trail/MST. The path breaks into steep sections of log steps before emerging onto crags with dramatic views. Past the views, soon turn right onto the red-blazed Bluff Ridge Trail (left, the Bluff Mountain Trail/MST goes to the picnic area). Not far beyond is the three-sided trail shelter atop Bluff Mountain (no camping).

The shelter and nearby clifftop make one of the Parkway's best easy hikes from the end loop of the picnic area. Take the path through the expansive meadow; in about 0.2 mile, turn right to the rocky clifftop then return and stay straight on the Bluff Ridge Trail to the shelter. Retrace your steps.

Key Points from Alligator Back Overlook

0.0 Start at Alligator Back Overlook.

0.2 Trail starts to climb.

0.5 Clifftop views.

0.6 Turn right onto Bluff Ridge Trail. (From picnic area, turn left at 0.2 mile.)

0.8 Reach trail shelter view (0.3 mile from picnic area).

1.6 Arrive back at the starting point (0.6 mile from picnic area).

The rest of the Bluff Mountain Trail is best strolled out and back from your choice of starting points—or invite friends and spot another car. This trail is one of those "transportation" paths that link roadside facilities but don't form loops. Nevertheless, its ridgeline location makes for nice views. Just see the map, check the mileage log for overlook access points, and pick a section. One starting point stands out:

Brinegar Cabin

Leave the end of the cabin's parking area (Milepost 238.5) and take the trail up the hill. Turn right in about 0.2 mile where the Cedar Ridge Trail goes left into Basin Cove. There are nice meadow views at about 0.4 mile for a turnaround (an

0.8-mile round-trip). It's also just over a mile from the Brinegar Cabin to the park's campground and facilities, another nice turnaround. Campers could hike to Brinegar and back for round-trip hikes of 2.8 or 2.2 miles (from the tent and RV campsites, respectively). It's 2.7 miles to Doughton Park's now-closed restaurant, a perfect place to head back to your car after a diverse sampling of the forests and fields that so recommend the Bluff Mountain Trail.

Option 3: Basin Cove Circuit Hikes

The Flat Rock Ridge Trail–Grassy Gap Fire Road circuit is the easiest Basin Cove loop hike (though harder ones are covered). This is a moderate backpacking trip, one of the best on the Blue Ridge Parkway. It can easily include a side trip to Caudill Cabin.

Parkway mile: 244.7
Distance: Flat Rock Ridge Trail–Grassy Gap Fire Road circuit, 11.1 miles; Bluff Ridge Trail–Grassy Gap Fire Road route, 8.7 miles; Bluff Ridge Trail–Flat Rock Ridge Trail circuit, about 13.0 miles
Difficulty: Strenuous, largely due to distance

Elevation gain: 1,800 to 1,900 feet
Maps: *USGS Whitehead*; Parkway handout map, available at the ranger station (Milepost 245.5), campground kiosk in season (Milepost 239.2), and online at nps.gov/blri/planyour visit/doughton-park-trails.htm

Finding the trailhead: Park at Basin Cove Overlook, Milepost 244.7 (GPS: 36.390807 / -81.199823). Bluff Mountain Overlook is at 243.4 (GPS: 36.408531 / -81.195604). Acquire backcountry camping permits in season at the Doughton Park Campground kiosk, Milepost 239.2. If you have a few weeks before your trip, call (336) 372-8877 and request a permit by mail. In winter you can also call the Bluffs District office at Doughton, Milepost 245.5 (828-348-3487).

The Hikes

Basin Cove is nicely configured for a lengthy circuit hike or a backpacking trip. The Bluff Mountain Trail gradually parallels the Parkway along the upper rim of the cove and four trails plunge into the drainage to meet near the backcountry campsite. A fifth trail in the bottom of the cove, the Basin Creek Trail, provides a day-hike side trip to Caudill Cabin. Unless you're a hiking animal, the cabin won't be accessible from the Parkway, so start at the bottom for the cabin; see Option 4.

A downhill circuit from the Parkway is doable in a day, but the 10- to 12-mile distance makes it a challenge. Luckily for day hikers who don't expect to reach the cabin, the route back up to your car is a bona fide moderate grade—the Grassy Gap Fire Road.

Many hikes are possible; just look at the map. The best circuit for backpackers starts at the Basin Cove Overlook and drops 5.0 miles down the sky blue–blazed Flat

Rock Ridge Trail to the Grassy Gap Fire Road. Leave the overlook and in 0.1 mile go right on the Flat Rock Ridge Trail at the junction where the Bluff Mountain Trail goes left. The Flat Rock Ridge is rugged, with frequent ups and downs, but it's well maintained and has the best scenery and views at 0.7 and 1.7 miles. Pause at about 2.0 miles at a great viewpoint.

Exit onto Longbottom Road at 5.0 miles. Go left across the bridge and left again back into the woods past the "Doughton Park" backcountry sign on the easy stream-side stroll of Grassy Gap Fire Road. Soon pass the Cedar Ridge Trail on the right to Brinegar Cabin, then cross a new trail bridge on Basin Creek (sponsored by the

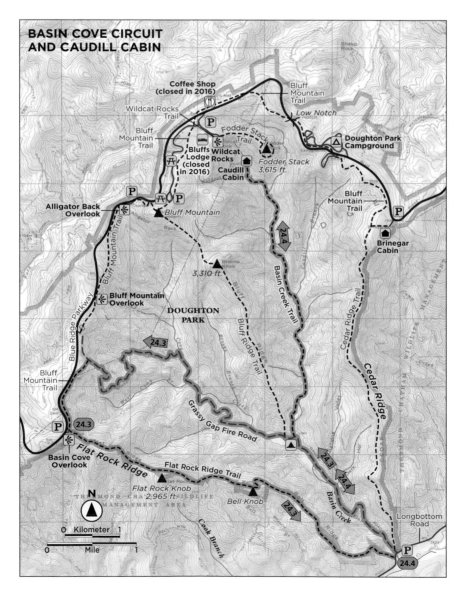

Piedmont Hiking and Outing Club and the Blue Ridge Parkway Foundation). The designated campsite appears just beyond on the left at 6.7 miles. This makes a premier base for a three-day camping trip with a hike to Caudill Cabin on day two and an easy fire road walk back to the Parkway on day three. (For more on camping, see Option 4.)

Day hikers just blow on by the campsite (or have lunch there). After a long gradual rise, go left on one of the easiest portions of the gradual Bluff Mountain Trail at 10.1 miles to Basin Cove Overlook at 11.1 miles.

There are two other nice circuits. The shortest in the area (and perhaps the best day hike without camping gear) also includes the Grassy Gap Fire Road but starts at the Bluff Mountain Overlook (Milepost 243.4). Take the gradual Bluff Mountain Trail and climb up to the Bluff Mountain Shelter and a rest at 1.9 miles. (See Option 2 for more suggestions.) Backpackers with heavy packs could defuse the uphill to the shelter by parking on the end loop of the picnic area (saving the climb back up for a later day with a lighter pack). From the shelter descend the steep and forested Bluff Ridge Trail 2.8 miles to the campsite—4.7 miles from the start. That leaves an easy return leg of 5 miles on the fire road and 0.6 mile on the Bluff Mountain Trail back to the Bluff Mountain Overlook—only 10.3 miles if done in a day.

The most rugged loop—done the easiest way—deletes the gradual fire road and starts at the Basin Cove Overlook. Head left on the Bluff Mountain Trail and descend to the campsite on the Bluff Ridge Trail for a 6.3-mile first leg. Descend the fire road to Longbottom Road for a right turn, then make another right across the bridge onto Flat Rock Ridge Trail. Flat Rock Ridge is the best of the difficult uphill hikes because it's longer, sections switchback, and there are views to admire during rest stops. Return to your car for a 13.0-mile round-trip.

For backpackers on any of these circuits, Caudill Cabin becomes a day hike from the designated campsite beside Cove Creek.

Key Points for Basin Cove Overlook Circuit

0.1 Go right on Flat Rock Ridge Trail where the Bluff Mountain Trail goes left.

2.0 Ridgetop view.

5.0 Left at road to another left on Grassy Gap Fire Road.

6.7 Pass campsite—or set up a tent.

10.1 Left on Bluff Mountain Trail.

11.1 Arrive back at trailhead.

Option 4: Caudill Cabin via Grassy Gap Fire Road and Basin Creek Trail

This is the easiest way to get to Doughton Park's most isolated and evocative spot—Martin Caudill's late-nineteenth-century cabin. It's a great but lengthy day hike and an easy backpacking trip.

See map on page 166.
Parkway mile: Milepost 248.1
Distance: 10.0 miles out and back
Difficulty: Strenuous due to distance and stream crossings
Elevation gain: 1,400 feet

Maps: *USGS Whitehead*; Parkway handout map, available at the ranger station (Milepost 245.5), campground kiosk in season (Milepost 239.2), and online at nps.gov/blri/planyour visit/doughton-park-trails.htm

Finding the trailhead: At Parkway Milepost 248, go east (downhill) on NC 18. At 6.2 miles, turn left onto Longbottom Road. At 4 miles, stay left on Longbottom Road. Three miles from that turn, park on the right just past a bridge across Basin Creek (GPS: 36.375212 / -81.144729). The Grassy Gap Fire Road enters the woods directly across the road from the parking area; the Flat Rock Ridge Trail does the same on the far side of the bridge.

The Hike

The heart of Basin Cove, including Caudill Cabin, is most easily reached from below the Parkway. Luckily, easy access to the lower trailhead makes it painless.

Start on the green-blazed Grassy Gap Fire Road—a gradual, wide trail over its entire length. Follow the fire road along Basin Creek, past the junction of Cedar Ridge Trail on the right (at 0.1 mile). The fire road crosses Basin Creek on a new bridge, passes campsites on the left, and reaches a pair of trail junctions on the right at 1.6 miles. The two-acre primitive camping area beside Cove Creek contains eight widely spaced sites with fire grills. Maximum group size is twenty; maximum site capacity is forty. Until a privy is built, regulations require that campers keep toilet sites well away from camp and not closer than 200 feet from water. Campfires must be confined to existing fire sites, and no living or standing wood can be cut; use dead-and-down wood only. Water should be treated or boiled and all trash packed out. Quiet hours at the site are from 10 p.m. to 6 a.m.

Turn right from the Grassy Gap Fire Road onto the blue-blazed Basin Creek Trail and consider that this was once an old wagon road into an isolated community. Over the 3.3 miles from this junction to the cabin, the grade crosses Basin Creek or tributaries two dozen times—many likely to require wading in wet weather. (No big deal—bring Crocs or water shoes.)

You'll pass a millstone in the creek after the first steep section and an old chimney and remnants of fence in the first mile (about 2.6 miles from your car). Rhododendron and hemlocks line the stream. The old grade deteriorates, and there's a waterfall with a swirling cold water pool to soak in at 2.5 miles (4.1 miles from your start). Pass the second easily seen chimney not too far below the cabin as the trail wanders the streamside, rising and falling more frequently. The cabin sits in a clearing 3.4 miles from the campsite, 5.0 miles from Longbottom Road. Towering 800 feet above are Wildcat Rocks, Fodder Stack, and surrounding ridges. Have a picnic, plan which pool you'll chill out in on the way back, and try to imagine the hardships and rewards of a life lived in such a secluded, hardscrabble place.

THE CAUDILLS' CABIN

When Parkway visitors gaze down at Caudill Cabin from Wildcat Rocks, they see Appalachian isolation. Lenny and Larry Caudill look down and see where their great-grandfather Martin Caudill raised fourteen children.

The men came to their family history at different times. Larry helped build the trail to the cabin in the 1980s with a local trail club after attending family reunions as a kid and "promising myself one day I'd visit that cabin far below." Lenny has delved deeply into genealogy—and he maintains the family history booklet he placed at the cabin for hikers.

Both men visit the rough-hewn 20- by 20-foot log structure a few times a year. On a 2009 hike they took along Lenny's then fourteen-year-old son, Alex, who was "born exactly one hundred years and one day after his grandfather Famon Caudill, the first child born in the cabin in 1895," says Lenny. Famon was one of the last residents of the Cove. He and most of the seventy-five residents left after the 1916 flood, which was caused by repeated hurricanes. His wife, Alice, her mother, and his brother were killed in the flood. Alice's grave is located at the backcountry campsite between the Basin Creek and Bluff Ridge Trails, not far from the foundation ruins of Basin Creek Baptist Church just beyond Grassy Gap Fire Road.

Some chimneys you see along the hike to Caudill Cabin mark the former cabins of other Caudills; Lenny and Larry call each by a relative's name. At the drop of a hat, they exit the trail to other ruins—including pristine "Perfect Chimney." They're actively GPS-ing their discoveries.

Sadly, the Caudill family cemetery still eludes them. "We'll find it. I promise," Lenny says. "To have a place where your family history is preserved is a rare opportunity," he continues. "We're particularly grateful to the Park Service for preserving our heritage."

As the National Park Service turned 100 in 2016, every citizen can say that the national parks are doing that for all of us.

Backpackers who use the designated campsite have the easiest day hike. A free camping permit is required and is available in season at the Bluffs District office, Milepost 245.5 (828-348-3487), or the campground kiosk in warm seasons, Milepost 239.2 (336-372-8877). Call to request a permit by mail.

Key Points

1.6 Turn right at campsite onto Basin Creek Trail from Grassy Gap Fire Road.

2.5 Pass first old chimney.

4.0 Pass another chimney.

5.0 Reach Caudill Cabin.

25 Jumpinoff Rocks Trail

Milepost 260.3

A classic leg-stretcher with a little up and down leads to a secluded stone observation platform atop rocks you should definitely not be "jumpinoff."

Parkway mile: 260.3
Distance: 1.0 mile out and back
Difficulty: Easy

Elevation gain: 196 feet
Maps: *USGS Horse Gap*; no Parkway map available

Finding the trailhead: Climb the flight of steps beside a picnic table on the right side of the Jumpinoff Rocks Parking Area (36.324304 / -81.368028).

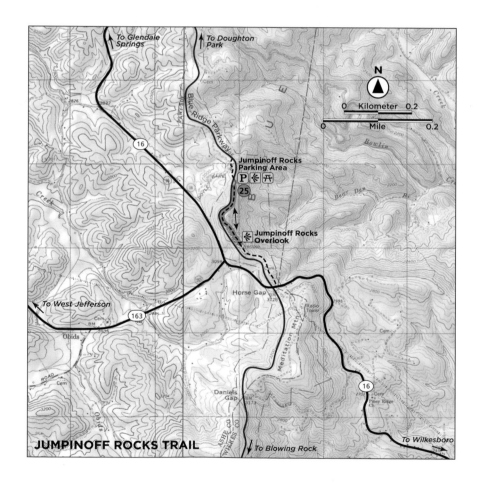

The Hike

The trail starts off in a rhododendron forest, slabbing to the right of a rising ridge. Reaching a small gap, the path levels then turns right, ascending around the high point that rises off to the left. The rooty path eventually bears left around the ridge and gradually dips to join an old road grade from the right. There's a bench at 0.3 mile, with short spurs left to limited views.

The trail bears right and dips gradually through pines and a carpet of galax into a quiet glade of white pines. Turning left, the route again reaches the edge of the drop-off beyond and steps down into a rock observation deck at 0.5 mile.

The view is expansive—and illustrative. Summer foliage softens the evidence of increasing timber harvesting, development, and second-home construction. The National Park Service and private organizations such as the Blue Ridge Parkway Foundation and Friends of the Blue Ridge Parkway are attempting to influence the future of surrounding lands.

Like other trails along this section of the Parkway, Jumpinoff Rocks Trail links north and south to North Carolina's now completed Mountains-to-Sea Trail.

Key Points

0.3 Bench.
0.5 Viewpoint.

Snowless sections of the Parkway may be open in winter, but in the most lofty locations, the snow-covered road is usually gated. A few stretches may be plowed, such as this one near Blowing Rock, North Carolina, and its neighboring High Country ski areas.

26 E. B. Jeffress Park

Mileposts 271.9–272.5

One of the Parkway's best self-guiding interpretive trails and evocative artifacts of human habitation make Jeffress Park a truly wonderful stop.

In 1933 E. B. Jeffress, chairman of the North Carolina State Highway and Public Works Commission, was one of the North Carolinians working to exclude Tennessee from the route of a mountaintop motorway between Shenandoah and Great Smoky Mountains National Parks. He also left no doubt that he and then Governor J. C. B. Ehringhaus were set against permitting the Parkway to be a toll road—as was Skyline Drive that had just opened through Virginia's Shenandoah National Park. Jeffress Park, one of the Parkway's smallest roadside recreation areas (600 acres) memorializes the man who made that "No fee" message clear to Parkway planners.

Just south of Jeffress Park, newly four-laned US 421 courses up to Deep Gap, a major Parkway access point 10 miles east of Boone, North Carolina.

Option 1: The Cascades Trail

One of the Parkway's best interpretive nature trails leads to a wonderful waterfall.

Parkway mile: 271.9
Distance: 1.0-mile loop
Difficulty: Moderate

Elevation gain: 170 feet
Maps: USGS *Maple Springs*; no Parkway map available

Finding the trailhead: Park in the Cascades parking area at Parkway Milepost 271.9 (GPS: 36.245555 / -81.458016). The trail goes left at the restroom building. A picnic area surrounds the opposite end of the parking lot, where the Tompkins Knob Trail connects. Both these trails are part of the Mountains-to-Sea Trail.

The Hike

This trail offers a great sense of the ecological community that teeters on the escarpment of the Blue Ridge. The path wanders the crest of cliffs overlooking the Piedmont and brings hikers to Falls Creek just as a waterfall leaps over the edge. You'll marvel at the meadow-covered farming community suspended on lower mountains below the Blue Ridge.

Trees are the subject of the trail's twenty interpretive plaques—a great tour to take for anyone getting familiar with the Parkway ecosystem. Between the drier location at cliffside and the well-watered stream drainage, hikers will encounter many of the tree species that populate Blue Ridge forests.

The Cascades plummets past one of the Parkway's classic old stone observation platforms.

Leave the parking lot on a paved trail that becomes gravel. There's a bench where you can ponder what you're learning about dogwood, tulip tree, pignut, black locust, serviceberry, mountain laurel, white oak, flame azalea, minnie bush, highbush blueberry, and chestnut oak.

The trail dips left into the rhododendron and arcs across a rustic log bridge over Falls Creek. The return loop trail goes left, so turn right and quickly descend stone steps to an upper rock wall–encircled observation platform where the stream jumps over the edge. The lower platform affords an even better view. Stay behind the guardrail—people have fallen to their death at these falls.

Go right at the return loop junction, pass the MST heading right, and follow the stream on your left. Cross a bridge across the stream and pause at one of the two upcoming benches. Birches, rhododendron, sweet birch, witch hazel, eastern hemlock, black gum, and red maple are all species that favor these shady streambanks. The trail rises to the junction you passed earlier, so head right to the parking area.

There's evidence here of increasing off-trail wandering: Please heed the Park Service sign asking that hikers stay on designated trails.

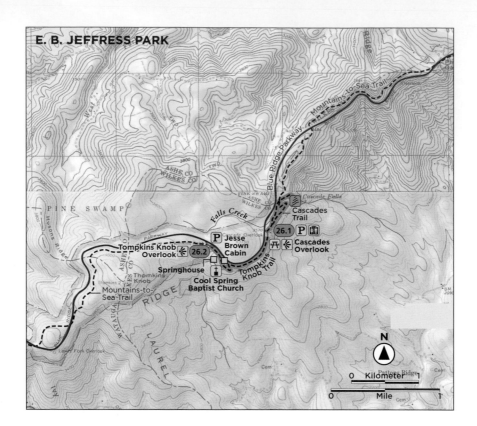

Key Points

0.05 Go right where loop splits.

0.3 Cross log bridge over stream and go right at junction.

0.4 Upper falls view with lower platform 150 feet below.

0.5 Bear right at junction.

0.9 Bear right at final junction to parking lot.

Option 2: Tompkins Knob Trail

This trail through a white pine forest inspires appreciation for early mountain structures.

See map above.
Parkway mile: 272.5
Distance: 1.2 miles out and back
Difficulty: Easy
Elevation gain: Negligible
Maps: *USGS Maple Springs*; no Parkway map
available

Finding the trailhead: Park at the Tompkins Knob Parking Area, Milepost 272.5 (GPS: 36.244276 / -81.465850) and take an immediate left from your car on a less-than-obvious path that dips across the grassy decline into the woods.

The Hike

This pleasant path offers three interesting historic structures and a longer walk to the Cascades Trail's picnic area. You could include the Cascades loop for an even longer option.

Among structures from the last century are a cabin, an adjacent springhouse, and a shelter that served as a rustic church (don't expect a steeple). No elaborate living-history displays take place here—just quiet aplenty to imagine life a hundred years ago.

Head through the woods along the Parkway and emerge below Jesse Brown's cabin—a late-nineteenth-century residence moved here to be closer to Cool Spring,

Besides the Jesse Brown Cabin, the Tompkins Knob Trail showcases a rustic church and a spring-house just to the left of this couple.

the lofty seepage trickling out of the ground in two places to your right beside a tiny decaying springhouse. Head down the short distance to examine this vanishing structure. Water gurgles out of the mossy rocks and is artfully funneled through the springhouse along one channeled-out log and into a larger log that directs the flow through the structure. The water's summertime temperature of 40-some degrees no doubt nicely chilled food stored inside the shady enclave.

The cabin and its impressive fireplace are worth a look, too. Farther up the gradual hill is the "Baptist church" named for Cool Spring—a shelter used when bad weather greeted circuit-riding preachers who dropped in to minister to high-hollow residents.

Head left at the sign describing the church and descend gently through shady hardwoods past a bench—the greatest elevation change on the whole walk. From here all the way to the Cascades Trail parking and picnic area, it's a largely level saunter under inspiring white pines where whispering trees mingle with the whoosh of a passing car. That last piney section of trail could be an out-and-back stroll from the Cascades Parking Area with the cabins as a nice destination.

The entire walk is part of the Mountains-to-Sea Trail, a stroll of 0.6 mile, a 1.2-mile round-trip.

Best of all, ambitious hikers can start from the Tompkins Knob Parking Area and hike to the Cascades, turning the 1.0-mile waterfall walk into a really pleasant 2.4-mile trek.

Key Points

0.15 Pass between Jesse Brown's cabin and springhouse.

0.2 Enter the woods beyond Cool Spring Baptist Church.

0.25 Pass first bench.

0.5 Second bench.

0.6 Jeffress Park Picnic Area and Cascades Trail parking.

The High Country

Mileposts 276.4 (US 421 at Deep Gap, NC) to 384.7 (US 74 at Asheville, NC)
From Deep Gap at US 421 (Milepost 276.4) to Asheville, North Carolina, at US 74 (Milepost 384.7), the Parkway traverses what can only be called the High Country corner of North Carolina. Ironically, the highest spot on the Parkway is not here—it's south of Asheville.

From Craggy Pinnacle, at Milepost 364.1, the Parkway winds north past Greybeard Mountain Overlook to where the Black Mountains soar into the Canadian forest zone. Mount Mitchell's summit tower is at top right.

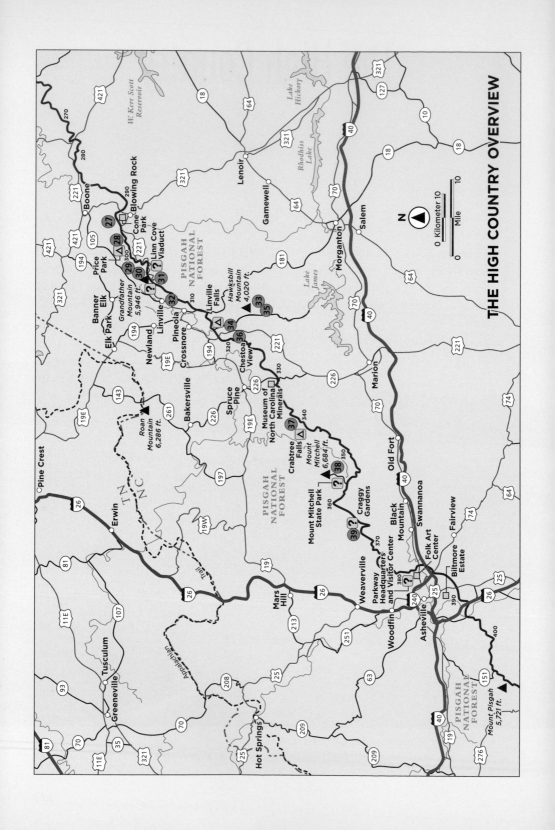

THE HIGH COUNTRY OVERVIEW

But everything else about this area says lofty, indeed, almost alpine. At Grandfather Mountain, the Blue Ridge escarpment rises to its greatest relief—nearly a vertical mile above the surrounding Piedmont. The computer-designed span of the Linn Cove Viaduct—the Parkway's newest section, opened in 1987—puts you right in the middle of it. Easily accessible just 5 miles off the Parkway is Mount Mitchell (6,684 feet), the East's highest summit. Trails at both locations deserve your attention.

But there are two sides to the High Country. The first half of this Parkway section is bordered by private lands, some of it developed and popular as a resort area. The second half is again wrapped in national forest.

The resort experience has been around since the 1880s, when the lowland rich first fled the summer heat to spark tourism in the mountains. They came for the South's coolest summer temperatures and, later, golf at classic, still popular hostelries like Blowing Rock's Green Park Inn and the chestnut bark–covered luxury of Linville's historic Eseeola Lodge.

The inns and shops of Main Street in the quaint town of Blowing Rock epitomize the appeal of the High Country tourist towns. The town's namesake destination, the Blowing Rock, is a crag with a great view that bills itself as "North Carolina's first travel attraction." Early history is the focus at Boone's summer outdoor drama *Horn in the West*, the inspiring, little-known story of how High Country mountaineers marched over the mountains to defeat Loyalists in one of the American Revolution's pivotal battles, King's Mountain.

Other area burgs include Linville, at the base of Grandfather Mountain, one of the United States' first planned resort communities. Banner Elk's license plates call it the ski capital of the South for Beech and Sugar Mountains, the region's southernmost major ski areas. And Boone, the "Hub of the High Country," is a granola-inclined college town that's home to Appalachian State University. The village of Valle Crucis claims the Mast General Store (circa 1880), which the late Charles Kuralt called "America's premier country store."

It goes without saying that there are copious craft shops and country clubs here, and the area's diverse dining is as good as or better than that in surrounding cities.

Parkway facilities in the High Country include Julian Price Memorial Park (Milepost 296.9), a major picnic area and campground memorably sited beside Price Lake. Linville Falls (Milepost 316.4) also has a campground and a large picnic area. Crabtree Falls (Milepost 339.5) has a campground. The summit state park at Mount Mitchell (Milepost 355) has a restaurant and small tent-camping area (highest in the East).

Don't forget camping in the Pisgah National Forest. Nearer to Mount Mitchell are classic campgrounds such as Black Mountain, nestled in the virgin forest at the base of the mountain. There are a few additional campgrounds far below Grandfather Mountain in a huge dirt road–laced region.

Environmental awareness is easy to cultivate on this stretch of the Parkway. The Museum of North Carolina Minerals (Milepost 330.9) is newly renovated and one of the best such exhibits anywhere. Just off the Parkway, Grandfather Mountain's Nature

Museum and environmental wildlife habitats are first rate. Mount Mitchell also has a nature museum and a new wheelchair-accessible summit tower with horizon-identifying plaques. Ten minutes east of the town of Linville Falls from the Parkway's US 221 exit is Linville Caverns—North Carolina's only commercial cavern. Just a minute west of that exit, Linville Falls Winery's vineyards sprawl across scenic hillsides. The winery's Tuscan-style tasting room is a top-notch place to sip award-winning vintages and hear live local music.

Museum-quality crafts are also in evidence. Between the Parkway Craft Center in Moses Cone's Manor House (Milepost 294) and the stunning original works of art for sale in the Folk Art Center (Milepost 382), you'll be astonished at the vibrancy of Appalachian handcrafts. The artisans who create these works get their training not far off the Parkway at the world-renowned Penland School of Crafts.

All in all, the High Country may be the high point of the Parkway experience.

Don't forget to check the Mileage Log for more detail about travel options and more trails in Boone and Blowing Rock.

For additional hikes in the area, read the author's FalconGuide *Hiking North Carolina*. For an inspiring overview of the history of the High Country and the area's most famous mountain, pick up the author's new book, *Grandfather Mountain: The History and Guide to an Appalachian Icon.*

Check appendix B for relevant websites and contact information.

Grandfather Mountain epitomizes the High Country's awesome scenery. The Tanawha Trail's boardwalks on Grandfather's view-packed Rough Ridge are just a 15-minute hike from your car.

27 Moses Cone Memorial Park

Mileposts 291.8–294.6

Moses Cone Memorial Park's 3,500 acres are quite simply one of the Parkway's best places to pause—in part because Cone Park so well exemplifies the tourism tradition of the mountains and in particular the surrounding region. This is the heart of the North Carolina High Country resort area, and the village of Blowing Rock is its crown.

Moses Cone (1857–1908) helped launch that resort tradition. His Parkway contribution started in Greensboro, North Carolina. Together with brother Cesar, Cone amassed a fortune in North Carolina's post–Civil War textile industry with his Proximity Textile Mills. He built an empire popularizing blue denim cloth and became known as "The Denim King." Cone moved to his lake-dotted mountain estate at the turn of the twentieth century and offered jobs to locals in his apple orchards and fields.

He crowned his holdings with a Victorian mansion on the crest of the Blue Ridge. His Flat Top Manor celebrated its fiftieth anniversary as the Parkway Craft Center in 2001. The estate sprawls from the mansion down across white-pine forests to Bass Lake, up to the peaks of Rich and Flat Top Mountains, and into hardwood and hemlock–filled drainages toward Grandfather Mountain—quite simply one of the most beautiful places on the Parkway.

Cone exemplified the role of wealthy benefactors in the high road's history, recalling John D. Rockefeller Jr.'s purchase of Linville Falls, and Julian Price's donation of land just south of Cone Park. Cone died in 1908, less than a decade after acquiring his estate; his wife donated the land to the new Parkway. Today he and his wife lie in graves on the Flat Top Trail.

Cone built more than 25 miles of road-width carriage paths that wander—at times corkscrew (one section is called "The Maze")—at very gradual grades with flat footing that create easy avenues for carefree strolls. These paths are perfect for families and are Nordic nirvana to cross-country skiers. Hard-core hikers will enjoy very long walks that gobble up the miles. Cone Park is a superb place to reach an energetic easy stride and just enjoy the woods.

Today portions of this massive white-pine forest appear virgin in size and grandeur—though very sadly, the hemlock woolly adelgid is killing towering trees. Under the cathedral-like canopy, hikers experience a silent and beautiful setting that dazzles cross-country skiers in winter. When snow is on the ground, walkers should take care to help preserve smooth skiing conditions by not walking in ski tracks. Please create a hikers' path on one side of the trail.

Cone attracts both horseback riders and walkers, so you may find yourself stepping around piles of equine passage. These are, after all, carriage paths, and the National

Park Service encourages horseback riding while prohibiting the more widely popular sport of mountain biking.

With so many junctions, Cone Park's system of carriage roads can be confusing, despite improved signage in recent years. The following descriptions recommend carefully described circuits that many hikers and skiers only encounter by chance.

Between the lakes of Cone and neighboring Price Park, this is the Parkway's best place for a "golden pond" experience of hissing breezes through lakeshore leaves, golden high–altitude summer light, and sunshine reflecting off the scintillating surface of a mountain lake. You can hike or camp by the water's edge; don't miss the A loop of Price Lake Campground for the quintessential lakeshore camping experience. Bass and Trout Lakes are among the most popular fishing sites in the High Country area.

Today Cone's Flat Top Manor is an impressive crafts center, visitor center, and gift shop, with frequent demonstrations by crafters and interpretive programs by park rangers (including popular tours of the mansion's upstairs). The seasonal visitor center phone number is (828) 295-3782.

Option 1: Figure Eight Trail

One of the Parkway's most successful, intriguingly designed interpretive trails explores a Northern–type forest.

Parkway mile: 294
Distance: 0.7-mile loop with figure eight
Difficulty: Easy
Elevation gain: Negligible

Maps: *USGS Blowing Rock*; Parkway handout map, available at the Cone Manor House/Parkway Craft Center and online at nps.gov/blri/planyourvisit/moses-cone-trails.htm

Finding the trailhead: Park at the Cone Manor House/Parkway Craft Center and descend to the Manor House (GPS: 36.149466 / -81.692533). Cross the front porch and descend the front steps; turn right across the lawn to the sign by the woods.

The Hike

This very easy hike should be your first walk in Moses Cone Park. At least briefly explore the craft center in the Manor House, then take in the path Mr. and Mrs. Cone shared with guests. The often evocative wording of the plaques "endeavor to interpret for you" the forest and the culture of their mountaineer neighbors.

When the gravel path splits, take the left turn at 0.1 mile through impressive rhododendron. The trail is underpinned by stonework, then turns right and heads back the way it came. Halfway back, a right turn at 0.3 mile leads into the namesake figure eight that's hidden within the loop. Like the much larger "Maze" section of carriage road above Bass Lake, this little detour through dense rhododendron is instantly disorienting—and no doubt reflective of what the Cones loved about their densely

Try the Cones' favorite path for introducing their guests to the natural beauty of the High Country.

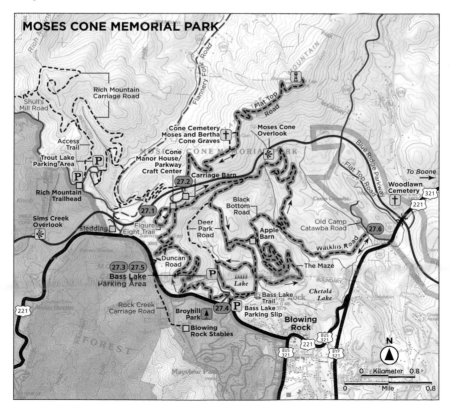

MOSES CONE MEMORIAL PARK

Rich Mountain Carriage Road

Shull's Mill Road

Flannery Fork Road

Flat Top Road

Cone Cemetery Moses and Bertha Cone Graves

Moses Cone Overlook

Access Trail

Trout Lake Parking Area

Cone Manor House/ Parkway Craft Center

Blue Ridge Parkway

To Boone

Flat Top Road

Woodlawn Cemetery

321

221

Carriage Barn

27.2

Rich Mountain Trailhead

Sims Creek Overlook

Sledding

27.1

Figure Eight Trail

Deer Park Road

Black Bottom Road

Old Camp Catawba Road

Apple Barn

27.6

Watkins Road

Duncan Road

The Maze

27.3 27.5

Bass Lake Parking Area

Bass Lake

Chetola Lake

221

Rock Creek Carriage Road

Broyhill Park

27.4

Bass Lake Trail

Bass Lake Parking Slip

Blowing Rock Stables

Blowing Rock

BUS 321

321

BUS 321

BYP 321

221

N

0   Kilometer   0.8

0   Mile   0.8

wooded Blue Ridge estate. Follow the arrows, taking a right back on the main path at 0.4 mile.

Impressive hardwoods such as oak, red maple, hickory, and black cherry cluster inside the trail loop. Toward the end, spruce and fir mix in to lend a Northern feel. That and the flat terrain make this a good cross-country ski trail.

Signs tell how the mountaineers used the trees (tea made from black cherry bark was good for coughs, and the wood "warps not at all"). By the time you leave the woods behind the massive Manor House at about 0.7 mile, you're in the perfect frame of mind to pause at one of the final plaques and "visualize the feudal elegance of this elite estate set down in the midst of mountaineer country."

Key Points
0.1 Turn left onto loop.
0.3 Turn right into figure eight.
0.4 Turn right out of figure eight.
0.7 Arrive back at Manor House.

Option 2: Flat Top Road

This is the best hike to summit views of the Moses Cone Park area.

See map on page 183.
Parkway mile: 294
Distance: 5.6 miles out and back
Difficulty: Moderate
Elevation gain: 580 feet

Maps: USGS *Blowing Rock*; Parkway handout map, available at the Cone Manor House/Parkway Craft Center and online at nps.gov/blri/planyourvisit/moses-cone-trails.htm

Finding the trailhead: Park at the north end of the Moses Cone Manor House parking area, away from the house and above the Carriage Barn (GPS: 36.149989 / -81.691726). Descend past the Carriage Barn on a wheelchair-accessible route to the gravel path below; go left.

The Hike

Flat Top Road, unlike the lower trails of Cone Park, climbs through open meadows to spectacular views from a tower on the summit of Flat Top (4,558 feet). Views encompass the entire North Carolina High Country.

Turn left below the Carriage Barn on Flat Top Road and go under the Parkway via a tunnel to emerge at a junction amid meadows. The Rich Mountain Road goes left; bear right and go uphill into woods. Enter more meadows at 0.9 mile; a spur leads left to graves where Cone and his wife lie sheltered by a grove of evergreens. Mrs. Cone lived four decades after her husband's death, long enough to see his grave broken into in 1924. The *Watauga Democrat* headline read "Ghouls Enter Grave of Moses H. Cone."

Like Flat Top Road shown here, Cone Park's carriage trails often wind into spacious flower-filled meadows.

The road continues across the meadow, switchbacks right, and enters the woods. At one point the route swings just above cliffs that drop off into the forest. The trail makes very tight turns at 2.0 miles and then curves around the summit to reach the tower at 2.8 miles (5.6 miles out and back).

The tower was nicely restored in 2001. Expect a touch of acrophobia on the breezy climb to the top. Grandfather Mountain dominates the vista.

Key Points

0.1   Keep right at junction to climb along edge of meadow.

0.9   Cone family gravesite.

2.8   Summit tower.

Option 3: Bass Lake Loop Hike

This hike is a circumambulation of Cone Park's prettiest lake.

See map on page 183.
Parkway mile: 294.6

Distance: 0.8-mile loop from the lakeshore parking lot; 1.2-mile loop from US 221 trailhead

4.7 Turn right onto Watkins Road and retrace route to car.

5.7 Old Camp Catawba Road.

Option 7: Rich Mountain Summit

This is the best hike to Cone Park's upland meadows.

Parkway mile: 294.6

Distance: 5.2 miles out and back from Rich Mountain trailhead; 3.6 miles from Mountains-to-Sea Trail

Difficulty: Moderate

Elevation gain: 510 feet from first trailhead

Maps: *USGS Blowing Rock*; Parkway map available online at nps.gov/blri/planyourvisit/moses-cone-trails.htm and seasonally at Cone Manor House/Parkway Craft Center

Finding the trailhead: Both starts are on Shull's Mill Road, best reached from the US 221/Parkway junction 0.5 mile south of Cone Manor. Exit the Parkway at Milepost 294.6 and take the first right on Shull's Mill Road (trip your odometer). Descend under the Parkway tunnel and bear left uphill to a trailhead on the right at 0.5 mile (GPS: 36.151772 / -81.705153). The paved road downhill there is the exit (one way) for the Trout Lake parking area. For the Mountains-to-Sea Trail, drive another 1.3 miles and park on the left in the curve (GPS: 36.159649 / -81.717901). Walk north on the roadside and the trail goes left up the bank across the road on a new staircase. (South, the Mountains-to-Sea Trail descends in 1.5 miles to a newly bridged junction with the Boone Fork Trail close to Price Park's backcountry campsite—a nice overnighter where a permit is required from the Price Park Campground kiosk. See the Old Johns River Road walk described in the Mileage Log at 296.1.)

The Hike

Called "Nowhere Mountain" by baby-boomer locals of the Boone area, Rich Mountain is a great hike or ski tour. The corkscrew ascent to its summit is an ongoing scenic experience as you preview the peak's summit view on the way around and around the peak. The hike described here is from either of two trailheads on Shull's Mill Road, but an even lengthier ascent can start at the Trout Lake Trail (see Option 8).

From the first trailhead on Shull's Mill Road, the carriage path access trail climbs steadily to a crest at about 0.6 mile. Bear left across the meadow on the upper part of Rich Mountain Carriage Road. (Don't bear right; a lower section also descends to Trout Lake, a longer hike below.)

The trail leaves the meadow and wanders through a wonderful rhododendron tunnel, and passes a junction on the left where the Mountains-to-Sea Trail crosses a stile at 1.2 miles (0.4 mile to the second trailhead on Shull's Mill Road). Continuing, you leave the forest into a meadow at 1.7 miles. The peak is up to your right amid wind- and ice-damaged trees. The trail corkscrews to the summit (4,370 feet) at 2.6 miles. Advanced hikers can wander the meadows going up or down—but stay on the trail to avoid the obvious, eroding routes.

Cone's carriage trails turn into perfect cross-country ski trails in winter. Here the Mountains-to-Sea Trail branches off to a favorite trailhead on Shull's Mill Road.

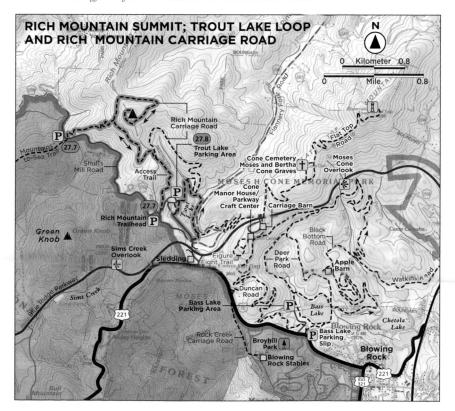

From the second trailhead, the steeper Mountains-to-Sea Trail climbs to the main path at 0.4 mile. Turn left—the peak is 1.4 miles distant, 1.8 miles from your car—for a 3.6-mile round-trip.

There's another option. Just before the trail leaves the forest at 1.7 miles, a carriage road goes left at a gate that makes a nice quiet side trip (it's not shown on Parkway maps). A branch goes left not far from the gate that circles to the top of a tiny summit. The main road runs out a ridge to a few nice meadow views, the last down on one of Moses Cone's apple orchards. Turn around there for a 0.6 mile round-trip diversion. Be sure to retrace your steps—there is no formal connection from this area back to your starting point.

Key Points

0.0 Start at the trailhead on Shull's Mill Road.

0.6 Take a left at the meadow onto Rich Mountain Carriage Road.

1.2 Mountains-to-Sea Trail goes left over stile, also to Shull's Mill Road.

1.7 Enter summit meadow.

2.6 Reach the peak.

Option 8: Trout Lake Loop and Rich Mountain Carriage Road

Unlike popular Bass Lake, with its grassy banks and deciduous trees, Trout Lake—its shores covered in a forest of towering hemlocks—is far less visited. This is also a great starting point for a long and quiet hike higher on Rich Mountain.

Parkway mile: 294.6
Distance: 1.0-mile lakeshore hike; 2.6-mile circuit of lower Rich Mountain Carriage Road; 6.6-mile circuit to Rich Mountain summit
Difficulty: Easy for lakeshore; moderate to strenuous for the longer walks

Elevation gain: Negligible around lake; 610 feet to Rich Mountain
Maps: USGS Blowing Rock; Parkway map available online at nps.gov/blri/planyourvisit/moses-cone-trails.htm and seasonally at Cone Manor House/Parkway Craft Center

Finding the trailhead: Exit the Parkway at Milepost 294.6 and turn right onto Shull's Mill Road. Pass through the Parkway tunnel, avoid the sharp right onto unpaved Flannery Fork Road, and take the second, oblique right onto a one-way road to the Trout Lake parking area (GPS: 36.152788 / -81.702959). The exit road returns to Shull's Mill Road at the first trailhead for the Rich Mountain hike (go left 0.5 mile back to the Parkway).

The Hike

Trout Lake makes for a memorable lakeshore walk or ski trip.

From the edge of the Trout Lake Parking Area, take one of the two access trails that dip to the carriage road below and go right. In a short distance turn left onto the road you just drove in on. As you near Shull's Mill Road, turn left and dip down into the woods again. You'll pass a junction at 0.4 mile where the Rich Mountain Carriage Road comes in on the right (the Cone Manor House is 1.0 mile to the right). At 0.5 mile reach Flannery Fork Road and turn left to cross the dam. Some Trout Lake hikers park here on the Flannery Fork Road (a secluded unpaved byway to Boone that's worth the detour).

Across the dam, the trail enters a towering, centuries-old hemlock forest that's fading as the hemlock woolly adelgid kills the trees. At 0.7 mile, left where the Rich Mountain Carriage Road goes right, cross the bridge, through tall trees and a northern lakeshore scene. Take either of the two side trails right and uphill to the parking area for a 1.0-mile hike.

The proximity of the trailhead for the Rich Mountain Carriage Road hikes—only a 100-yard walk up the exit road—makes this a nice start for more ambitious hikes. To make a loop of the lake and lower Rich Mountain Carriage Road, go left from the parking area on the lakeshore for 0.3 mile, then turn left at the first junction with the Rich Mountain Carriage Road past a scenic water impoundment with a splashing spillway. Pass through a gate at 1.6 miles and exit the woods and at 1.9 miles enter the meadow at a junction just above the main Rich Mountain trailhead on Shull's Mill Road. To the right, the Rich Mountain Carriage Road goes across the meadow to the summit. Turn left and descend the carriage road access trail to Shull's Mill Road at 2.5 miles. From there, go left down the parking area exit road for a 2.6-mile hike.

Or go right at the meadow above the Shull's Mill Road trailhead and reach the Rich Mountain summit at 3.9 miles. Retrace your steps from there, turn right down to Shull's Mill Road, and it's a 6.6-mile hike at the Trout Lake Parking Area.

Key Points on Trout Lake Loop
- **0.4** Rich Mountain Carriage Road comes in on right.
- **0.7** Rich Mountain Carriage Road goes right.
- **1.0** Parking area.

Near Blowing Rock, pass by fields of flowers in Moses Cone Park.

28 Julian Price Memorial Park

Mileposts 295.9–297.2

Julian Price Memorial Park is one of the scenic high points of the Blue Ridge Parkway. Its 4,200 acres contain a golden 47-acre lake, the Parkway's second-largest picnic area, and its largest campground, with superb lakeside camping. You can reserve sites at Price Park Campground in advance online at recreation.gov or by calling (877) 444-6777.

Price Lake is the park's centerpiece. Grandfather Mountain towers in the distance, the source of the lake visible as a bowl-shaped valley scooped out high on the peak. When the lake is frozen into jagged, jumbled sheets, access is still easy for winter hikers and cross-country skiers—the Park Service plows the road from the US 221/Holloway Mountain Road exit (Milepost 298.6), easily reached from Blowing Rock.

A trail circles the lake, and another path delves into the waterfall-filled Boone Fork drainage. The Greensboro-based Jefferson Standard Insurance Company donated the land to memorialize its founder and president, Julian Price, after his death in an automobile accident—an ironic tribute in a park dedicated to experiencing nature by car.

Autumn is a great time to hike Price Lake—or rent a boat. There's a watery TRACK Trail for paddlers peering at hikers on the trail.

In summer, canoes, rowboats, and kayaks dot the lake. Bring your own or rent at the park's boathouse at Milepost 297 (no sails or motors).

Option 1: Green Knob Trail

This loop hike is a microcosm of one of the most scenic sections of the Parkway. It follows a stream from a lakeshore through towering trees to meadow-capped hilltops and panoramic views.

Parkway mile: 295.9
Distance: 2.1-mile loop
Difficulty: Moderate
Elevation gain: 460 feet

Maps: *USGS Boone*; Parkway handout map, available at Price Campground contact kiosk and online at nps.gov/blri/planyourvisit/julian -price-trails.htm

Finding the trailhead: Park at Sims Pond Overlook (Milepost 295.9), 1.3 miles south of the US 221 exit near the town of Blowing Rock (GPS: 36.142480 / -81.719718). You could also use the Sims Creek Overlook at Milepost 295.3.

The Hike

This hike takes the scenic gamut of the Julian Price and Moses Cone Parks and brings it together in one walk.

Cross the spillway bridge and dam of Sims Pond and turn left along the rhododendron-lined shoreline passing fishing trails to the water's edge.

The trail rises along the feeder stream through a long grove of towering hemlocks, sadly now dying or dead due to the hemlock woolly adelgid. The trail rises above the stream as the ka-thump of cars can be heard above on the Sims Creek Viaduct.

At a bridge and bench (0.6 mile), a side path climbs steeply right to Sims Creek Overlook (an alternate start). The trail steepens and rises out of the drainage to arc left into a broad meadow at 1.0 mile (follow concrete posts with blue directional arrows). Exit the meadow through a fat-man squeeze and dip into hardwoods past a weathered bench to a view of Price Lake and Grandfather Mountain. Descend more steeply down a scenic ridgeline route through woods and smaller meadows to another spectacular view at the bottom. The ridgeline route dips in and out of intimate swales, where the fringed green carpet of ferns runs off into open woods. Go left through a fat-man squeeze; a rhododendron tunnel brings you to the Parkway and the sound of cars. Walk left 150 feet to Sims Pond Overlook.

Key Points

0.0   Start at Sims Pond Overlook.

0.4   Bench beside a pool in towering forest.

0.6   Access trail to Sims Creek Overlook.

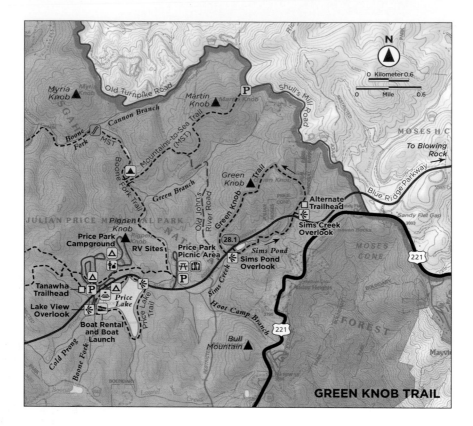

GREEN KNOB TRAIL

1.0 Leave woods into first meadow.

1.4 Exit meadow near summit of Green Knob.

2.1 Arrive back at overlook.

Option 2: Boone Fork Trail

One of the Parkway's longer trails wanders a significant distance away from the road and for much of its length follows a scenic mountain stream with rocky plunges and deep pools.

Parkway mile: 296.4
Distance: 4.9-mile loop
Difficulty: Strenuous
Elevation gain: 440 feet

Maps: *USGS Boone*; Parkway handout map, available at Price Campground contact kiosk and online at nps.gov/blri/planyourvisit/julian -price-trails.htm

Finding the trailhead: Turn into the Price Park Picnic Area at Milepost 296.4; park in the first lot on the right, opposite the restroom (GPS: 36.139423 / -81.727161).

The Hike

The Boone Fork Trail is a standout for many reasons. Don't expect the Parkway's typical distant views. This is an "in the trees" trail that substitutes a stream full of cascades and pools for vistas. And it's long by Parkway standards, so give this hike some time.

Pass the restroom and cross Boone Fork Creek where a map sign marks the start of the loop. Grab a TRACK Trail brochure at the kiosk and go right along the creek through beautiful, flower-filled boggy areas favored by beavers. Obvious railroad ties in the rhododendron tunnel treadway attest that this was the old railroad grade of the Boone Fork Lumber Company, which logged part of Grandfather Mountain (for more, see the author's new book, *Grandfather Mountain: The History and Guide to an Appalachian Icon*).

At about 1 mile, the Mountains-to-Sea Trail (coming from ahead of you) turns to your right and crosses the stream going north on a long bridge built in 2016. This is where the TRACK Trail ends, requiring a return to your car.

Don't be disappointed if you get a wet gray day to enjoy Price Park. The lake itself can be spellbindingly beautiful, and the water gushing from it feeds all the waterfalls on the Boone Fork Trail below the dam.

The new bridge opens up other options. North across the bridge, the trail immediately reaches Price Park's once isolated backcountry campsite, then traverses portions of the Old Johns River Road 1.5 miles to the MST crossing on Shull's Mill Road (featured in Moses Cone's Rich Mountain hike; see Hike 27 Option 7). Starting at Shull's Mill Road makes the Boone Fork hike 7.9 miles. The campsite also makes an easy overnighter from the Price Park Picnic Area, and via the scenic Old Johns River Road from the Parkway near Sims Pond Overlook (see Mileage Log Milepost 296.1 for more).

Continuing straight on the combined Boone Fork/Mountains-to-Sea Trail (avoiding the bridge), the path passes a side trail to Hebron Falls, a popular sunning and swimming spot, then levels through woods and negotiates a ladder before turning sharply downhill to the stream and the best waterfall on the trail at 1.8 miles.

The trail repeatedly climbs up to, then down from, sections of old railroad grade; trestles once carried logging trains across the space between the grades. Switchback left out of the Boone Fork drainage at about 2.5 miles along Bee Tree Creek. After a bridge, the trail leaves the stream on a section of new trail built in 2013.

Passing beneath a rock outcrop, the new trail bears left (please do not go straight up the eroding old trail that managers are trying to close). The new trail climbs into a meadow to a sign at 3.5 miles. (A right turn here is the Holloway Meadow Loop

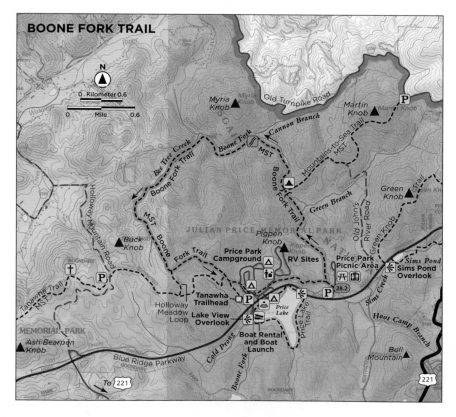

covered in the upcoming Tanawha Trail section, Hike 29 Option 1.) Turn left across the meadow and descend into white pines to a junction on the right at 3.9 miles. Here the Mountains-to-Sea Trail/Tanawha turns right for Grandfather Mountain and the Tanawha Trail joins you. Continue on Boone Fork/Tanawha to a split at 4.1 miles where Tanawha turns off right to its terminus near site 46 of the B loop in Price Park Campground. Stay left through the campground, cross the road, and pass restrooms on a paved trail. The trail becomes gravel, passes between a ranger residence and campground kiosk at about 4.5 miles, crosses the RV campground road, and descends into the meadow to the loop sign. Cross the bridge to your car.

Key Points

0.0 Start at Price Park picnic area.

0.5 Beaver activity may be seen along stream.

1.0 Mountains-to-Sea Trail branches right to Moses Cone Park.

1.8 Rejoin Boone Fork Trail near hike's biggest waterfalls.

2.5 Trail enters drainage of Bee Tree Creek.

3.9 Mountains-to-Sea and Tanawha Trail junction right from Grandfather Mountain.

4.1 Tanawha Trail branches right toward its Price Park Campground terminus.

4.5 Pass between a ranger residence and the campground check-in kiosk.

4.9 Arrive back at picnic area.

Option 3: Price Lake Trail

A lakeside loop of the Parkway's largest body of water. An out-and-back walk here is Price Park's second TRACK Trail for hikers (also see Boone Fork Trail). Or bring, or rent, a boat. The first ever paddlers TRACK Trail follows the lakeshore. Both the walking and water brochures are scavenger hunts and beaver activity is seen here too. Visit kidsinparks.com/price-lake.

Parkway mile: 297.2
Distance: 2.5-mile loop
Difficulty: Easy to moderate
Elevation gain: Negligible

Maps: *USGS Boone*; Parkway handout map, available at Price Campground contact kiosk and online at nps.gov/blri/planyourvisit/julian-price-trails.htm

Finding the trailhead: Either of two lakeshore overlooks is a potential starting point. The preferred start, Lake View Overlook, is reached by a spur road at Milepost 297.2 (GPS: 36.135734 / -81.738382). Be aware, Lake View Overlook is the new name for former Boone Fork Overlook. Price Lake Overlook is at Milepost 296.7 (GPS: 36.138982 / -81.732288).

The Hike

Leave the southern end of the Lake View Overlook by the trail map sign and descend a wheelchair-accessible ramp behind the boat rentals (the start of both TRACK

Trails). The first 0.7 mile of this trail has been upgraded for wheelchair access to stream and lakeshore fishing spots. (Expect similar improvements soon on the rest of the trail.) The trail bridges Cold Prong then Boone Fork, the lake's main source, and crosses a boggy area on a boardwalk at about 0.7 mile. Turn around at a lakeside fishing deck opposite the boat launch for a 1.4-mile hike that's one of the best on the Parkway for the wheelchair-bound, very young hikers, and cross-country skiers.

From this point back to the Parkway, the trail around the longest arm of the lake is a woodsy and quiet walk punctuated by the hollow thunk of paddle on canoe or kayak. There's a new boardwalk and a bridge across a boggy area on the far end of the lake, where the trail crosses Laurel Creek to bear left back toward the Parkway (the walking TRACK Trail retraces its steps from here). A variety of rocks reach into the water, enticing boaters to land and anglers to cast, all with good views of Grandfather Mountain. Descend steps to the Parkway at 1.7 miles and go left across the dam through Price Lake Overlook. A lakeside deck creates another wheelchair-accessible place to fish or catch a view before leaving the open roadside and entering the tall white pines of the campground. The trail follows the lake then veers right to bisect Loop A—easily one of the premier places on the Parkway to set up a tent.

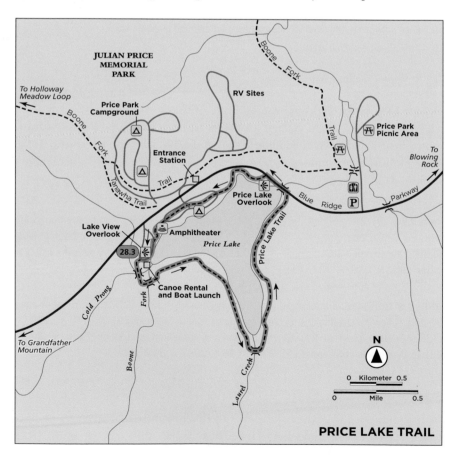

PRICE LAKE TRAIL

Just past a restroom at 2.2 miles, the trail crosses the road into the woods. At a junction go left; the trail to the right crosses the Parkway to the other campground loops and the Tanawha Trail Parking Area. The Price Lake Trail rises left to skirt the campground amphitheater and enter Lake View Overlook where you started your hike.

Key Points

0.0 Start hike at Lake View Overlook.

0.5 Cross lengthy boardwalk.

0.7 Fishing deck opposite boat ramp.

1.0 Bridge signals left turn along final side of the lake.

1.7 Turn left along Parkway to cross dam.

2.2 Pass restrooms.

2.5 Arrive back at Lake View Overlook.

Car camping and the Parkway just go together. On the Price Lake Trail, you'll literally pass this tent site in Price Park Campground, one of the Parkway's best places to pitch a tent.

29 Tanawha Trail and the Parkway at Grandfather Mountain

Mileposts 298.6–304.4

The Tanawha Trail—the Cherokee word means "great hawk" or "eagle"—lies along the entire length of the Grandfather Mountain "missing link" portion of the Parkway. The trail reaches from Beacon Heights all the way to Julian Price Memorial Park campground and is the crowning achievement of the Blue Ridge Parkway trail network. Tanawha is part of North Carolina's Mountains-to-Sea Trail and connects south to the Oisgah National Forest and north along the Parkway.

Hikers won't fail to notice the trail's intricate stone stairways, rock-paved treadways, and arching wood bridges (lowered here by helicopter), all designed to minimize hiker damage to this scenic environment. The federal government spent almost $750,000 in 1980s dollars on the 13.5-mile trail.

The Tanawha Trail's best views are from Rough Ridge, a high outcrop where boardwalks and handrails were required to keep the public from trampling the low, alpinelike vegetation, some of it rare and endangered. Dogs are permitted on-leash, but people and their pets should be careful to stay on the trails. Happily, substantial effort has been devoted to preserving a truly unique area.

The Tanawha Trail, like many other sections of the Mountains-to-Sea Trail in North Carolina and the Appalachian Trail in Virginia, will rarely be hiked end to end by Parkway motorists. The most worthwhile sections of these roadside paths are the places that provide loop opportunities or attractive turnaround points. The hikes described below focus on those parts of what planners called the "Parkway parallel trail" before it was renamed.

Option 1: Tanawha Trail Hikes near Holloway Mountain Road

Two opportunities—a circuit hike and an out-and-back walk—allow you to sample the Tanawha and Mountains-to-Sea Trails in an area noted for outstanding meadow views.

Parkway mile: 298.6
Distance: 2.4-mile circuit to the north of the road now named Holloway Meadow Loop by the Park Service; 1.6-mile out-and-back hike to the south (with greater distances and a higher-elevation hike possible)
Difficulty: Easy for the meadow hikes immediately north and south of Holloway Mountain Road; moderate for others

Elevation gain: 50 feet
Maps: *USGS Grandfather Mountain*; Tanawha Trail handout map available online at nps.gov/blri/planyourvisit/tanawha-trail.htm and in season at Linn Cove Information Station/Visitor Center (That map does not show the hike described first below; rely on the map provided here.)

Finding the trailhead: Leave the Parkway south of Blowing Rock at Milepost 298.6–the Holloway Mountain Road/US 221 exit. Turn immediately right onto the dirt road and park on the left in 1 mile at the new Tanawha Trail/MST parking area (GPS: 36.139853 / -81.757517).

The Hikes

The circuit hike to the north patches together an easy sampling of the Tanawha, Boone Fork, and Mountains-to-Sea Trails without requiring that you completely retrace your steps.

Cross the road and head through the fat-man squeeze going north on the combined Tanawha and Mountains-to-Sea Trail. Cross the first stretch of meadow, pass through another squeeze at 0.1 mile, then turn right onto an old gravel farm road. At 0.4 mile veer left up a few log steps as the trail leaves the grade. At 0.5 mile cross the next fence and pass a Tanawha Trail signpost just beyond to rejoin the old road grade.

Pause 200 feet beyond the sign, at about 0.6 mile, where the loop splits near the edge of a meadow. Your hike returns on the grade to the right, so go left, veering uphill where the road grade rises left. Emerge into the meadow and follow the obvious but faint, now-grassy old roadway left through the grass for 100 feet parallel to rhododendron at the edge of the woods. The roadway wanders across the meadow, under the power line in the distance, and to the right of the rise beyond. Leave the meadow under an arch of rhododendron.

Leave the meadow as the grade dips under arching rhododendron. At about 0.9 mile the grade re-emerges into the meadow to a junction where the Boone Fork Trail comes in on the left. The junction is marked by a Mountains-to-Sea Trail signpost and signs. Keep straight; the Boone Fork Trail joins the road grade you're walking. Continuing into the meadow, arc to the right across the field, and descend into white pines to a signed junction at 1.3 miles. This is the Mountains-to-Sea Trail/Tanawha Trail combination that you started on but left back at the meadow. Turn right off the Boone Fork Trail and head south along this section of the MST you missed.

North of Grandfather Mountain, feather-routed posts lead hikers through meadows on the combined Tanawha and Mountains-to-Sea Trails. One hiker added the real thing.

Ferns, moss, and pine needles cover the ground under a grove of white pines. The path crosses two small bridges, and follows a fenceline, then gradually climbs right to reenter the meadow at an old apple orchard. Leveling off, the trail switchbacks left (keep your eye out for this jog left) and passes a grove of white pines flanked by another apple orchard—a long-ago mountaineer homesite. The trail swings past the site and enters the woods at a trailside pit where an underground stream threatens to collapse the path.

Heading back into the woods at 1.8 miles, the loop closes as you immediately rejoin the grade you walked in on. Heading back the way you came, go left off the road grade through the first tiny meadow. If you miss the last left to your car, don't sweat it. The gravel roadway empties onto Holloway Mountain Road 200 feet west of where you parked (turn left), for a total hike of about 2.4 miles.

Just across the road from the hike above lies an even easier meadow walk to the south where the Tanawha Trail heads toward Grandfather Mountain and views of the peak dominate the horizon.

The trail leaves the parking area through two fence gates—one route gently arcs up the edge of the meadow beside Holloway Mountain Road on the Parkway side of the parking area, the other goes straight up the grassy hill and is causing erosion. Take the gradual path and cross another fence at 0.4 mile below an old cemetery (just out of sight on the high right). It swings into the bowl of the next meadow then wanders

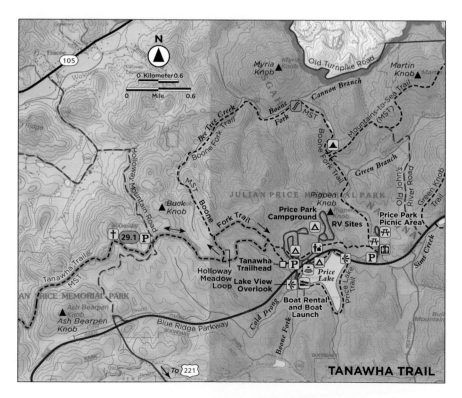

through a grove of white pines with views down on the Holloway Mountain Road. When you reach a power line toward the end of the meadow at about 0.8 mile, a return from there creates an easy meadow stroll that's perfect for a picnic or ski tour of 1.6 miles.

Beyond that meadow turnaround point, the trail continues, descending into the woods and passing through a meadow at 1.1 miles and a nice clifftop view up to Grandfather Mountain's northernmost ridge at 1.6 miles. It crosses a small stream at 1.9 miles then rises to a junction at 2.0 miles where a side trail goes left 0.2 mile to Cold Prong Parking Area (Milepost 299.0). Spot a car there for a 2.2-mile hike, or head back for a 4.4-mile out-and-back hike from Holloway Mountain Road. (For much more on the above hike and the history of this area, see the author's new book, *Grandfather Mountain: The History and Guide to an Appalachian Icon.*)

Key Points for the Circuit to the North

0.0 Cross road from the parking area.

0.4 Veer left off the grade and up log steps.

0.6 Turn left (north) onto the faint roadway to cross the meadow.

0.9 Join Boone Fork/Mountains-to-Sea Trail.

1.3 Turn right onto Mountains-to-Sea/Tanawha Trail.

1.8 Close loop, rejoining portion of trail you've already walked.

2.4 Holloway Mountain Road.

Option 2: Tanawha Trail from Cold Prong Parking Area

An out-and-back hike or two-car shuttle heads uphill from Cold Prong Overlook to Boone Fork Parking Area.

Parkway mile: 299
Distance: 3.8 miles out and back
Difficulty: Moderate
Elevation gain: 360 feet
Maps: USGS *Grandfather Mountain*; Tanawha Trail handout map available online at nps .gov/blri/planyourvisit/tanawha-trail.htm and in season at Linn Cove Information Station/ Visitor Center. Parts of this hike are shown on Grandfather Mountain hiking map, free at Grandfather Mountain entrance (south from Cold Prong Overlook 6.1 miles to US 221 exit; right 1 mile to entrance).

Finding the trailhead: Park at Cold Prong Overlook (GPS: 36.119883 / -01.781640). The trail starts near the middle of the lot and dips left and down directly to the Tanawha Trail in 0.2 mile. Avoid the trail that leaves the north end of the parking lot. The poorly maintained loop used to circle now-drained Cold Prong Pond in 0.5 mile. (Be aware that this trailhead used to be called Cold Prong Pond Overlook.)

The Hike

Cold Prong Overlook is the start of a noteworthy hike up to Boone Fork Parking Area. It's uphill, which means it's downhill on the way back, and has a logical destination—a scenic bridge over rushing Boone Fork, where a variety of hikes to the Grandfather summit region start. Another plus is that few people hike this scenic section of trail.

Take a left 0.2 mile below the parking area on the Tanawha Trail. The path crosses a wet slab of rock and a few bridges to turn right well away from the Parkway. At 0.5 mile cross another bridge to a right turn that deftly surmounts a crag to leave the drainage.

The trail rises past hemlocks, sharply switchbacks left, and enters an impressive cove hardwood forest with plentiful wildflowers at about 1.2 miles. The road can't be heard from here—this would be a great place for one of those (nearly) ubiquitous Parkway benches. The trail dips out of the cove and turns right around a ridge to enter the old railroad grade of the Boone Fork Lumber Company that logged Grandfather Mountain circa 1916–1924. The trail leaves the railroad grade to the left. At about 1.9 miles bear right at the junction (the trail going left reaches Boone Fork Parking Area in 0.1 mile); the Boone Fork trail bridge is a few hundred feet away. Nice pools lie below.

Key Points

- **0.0** Leave Cold Prong Overlook.
- **0.2** Junction with Tanawha Trail; go left.
- **1.2** Nice cove hardwood forest.
- **1.9** Boone Fork trail bridge.

Option 3: Tanawha Trail to Rough Ridge

Quite possibly the Parkway's easiest path to a spectacular view, here the Tanawha Trail traverses the alpine-appearing crest of a leading ridge to Grandfather Mountain. This cliff-bordered crag is popular with rock climbers, who call it Ship Rock.

Parkway mile: 302.8
Distance: Entire section is 1.5 miles, but the closest view is only a 0.6-mile round-trip. Out-and-back hikes of 1.2 and about 2.0 miles lead to the peak of Rough Ridge.
Difficulty: Moderate to strenuous
Elevation gain: 540 feet from Wilson Creek Overlook; 480 feet from Rough Ridge Parking Area

Maps: USGS Grandfather Mountain; Tanawha Trail handout map available online at nps.gov/blri/planyourvisit/tanawha-trail.htm and in season at Linn Cove Information Station/Visitor Center. The Grandfather Mountain hiking map shows the trail best and is available free at the Grandfather Mountain entrance (south from Rough Ridge Overlook 2.3 miles to US 221 exit; right 1 mile to entrance).

Finding the trailhead: This hike is accessible from Wilson Creek Overlook (Milepost 303.6; GPS: 36.100526 / -81.808748); and Rough Ridge Overlook (Milepost 302.8; GPS: 36.098359 / -81.797124).

The Hike

The most direct route to the summit of Rough Ridge is from the parking area of the same name. Ascend new steps and decking and turn left on Tanawha across an arching wooden bridge above a cascading stream. A right turn leads 4 miles north on the Tanawha Trail, around Pilot Knob and down through luxuriant spruces, to Boone Fork Overlook.

Cross the bridge and the trail climbs amid blueberry bushes and galax and then turns a corner, passes a fascinating stack rock formation, and wanders 200 feet of boardwalk designed to keep hikers from trampling the low vegetation. This may be the easiest Parkway path to an awesome view. From this boardwalk, just 0.3 mile from the parking area (0.6 mile round-trip), the view is remarkably similar to that from the summit—another 0.3 mile ahead up rocky, moderate switchbacks (1.2 miles round-trip). From either location, it's easy to watch a sunset and get back to your car quickly. This vista engulfs you. Above, the three highest summits of Grandfather Mountain

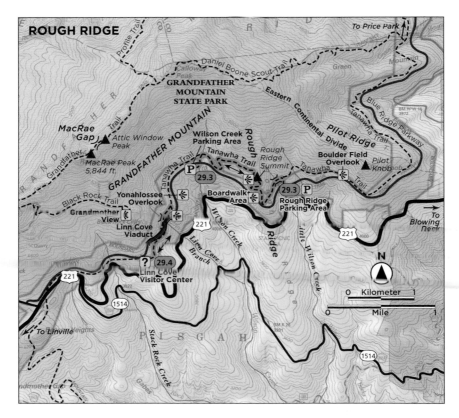

reach a dramatic climax. From the highest, Calloway Peak (5,964 feet, farthest right), the Wilson Creek drainage drops like a chute past Rough Ridge (where you're standing), Black Rock Cliffs (to the south, above the viaduct), and Pilot Knob (behind you). Mount Mitchell lies on the horizon. This is the greatest single rise of the Blue Ridge escarpment. The Piedmont lies almost a vertical mile below the peaks, beyond the rippling corduroy of Pisgah National Forest.

For a longer hike that avoids the crowds, start at Wilson Creek Overlook and hike under the bridge and into the woods above the road. At the Tanawha Trail, go right and cross Wilson Creek. The trail dips below an outcrop within sight of the road and then climbs across a boulderfield forest ecosystem, one of the rarest on the mountain, with towering trees and inspiring spring wildflowers. You'll reach a saddle where stone steps artfully surmount the crag-capped summit of Rough Ridge, about 1 mile from the Wilson Creek parking area (2 miles round-trip).

At the summit, cable-defined pathways keep people on the paths amid fragile Allegheny sand myrtle and turkey beard. Unfortunately, even dogs that are on-leash may not stay within the barriers, so the Park Service urges dog owners to use care on this trail.

If you left another car below at the Rough Ridge parking area, descend for a 1.6-mile hike. If you didn't leave a car there, it's a still-pleasant 0.8-mile roadside walk back to Wilson Creek Overlook and a 2.4-miler.

Key Points from Rough Ridge Parking Area

0.0 Ascend deck steps from parking area.

0.3 Boardwalk views.

0.6 Views from the summit of Rough Ridge.

Option 4: Linn Cove Viaduct

A wheelchair-accessible paved path leads under this stunning span of the Parkway's Linn Cove Viaduct and then continues as a rougher trail through beautiful Linn Cove. The turnaround point is a classic postcard view of the viaduct.

See map on page 207.
Parkway mile: 304.4
Distance: 0.3 mile out and back for barrier-free trail; 1.0 mile out and back to classic views of the viaduct
Difficulty: Easy and barrier-free to moderate
Elevation gain: Virtually none for the paved trail; 50 feet for the moderate hike

Maps: USGS Grandfather Mountain; Tanawha Trail handout map available online at nps.gov/blri/planyourvisit/tanawha-trail.htm and in season at Linn Cove Information Station/Visitor Center. The Grandfather Mountain hiking map shows the trail best and is available free at the Grandfather Mountain entrance (south 0.7 mile to US 221 exit; right 1 mile to entrance).

Finding the trailhead: The trail starts at the end of the Linn Cove Parking Area opposite the small visitor center at Milepost 304.4 (GPS: 36.090784 / -81.814063).

The Hike

The easiest walk to a view of the Linn Cove Viaduct begins at the Linn Cove Visitor Center, where displays explain the technical and natural history behind this amazing portion of the Parkway. A paved and barrier-free trail winds from the far end of the parking lot for 0.15 mile to a viewpoint beneath the viaduct.

For the next-easiest viaduct walk, stay on the trail beyond the pavement to the level of the bridge and zigzag under cliffs amid towering hemlocks. It undulates over impressive stone stairways among the jumble of huge boulders that tumble down from Grandfather Mountain's Black Rock Cliffs. This is the terrain that prompted the choice of span you see arcing beside you, evidenced by the occasional whoosh and thump of a passing car. The trail leaves the Linn Cove stream drainage; at 0.5 mile, turn right at a sign amid rhododendron to a roadside boulder for an oft-photographed postcard view back at the bridge (1-mile round-trip).

To reach the postcard view from a far less popular direction, start 0.8 mile north at the Wilson Creek Overlook, trailhead for the recommended hike to Rough Ridge. Head south to this view of the viaduct for a quiet 1.6-mile hike.

Key Points

0.0 Leave visitor center parking area.

0.15 End of paved path.

0.5 Postcard view of viaduct.

Grandfather Mountain's Linn Cove Viaduct is a spectacular span. This viewpoint on the Tanawha Trail not far from the Viaduct Visitor Center offers this postcard perspective.

30 Grandfather Mountain

Mileposts 299.9–305.1

Grandfather Mountain's public image has evolved over the years. Once almost exclusively seen as a tourist attraction, Grandfather has become synonymous with its spectacular backcountry. The Mile-High Swinging Bridge is still a popular attraction reached by car, but there have been plenty of changes since owner Hugh Morton passed away in 2006. Morton's heirs sold the backcountry as a North Carolina state park in 2009, and tourist development transitioned to a nonprofit stewardship foundation. The mountain's now publicly owned highest peaks are laced with a wonderful network of trails that tower over the attraction. The once-ignored backcountry hiking network experienced a renaissance in the late 1970s, when a fee-based hiking program reclaimed deteriorating trails that had been closed after a hiker died of hypothermia. Over the years, the pay-for-use trail system became an innovative example of wilderness management, and hiking grew as a part of the Grandfather Mountain experience.

Growing scientific research has since revealed the mountain to be eastern America's most ecologically significant summit. The mountain's 4,000 acres boast forty-three species of rare or endangered plants and animals, more than Great Smoky Mountains National Park. That's just the latest chapter in the mountain's long history—a stirring

Grandfather Mountain may be the scenic high point of the Parkway, and you won't get a better view of it than from MacRae Peak on the Grandfather Trail.

saga related in the author's new book, *Grandfather Mountain: The History and Guide to an Appalachian Icon.*

Hikers should keep in mind that the state park and the attraction are different entities with different policies (visit the park and attraction websites). Under state park management, the trail fees were ended, but a camping fee has been reinstated for group campsites along with a campsite reservation system. Currently campers also choose smaller sites at trailhead registration signs. A hiking permit is still required, but it's free and available at trailheads (except on the trails that start inside the attraction, where a hiker register form is handed to motorists when a fee is charged for access). The attraction closes at night, so no camping is permitted there—do not leave your car overnight inside the attraction, and be sure to return from your hike by the time noted on the signs. Hikers walking into the attraction from the state park are not charged, but be aware that it's a very long day hike and there is no walking allowed on the road. Hikers reaching the attraction must expect to hike back or be picked up (their ride will be charged to enter).

Hikers should be alert to weather conditions at Grandfather Mountain. People have died on the mountain from exposure, lightning strikes, falls, and heart attacks. The mountain is known for its snowy winters and year-round high winds.

Another new aspect of Grandfather Mountain: It has shrunk. No, the "Grandfatherly" old summit isn't slumping, but it was remeasured in 2008. Calloway Peak became 5,946 feet (not 5,964—the elevation published by the state in 1917); MacRae Peak is now 5,844 feet (not 5,939). Also be aware, a new parking area and connector path at the Profile Trail, and reroutes elsewhere, may change trail mileages.

For more information: Grandfather Mountain State Park: (828) 963-9522; ncparks .gov/Visit/parks/grmo/main.php; attraction: (828) 733-4337; grandfather.com.

Option 1: Tanawha Trail and Daniel Boone Scout Trail to Calloway Peak

Tracking up the back side of Grandfather Mountain, the Daniel Boone Scout Trail climbs to Calloway Peak. Two other view-packed trails, one a nice beginning backpacking trip, also start on the Tanawha Trail from the Blue Ridge Parkway.

See map on page 215.
Parkway mile: 299.9
Distance: 5.8- or 4.9-mile out-and-back hike to Calloway Peak and a great view on the Boone Trail; 3.6-mile hike on the Cragway Trail; 3.2 miles on the Nuwati Trail
Difficulty: Strenuous for the Boone Trail to Calloway Peak and for the Cragway circuit; moderate for the Nuwati Trail

Elevation gain: 2,026 feet for the climb to Calloway Peak; 920 feet for the Cragway circuit; 580 feet for the Nuwati Trail
Maps: *USGS Grandfather Mountain.* The best map for the hike is the Grandfather Mountain attraction trail map, downloadable from the attraction website and available free at the Grandfather Mountain entrance (south on the Parkway from Boone Fork parking area 5.2

THE "MISSING LINK"

Motorists are invariably attracted to this "newest" part of the Parkway in the Grandfather Mountain area. In addition to the scenic grandeur, they're wowed by the Linn Cove Viaduct, a multimillion-dollar, space-age span made famous in nationally televised automobile advertisements.

The costly and curving Linn Cove Viaduct literally leaps away from the mountain. The segmented bridge was built with each ensuing section lowered out over thin air and affixed to the one before it. A small visitor center, the Parkway's Linn Cove Visitor Center, tells the inspiring technical story of the viaduct's construction. A portion of the Tanawha Trail takes you right beneath the viaduct.

The story of this long-awaited "missing link" in the Blue Ridge Parkway began after World War II, when young combat photographer Hugh Morton returned to his family's lands on Grandfather Mountain and built a "Mile-High Swinging Bridge" between two rocky peaks. Over the years, Morton's promotional genius and his gift for scenic photography made the mountain a high point of North Carolina tourism.

Not everything went smoothly. For thirty years the Department of the Interior wrangled with the private landowner over where the Blue Ridge Parkway would cross "his" mountain. Eventually, precluded from condemning land for a high route across private land, the National Park Service agreed on a lower route and the Parkway battle came to a close.

After decades of controversy, the technical difficulties of road building on the rocky route had to be addressed. Lucky for everyone involved, including the public and the spectacular mountain, during the delay in the Parkway completion, computer technology arrived that permitted a soaring viaduct span to bridge a fragile mountainside. The National Park Service spared no expense to minimize the road's environmental impact.

The two protagonists in the latter part of the controversy—Morton and longtime Parkway superintendent Gary Everhardt, who retired in 2001 after twenty-three years as the longest serving head of the Parkway—ended up as friends who cooperated often for the benefit of the environment. Under Everhardt, a former director of the National Park Service, landmark Parkway facilities were conceived or completed, including the Folk Art Center, Blue Ridge Music Center, Asheville's Parkway Visitor Center, park headquarters, and the Grandfather part of the road with its radical viaduct. Today the high peaks of Grandfather Mountain are known as the East's most ecologically significant summits, a nationally important site. For much more on the history of the mountain and the Parkway, see the author's 2016 book, *Grandfather Mountain: The History and Guide to an Appalachian Icon*.

miles to US 221 exit, right 1 mile to entrance). The state park trail map is available at trailhead registration signs. The Parkway's Tanawha Trail handout map is available at the Linn Cove Visitor Center and online at nps.gov/blri/plan yourvisit/tanawha-trail.htm.

Finding the trailhead: The best starting point for all these hikes is the Boone Fork parking area on the Blue Ridge Parkway (GPS: 36.119889 / -81.781553). An alternative, especially in winter when snow closes the Parkway, is the Asutsi Trail, which starts on US 221, 8.5 miles north of the Grandfather Mountain entrance and 1.5 miles south of the US 221/Holloway Mountain Road junction south of Blowing Rock (GPS: 36.116333 / -81.777285).

The Hikes

Looking east from Calloway Peak, the dramatic vertical drop of nearly a mile is one of the South's most noteworthy vistas. Part-time Parkway ranger Clyde Smith and a Blowing Rock Boy Scout troop built a primitive trail up this wild side of the mountain during World War II, but it had become only a memory until Grandfather Mountain's trail program reclaimed it in 1979 along with a half-century-old back-packing shelter. By the early 1980s, two new trails were added in the bowl-shaped valley beneath Calloway Peak that was once thought to be a glacial cirque like those in New England. That conclusion was based on "glacial grooves" that were later discovered to have been left by logging cables.

Hike to Boone Fork Bowl

Starting at the Parkway's Boone Fork parking area, the connector to the Tanawha Trail leaves the lot, goes right at the first junction, then left at the next on the Tanawha Trail to cross the laminated bridge spanning the creek. The Asutsi Trail connector to US 221 branches left just over the bridge (0.4 mile to US 221) and just before the state park registration sign. At 0.4 mile, take a right on the blue circle−blazed Nuwati Trail and follow the level but rocky trail up an old logging railroad grade. A spring gushes at 0.7 mile as the trail becomes a scenic rhododendron tunnel fringed by ferns. At 1.1 miles the Cragway Trail goes left. The trail crosses numerous streams and campsites on the left (where a large logging cable like those that created the "ice-carved" grooves is held firm in the V of a tree).

Cross Boone Fork at 1 mile. A tent platform is off to the left before a fork. A right dead-ends at a campsite; a left rises steeply to prominent Storyteller's Rock, project-ing above the valley floor at 4,500 feet, 1.6 miles from the trailhead, the supposed site of the glacial grooves. The 360-degree panorama encompasses the entire high mountain valley—the upper bowl and headwall of the supposed "cirque," Calloway Peak above it, and the cliffs of White Rock Ridge above on the right.

The Nuwati Trail gains only about 600 feet in 1.6 miles, so it's a good beginning backpacking trip for trailside campsites and spectacular scenery. Storyteller's Rock makes a nice evening viewpoint.

Cragway Loop

The best way to hike the steep, orange circle—blazed Cragway Trail is down. Where the Nuwati Trail turns right off the Tanawha Trail (above), continue on Tanawha and at 0.6 mile go right on the white diamond—blazed Daniel Boone Scout Trail. After a gradual, switchbacking climb, the trail emerges between two rock outcroppings at 1.6 miles. The Daniel Boone Scout Trail continues left 0.1 mile to a group of tent platforms at about the centerpoint on the trail. To the right, Cragway descends to the Nuwati Trail. Go right, but first ascend Flat Rock View, a table-flat vantage point and perfect lunch spot.

Going right on Cragway, the trail winds along open crags, reenters woods, and emerges into a heath bald of blueberry bushes and rhododendron at Top Crag. Be careful to avoid further impact on the alpine-like Allegheny sand myrtle growing here. This view is one of the best on the mountain.

The path descends rocky crags with great views. Take a right on the Nuwati Trail (2.5 miles from the start), then a left on Tanawha, and the round-trip back to the Boone Fork parking area is 3.6 miles. If you go left first and include Storyteller's Rock before hiking out, the round-trip is 4.6 miles.

The Hike to the Summit

To reach Calloway Peak, hike the Daniel Boone Scout Trail as above and at about 1.6 miles pause at the Daniel Boone campsite, where a side trail leads 100 yards to Bear Wallow Spring. The Boone Trail switchbacks higher in and out of a scenic red spruce forest. At the crest of Pilot Ridge is a nice campsite on the left. Continuing, the trail enters the spruce-fir forest zone—a dark, cool evergreen area carpeted with moss and wood sorrel. After a side trip to Viaduct View, a second side trail left, at about 2.6 miles, leads to Hi-Balsam Shelter, a tiny low-lying lean-to that sleeps five (no tent camping or fires).

The Daniel Boone Scout Trail continues past a tent platform campsite on the left (no fires permitted). Opposite the campsite, off in the woods, lie the remains of a single-engine plane that crashed in 1978. Past this point the trail suddenly stands on end, climbing steeply with ladders to Calloway Peak (5,946 feet; marked by a white X), 2.8 miles from the trailhead. The panoramic view takes in the dramatic drop to the Piedmont.

The Boone Trail terminates about 0.1 mile away at the Grandfather Trail and Watauga (wa–TAW–ga) View, the best vantage point to the west. Between the peak and the junction, the summit area is a rocky, evergreen-covered crest.

Retracing your steps, the entire hike is just under 6.0 miles with a visit to Watauga View. If you go left on the Cragway Trail on the way down, the route is just under 5.0 miles, again assuming a Watauga View turnaround.

Key Points to Calloway Peak

0.0   Boone Fork Parking Area.

0.4   Tanawha Trail junction with Nuwati Trail.

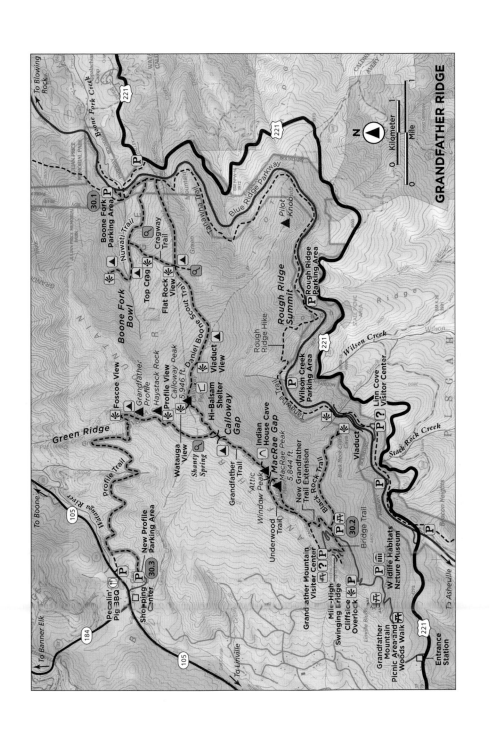

GRANDFATHER RIDGE

0.6 Right onto Daniel Boone Scout Trail.

1.6 Junction with Cragway Trail.

2.6 Hi-Balsam Shelter.

2.8 Calloway Peak.

5.8 Arrive back at the parking lot.

Option 2: Grandfather Trail

One of the South's most rugged, spectacular, and storied trails traverses Grandfather Mountain's summit ridge. The route ascends peaks and scales ladders over cliffs to reach Calloway Peak, the highest summit in the Blue Ridge.

See map on page 215.
Parkway mile: 305.1
Distance: 2.0 miles out and back over the first major peak; 4.8 miles to Calloway Peak and back
Difficulty: Strenuous

Elevation gain: About 746 feet from the summit parking area for loop of MacRae Peak; 1,698 feet to Calloway Park and back returning on Underwood Trail
Maps: USGS Grandfather Mountain. The best map for the hike is the free trail map of Grandfather Mountain.

Finding the trailhead: Start at the top of the Grandfather Mountain motor road. The historic start is opposite the summit visitor center (GPS: 36.096179 / -81.831769), but to preserve parking for motorists, park lower down in the uppermost Black Rock Trail parking lot (GPS: 36.095456 / -81.829176)—right after the "5000 feet" elevation sign. Here the Grandfather Trail Extension reaches the Grandfather Trail. If you want to start at the top and see the visitor center and swinging bridge (no walking is permitted on the road), take the Bridge Trail to or from the summit parking lot (0.4 mile). That trail starts across the road from the Black Rock parking area.

The Hike

The gold circle—blazed Black Rock Trail is a 1-mile level path across the mountain's eastern flank. It passes a formation called Arch Rock on the way to an end loop with great views of the summits above and the Parkway and Piedmont far below.

For Grandfather Trail, take the red diamond—blazed extension spur as it rises left out of the upper parking areas (Black Rock Trail goes right) and climbs to a junction with the Grandfather Trail. Or take the Bridge Trail and leave the summit lot at the visitor center. From there, the blue diamond—blazed Grandfather Trail scrambles up a rocky pitch, turns right, and levels through spruce forests under so-called Head Bumpin' Rock. The crag-top view just beyond is a nice turnaround for a family stroll. Left (west) is the resort development of Sugar Mountain (with the ten-story condominium now prohibited by state law). Right (east), the land plummets to the Piedmont. MacRae Peak (5,844 feet) is the cliff-faced, evergreen-covered summit straight ahead. Peer closely at about ten o'clock to see hikers on a series of ladders that you'll climb.

Between Calloway and Attic Window Peaks, the Grandfather Trail affords an alpine hiking experience.

Descend along cables (you'll see many), and pass the spur trail from the Black Rock parking area at 0.4 mile. (If you climb the extension trail, add 0.3 mile to all mileages below.) Pass a meadow to a junction at 0.5 mile, where the yellow diamond–blazed Underwood Trail goes left to the gap beyond MacRae Peak (the return route on a great loop, one of the truly spectacular short hikes in the region; 2 miles round-trip).

Stay right on the Grandfather Trail, climb more cables, then climb the first ladders, one in a fissure. A truly adventurous section of trail leads up more ladders to the clifftops above. Pause on the large ledge before the upper ladder. The visitor center is now far below.

Above that ladder, the clifftop becomes a knife-edge with a house-size boulder atop it—MacRae Peak. Climb the unnerving ladder that leans against the peak and have lunch. To the east, the Blue Ridge escarpment plummets past the Blue Ridge Parkway to the distant Carolina Piedmont. Continuing, the trail descends a steep chute with cables and a ladder to MacRae Gap, 1 mile from the visitor center. Turn back left on the Underwood Trail, 0.5 mile through crags, cliffs, mossy defiles, and evergreens reminiscent of the far north. Back at the visitor center, it's an adventurous round-trip day hike of 2 miles (2.6 miles round-trip from Black Rock parking).

Remaining on the Grandfather Trail, pass through a wood sorrel–covered gap, more ladders, a boulder cave, and then straight up through the massive split in the peak. At the top of the couloir, a trail leads right to a tent platform atop the domes. To the left, the trail emerges from between rocks to a stunning western view from Attic Window Peak at 1.2 miles.

Follow the Grandfather Trail to the next gap and a side trail to Indian House Cave, a big overhang at 1.3 miles. The trail continues on an evergreen-, rhododendron-, and mountain laurel–covered knife-edge above a series of dramatic cliffs into a high, alpine-like meadow and fine campsite. Going over the next whaleback of crags, the trail winds into Calloway Gap at 1.9 miles, a traditional ridgetop campground. The orange diamond–blazed Profile Trail descends steeply left 0.3 mile to water at Shanty Spring.

Right, the Grandfather Trail climbs again, through a tiny meadow and past a campsite on the right, then through dense evergreens to the Grandfather Trail's last junction at 2.3 miles. To the left, a short spur leads to Watauga View, a west-facing ledge over Banner Elk. To the right, the white diamond–blazed Daniel Boone Scout Trail reaches Calloway Peak (5,946 feet).

Looking east from any of these peaks, you'll understand why in 1794 early botanist André Michaux thought he'd climbed "the highest mountain of all North America." The dramatic drop-off inspired him to sing the "Marseillaise" and shout "Long live America and the Republic of France. Long live liberty, equality, and fraternity."

The Grandfather Trail gives hikers the best glimpse of the kind of scenery that prompted Michaux's famous flub. They'll also observe many of the plants he found so interesting. On the high, rocky clifftops, hikers encounter the fuzzy reddish-green leaves of Michaux's saxifrage, a delicate boreal plant that he might have first noticed here.

Key Points

0.4 Junction with Grandfather Trail Extension.

0.5 Junction with Underwood Trail.

1.0 Junction with Underwood Trail in MacRae Gap.

1.2 Attic Window Peak.

1.3 Right turn to Indian House Cave.

1.9 Calloway Gap.

2.3 Watauga View.

2.4 Calloway Peak (2.7 miles from Black Rock trailhead).

4.8 Arrive back at visitor center (5.4 miles to Black Rock parking).

Option 3: Profile Trail

This hike climbs the western flank of Grandfather Mountain to Calloway Peak.

See map on page 215.
Parkway mile: 305.1
Distance: 1.8 miles round-trip to Shanty Spring Branch; 7.0 miles round-trip to Calloway Peak
Difficulty: Easy to moderate to Shanty Spring Branch; strenuous to Calloway Peak

Elevation gain: 2,084 feet to Calloway Peak
Maps: USGS *Grandfather Mountain*. The best map for the hike is the free trail map from the Grandfather Mountain attraction (see above). Free state park map available at trailheads.

Finding the trailhead: In 2016, a new trailhead parking lot was built and the original parking area was expected to be closed. Leave the Parkway at Milepost 305.1 and turn right onto US 221. Continue past the Grandfather Mountain entrance (at 1 mile) and turn right onto NC 105 in Linville at about 3 miles. Drive 4 miles north of Linville on NC 105. Pass the junction with NC 184, and in 0.2 mile turn sharply right on a new access road that diverges east from NC 105 just north of the shopping center (GPS: 36.119285 / -81.833165). This new parking area is expected to hold 125 cars and include restrooms and a contact/maintenance facility.

The Hike

The Profile Trail was built in the mid- to late 1980s to replace the ancient Shanty Spring Trail, a steep and eroding trail dating from the latter half of the nineteenth century that was in the way of a proposed development (most of which luckily never occurred).

A new parking area was built in 2016, and was expected to close the original parking area on NC 105. Keep in mind a new start to the Profile is expected to lengthen the trail and mileages by 0.7 mile.

The Profile Trail has dramatic views of The Profile, the multifaceted, west-facing namesake face of Grandfather Mountain. The face, or faces, is best seen north of the trailhead. (Grandview Restaurant, a few miles toward Boone, is a nice place to appreciate The Profile during a pre- or post-hike meal.)

The graded trail is largely level as it wanders for its first 0.9 mile along the beautiful Watauga River through a mature, New England–like forest. The trail leaves the river, climbs steeply for 0.2 mile or so, and winds into a scenic, dry drainage where you'll find the waxy evergreen-leafed ground plant Fraser's sedge, on the endangered list. (A new trail from the new parking lot will likely intersect in this area.) At about 0.9 mile the trail dips across Shanty Spring Branch, the source of which is Shanty Spring, 2 miles ahead. Returning to the trailhead from here makes a nice round-trip family hike of 1.8 miles—which is why this portion of the Profile Trail is Grandfather Mountain State Park's TRACK Trail. Pick up or download the "Uncovering Cove Forests" booklet, designed especially for this site (but useful elsewhere).

Past the stream, the trail squeezes through a fissure then winds higher in and out of the drainages above on its way around Green Ridge. Immediately below the Grandfather Profile, there's a nice view over the Watauga River Valley town of Foscoe to Mount Rogers and Whitetop, the first and second highest peaks in Virginia, respectfully, at about 1.7 miles.

The trail switchbacks again to numerous tent sites and a grandiose campfire pit with a small seep beyond on the left. The trail ascends pathways of natural stone and switchbacks to a huge boulder with a rock-paved shelter spot. Not far beyond, the trail turns a corner to Profile View. Early mountaineers thought winter hoarfrost turned the dramatic face into a grandfather looking west.

At 2.7 miles the trail reaches Shanty Spring, where water empties from below a cliff. In his classic 1890s book *The Balsam Groves of the Grandfather Mountain*, Shepherd Dugger claimed this is "the coldest water outside of perpetual snow in the United States."

Going right at the cliff, the rocky upper Profile Trail rises through increasing evergreens to Calloway Gap, at 3 miles, and a junction with the Grandfather Trail and nearby tent platforms.

Left, hikers reach a side trail at 3.4 miles onto the often-windy western prow of the peak called Watauga View. Right, Calloway Peak is 0.1 mile away. The new Profile Trail parking, and a new start for the trail, were not complete at press time so final mileages are unknown.

Key Points

0.0 Start at new trailhead.
0.9 Shanty Spring Branch.
1.7 Foscoe View.
2.3 Profile View.
2.7 Shanty Spring.
3.0 Calloway Gap.
3.4 Watauga View.
3.5 Calloway Peak.

31 Beacon Heights from the Parkway and via the Mountains-to-Sea Trail

Milepost 305.2

A short and popular leg-stretcher affords spectacular views of Grandfather Mountain and its nearly vertical-mile drop to the Piedmont. By adding either short or long stretches of the Mountains-to-Sea Trail, hikers can find solitude.

Parkway mile: 305.2

Distance: 0.7-mile out and back. Adding a short piece of the Mountains-to-Sea Trail creates a hike of about 1.1 miles. From Old House Gap the Mountains-to-Sea Trail hike is 4.8 miles out and back.

Difficulty: Mostly easy; strenuous from Old House Gap

Elevation gain: About 120 feet; 1,360 feet from Old House Gap

Maps: *USGS Grandfather Mountain*; Tanawha Trail/Beacon Heights handout map available online at nps.gov/blri/planyourvisit/tanawha -trail.htm and in season at Linn Cove Information Station/Visitor Center. The Grandfather Mountain hiking map shows the trail best and is available free at the Grandfather Mountain entrance (north 0.1 mile to US 221 exit; right 1 mile to entrance).

Finding the trailhead: The Parkway trailhead is located at Milepost 305.2, 0.1 mile south of the US 221 entrance to the Parkway and 3 miles east of Linville (GPS: 36.083831 / -81.830172). To reach the lower Mountains-to-Sea Trail parking area, exit onto US 221 at Milepost 305.1. At the stop sign, turn left and drive under the Parkway, immediately passing SR 1513 on the right. Continue about 0.4 mile and take the next right onto SR 1514. At about 4.2 miles from US 221, turn right onto FR 192. Park at Old House Gap at 3.5 miles (GPS: 36.064224 / -81.809058). The Mountains-to-Sea Trail enters the woods on the right. Its first white-dot blazes are not visible from the parking area.

The Hike

This is one of the Parkway's best leg-stretchers. The grades are gradual, the footing isn't very difficult, and the views are outstanding. It's a popular hike, but by adding a stretch of the Mountains-to-Sea Trail, hikers can easily outwit the crowds and picnic alone at scenic viewpoints.

From the trailhead (4,220 feet) walk across the state road that parallels the Parkway (SR 1513) and enter the woods where the sign says "Tanawha Trail Beacon Heights 0.2." At the next junction, the Tanawha Trail departs to the left. The Mountains-to-Sea Trail comes in from the right and goes left with the Tanawha Trail. Turn right on the Mountains-to-Sea Trail—that's also the Beacon Heights Trail to the top. Past an overhanging rain-shelter rock on the left, there's a bench on the right before the steepest, rockiest part of the trail.

A mother and daughters grab some quality time on Beacon Heights. The Pisgah National Forest ripples off below to the Piedmont.

The round white blazes of the Mountains-to-Sea Trail turn off right at 0.2 mile where the Beacon Heights Trail switchbacks left. (A right turn here on the MST leads to a nearby view; see below.) Continuing, the path reaches another bench and junction at the peak. Go right to the top of a south-facing dome with great views to the Piedmont and the high peaks south along the Parkway, including Mount Mitchell. To the left, the path ascends stone steps to another dome with spectacular views of the eastern flank of Grandfather Mountain and the Pisgah National Forest's Wilson Creek drainage. Retrace your steps to the bottom (0.7 mile).

Key Points for Easy Hike

0.0 Leave parking spot.

0.05 Go right; Tanawha Trail and MST go left.

0.2 Turn left; Mountains-to-Sea Trail goes right.

0.3 Reach crest with summit views, explore both vistas.

0.7 Return to parking area; 1.1 miles with side trail to ledge.

Options: The longest Beacon Heights hike starts below, at Old House Gap, and rises through a forest that sees little foot traffic. Leave the secluded, leafy parking area at Old House Gap and follow an eroded, then sandy and pleasant old logging

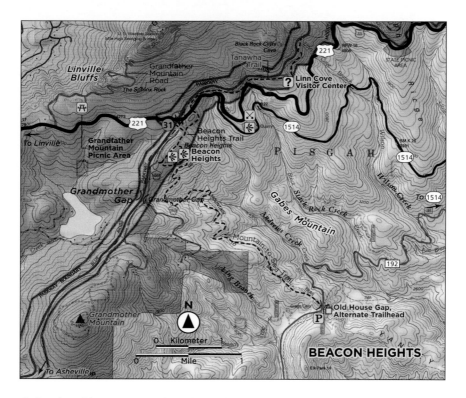

grade bordered by mountain laurel. At about 0.3 mile from the gap, go right on the Mountains-to-Sea Trail where the road grade goes left. The trail alternates between steeper and more gradual ascents as it climbs through towering hemlocks and rhododendrons to the upper drainage of Andrews Creek.

The trail reaches the top of the now-dry drainage and bears right up final switchbacks through sparser vegetation for Beacon Heights. A short, steep climb reaches a vista ledge on the flank of Beacon Heights (a private view for picnickers who'd rather not go any farther). Slabbing west and bisecting two boulders, the trail crests the ridge where the MST turns right on an old logging grade about 2.1 miles from Old House Gap. (To the left, the grade joins SR 1513, the dirt road you crossed from the Parkway trailhead). Go right on the MST for a short distance to the junction mentioned above with the Beacon Heights Trail from the Parkway. A right turn there leads to the top, about 2.4 miles from Old House Gap. The round-trip is just less than 5 miles.

The private view ledge mentioned above is also a nice and easy side vista from Beacon Heights when that trail is busy. Just turn right with the MST near the top, then head left into the woods to the ledge.

32 Flat Rock Self-Guiding Loop Trail

Milepost 308.3

This educational trail offers natural history interpretive signs and good distant views.

Parkway mile: 308.3
Distance: 0.7-mile loop
Difficulty: Moderate

Elevation gain: About 100 feet
Maps: *USGS Grandfather Mountain*; no Parkway map available

Finding the trailhead: The trail begins at Blue Ridge Parkway Milepost 308.3 (GPS: 36.050937 / -81.857435), 0.4 mile south of SR 1511, a side road to the Parkway from US 221 at Linville near the classic, historic accommodations of Eseeola Lodge.

The Hike

Here's a rare hike—one not to miss for serious hikers and more casual Parkway motorists alike. This is a quick walk to a good view or a wonderful hour-plus stroll for a family wanting nature study or a picnic.

Flat Rock's expansive ledges offer great views of Grandfather Mountain.

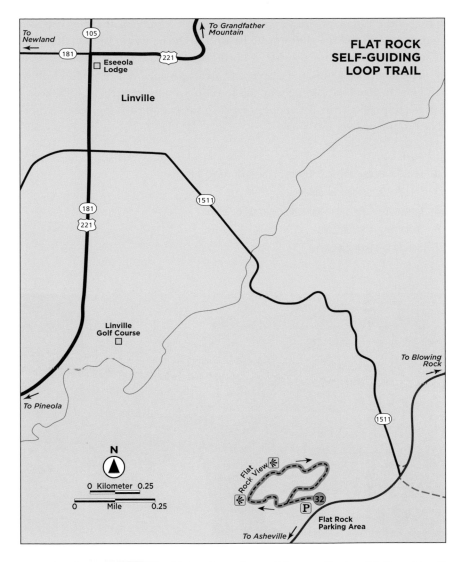

Not far above the parking area, where the trail loop splits, head left amid yellow jewelweed. Interpretive signs point out tree species and the shiny heart-shaped leaves of galax on the ground under the rhododendron. After passing a resting bench, step onto the quartzite outcrop of Flat Rock. The rhododendron woods quickly transition to a crag capped with gnarled pines, luxuriant moss, and lichen. Flat Rock's "bathtubs," the interesting bowl–size basins just ahead, often contain water that will eventually break down this solid shelf of rock.

Turn right to follow the yellow painted arrows that guide you across the breezy outcrop covered with wind-flagged hemlocks. The 180-degree view includes the Linville golf course below. The Appalachian Trail crosses the far western horizon on the meadow-covered peaks of Roan, Yellow, and Hump Mountains. Walk the ledge with one of the Parkway's best views of Grandfather Mountain ahead of you. Where the trail turns right off the clifftop, step beyond to the best view of Grandfather.

The trail continues into a sheltered northern hardwood forest past more tree ID signs, including hobblebush, red maple, and striped maple. All are found both here and in New England, explaining why this forest has a northern feel at 4,000 feet. The trail passes through a ferny flat and dips right to the end of the loop, where you head left back to the parking lot.

Key Points

0.0 Leave your car, and in 0.1 mile at the split, head left.

0.2 Trail heads onto rocky outcrop.

0.3 Continue in same direction after leaving outcrop.

0.6 Trail intersects; turn left.

0.7 Return to parking area.

In winter, Nordic skiers get one of Flat Rock's best views of Grandfather Mountain.

33 Linville Gorge Area

Milepost 312.2

Option 1: Hawksbill Mountain

Hawksbill Mountain is a crag-capped peak on the rim of the Linville Gorge Wilderness with panoramic summit views of Linville Gorge, a dozen major summits, and the Carolina Piedmont.

Parkway mile: 312.2
Distance: 1.4 miles out and back
Difficulty: Moderate
Elevation gain: 700 feet

Maps: *USGS Linville Falls* and *Ashford*. The best map is the USDA Forest Service map of the Linville Gorge Wilderness: www.national forestmapstore.com/category-s/1844.htm.

Finding the trailhead: Exit Blue Ridge Parkway at NC 181 near Pineola. Pass the NC 181/183 intersection, and 3 miles from there, turn right onto Gingercake Road, SR 1264 (where a sign reads "Pisgah National Forest Table Rock Picnic Area 8.7 Miles"). Measuring from there, bear left in 0.3 mile onto SR 1265 (signed "Table Rock Road"), which becomes gravel at 1.2 miles and becomes FSR 210. Pass trailheads for Sitting Bear and Devils Hole Trails at 2.7 miles. At 3.7 miles the Hawksbill Trail leaves the road on the right, with parking on the left (GPS: 35.914605 / -81.878331).

The Hike

Hawksbill is the less-jagged summit of the prominent duo of peaks, Table Rock and Hawksbill, that dominate the skyline of Linville Gorge. It has a sloping, rocky crest and low vegetation that permits expansive views. It also offers relative privacy, at least compared with Table Rock. This hike also avoids an additional 5-mile drive on steep, winding, and dusty roads to Table Rock. Views include Table Rock itself and the cliffs and crags that make this a world-class rock-climbing site.

The Hawksbill Mountain Trail enters the woods and climbs at a steady grade, then steepens. Take it slow in summer on the first 0.25 mile up the sunny side of Lettered Rock Ridge.

The path flattens, then slips off the sunny side onto a fern-bordered grade through a shady forest of rhododendron, maple, mountain laurel, and chestnut oak. The trail descends gradually, so be alert to make a sharp left at about 0.5 mile.

After the turn, the trail gradually steepens, undulating uphill through close vegetation and galax. Pass a shelter rock to the left of the trail and the path takes a hard right to the sandy soils and pines of the peak at 0.7 mile. Here, view trails fan out and trees give way to low vegetation such as Allegheny sand myrtle and sedges. Bear left on an obvious trail and wind down over prominent crags with fine views of Table Rock.

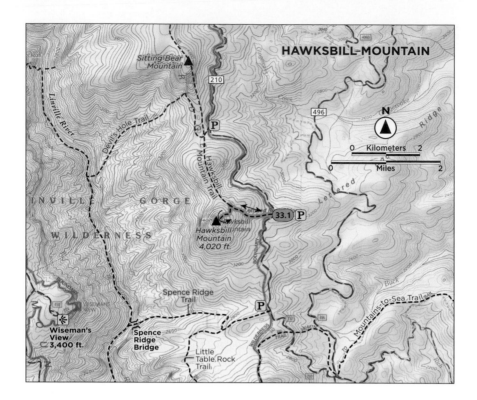

Key Points

0.0 Start at the parking area.

0.5 Sharp left toward summit.

0.7 Summit.

1.4 Arrive back at the parking area.

Option 2: Table Rock Trail and Shortoff Mountain

The most distinctive summit flanking the Linville Gorge Wilderness, Table Rock Mountain is a craggy peak popular with rock climbers. Hikers have panoramic views from the summit, and views from nearby Shortoff Mountain are even better. There is no better vista of the rugged chasm of Linville Gorge.

Parkway mile: 312.2

Distance: Table Rock, 2.2 miles out and back; Shortoff Mountain, 11.2 miles out and back

Difficulty: Moderately strenuous for Table Rock; strenuous for Shortoff Mountain

Elevation gain: 609 feet for Table Rock; 1,875 feet for Shortoff

Maps: *USGS Linville Falls and Ashford*. The best map is the USDA Forest Service map of the Linville Gorge Wilderness: www.national forestmapstore.com/category-s/1844.htm.

Finding the trailhead: Exit the Blue Ridge Parkway at the NC 181 junction near Pineola. Pass the NC 181/183 intersection, and measuring from there, turn right onto Gingercake Road, SR 1264, in 3 miles (where a sign reads "Pisgah National Forest Table Rock Picnic Area 8.7 Miles"). Measuring from there, bear left in 0.3 mile onto SR 1265 (signed "Table Rock Road"), which turns to gravel at 1.2 miles and becomes FSR 210. Pass the Hawksbill parking at 3.7 miles, and at 4.7 miles pass parking for the Spence Ridge Trail. At 5.7 miles turn right onto FSR 210B, following the sign to the Table Rock Picnic Area. At 6.3 miles pass the entrance to the North Carolina Outward Bound School. A paved, switchbacking ascent to the trailhead parking/picnic area starts at 7.25 miles. Reach the trailhead at 8.7 miles (GPS: 35.886492 / -81.884669).

The Hikes

The hike to Table Rock itself is far simpler than the drive to the trailhead. The Table Rock Trail parking lot is a lightly developed recreation area with tables and grills for picnicking and modern vault toilets. There's no water, and no camping is allowed. There are, however, great views; bring binoculars to watch climbers scale the cliffs.

The Table Rock Trail (combined with the Mountains-to-Sea Trail) leaves the north end of the parking area through profuse ferns and switchbacks right to the bottom of gradual steps. After a long stretch of rocky steps, the trail flattens and the

From Table Rock's summit, all the way to distant Shortoff Mountain at center left, the Linville Gorge shows off its ruggedest scenery. The Rock Jock Trail runs the clifftops on the ridge at right.

footing gets easier. At about 0.3 mile the trail switchbacks right as a side trail dips left into a little gap. This is the Little Table Rock Trail, which leads to the Spence Ridge Trail.

Continuing, the white circle–blazed Mountains-to-Sea Trail goes left and the Table Rock Trail makes switchbacks to the base of the first large crag. The trail squeezes between two boulders, then switchbacks twice past a shelter rock on the right as you near the crest, where views open up to the head of the gorge, toward Linville Falls. You're at the former site of a fire tower. North, Hawksbill Mountain is the rocky, gentle peak just across the gap; Grandfather Mountain rises on the right. The tinkling of rock-climbing hardware and climber conversation drifts up from Table Rock's North Ridge route. Summit vegetation waves in the gusts so typical of a cliff-edge environment.

If you're surefooted, go south where the summit descends along a spectacular spine of rocks. Many trails wander over and among the boulders to disintegrate into climbers' paths, working their way to stomach-churning drops. Find a private crag for lunch.

To the south, just past the Table Rock parking area, is the convoluted ridge called The Chimneys. Beyond, Shortoff Mountain drops off to Lake James. Across the gorge, the prominent cliff is Wiseman's View, a developed vista reached by road. Off to the right, the long crest of the Black Mountains includes Mount Mitchell.

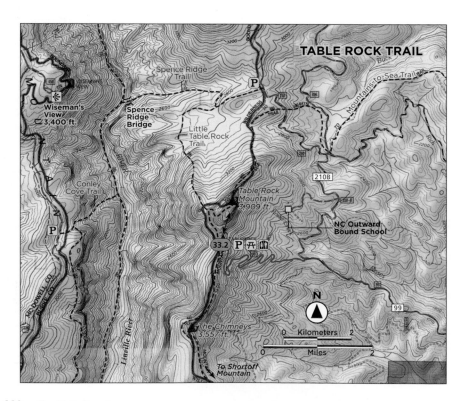

The Shortoff Mountain Trail leaves the same parking area but heads south. It follows a gradual ridgetop, then slabs to the west of The Chimneys (3,557 feet), rejoins the ridge, then swings southeast to descend 900 feet, much of it steeply, into Chimney Gap (2,509 feet). Continuing along the Shortoff Mountain Trail (part of the Mountains-to-Sea Trail), a wet-weather spring is located 150 feet left of the trail at about 2.3 miles. The trail reaches the summit of Shortoff Mountain at about 4.5 miles. A spring is located beyond the summit in a small gap. Paths reach clifftops where the most spectacular views in the gorge take in the deepest depths of the canyon (and reveal the impact of recent forest fires). Lake James sprawls below, a location for such memorable films as *The Last of the Mohicans* and the final scenes from *The Hunt for Red October*, where the escaped sub was supposed to be entering the coast of Maine.

Key Points to Table Rock

0.3 Trail switchbacks right at a side trail to the left (spring).

0.4 Mountains-to-Sea Trail goes right.

1.1 Summit.

Behind these hikers on Table Rock, Hawksbill appears as the crag-capped peak to the north.

34 Linville Falls Recreation Area

Milepost 316.4

Surrounded by one of those periodic bulges in the narrow corridor of the Blue Ridge Parkway, Linville Falls is the high road's biggest waterfall (by volume of water). This oft-photographed cataract gushes 100 foaming feet into the Linville Gorge, the USDA Forest Service wilderness canyon that lies below the falls. The Parkway's easy National Recreation Trails introduce this wild chasm.

Hikes on both sides of the Linville River offer views of the falls. The routes in two separate options below start at the same small visitor center (open seasonally, offering restrooms and a bookshop) on the Linville River near Linville Falls Campground and Picnic Area.

The remoteness of the gorge kept loggers out; John D. Rockefeller donated the inspiring, virgin-forested parcel to the National Park Service in 1952. Towering hemlocks and white pines soar above rhododendron that bloom profusely in late May. This lofty forest gives way to crags and rocky viewpoints, but rock climbing is off-limits. In winter, cross-country skiers will find that these gradual trails make inspiring ski tours. When snow closes the Parkway, a Forest Service spur trail provides access (un-skiably steep for the first 300 feet; see below).

Option 1: Duggers Creek Loop, Linville Gorge Trail, and Plunge Basin Overlook Trail

Three trails on the visitor center side of the river make the most scenic, least visited hike to Linville Falls.

Parkway mile: 316.4
Distance: 0.25 mile for Duggers Creek Trail; 1 mile round-trip to Plunge Basin Overlook; 1.4 miles round-trip into Linville Gorge; 1.8 miles round-trip to both Plunge Basin and Linville Gorge
Difficulty: Easy for Duggers Creek Trail; moderate for Plunge Basin Overlook; moderate to strenuous for Linville Gorge

Elevation gain: 190 feet for the Linville Gorge Trail
Maps: *USGS Linville Falls*; Parkway Linville Falls map available at trailhead visitor center and campground and online at nps.gov/blri/plan yourvisit/linville-falls-trails.htm

Finding the trailhead: Leave the Blue Ridge Parkway between Mileposts 316 and 317 on the spur road to the trailhead, about 1 mile north of the US 221/Blue Ridge Parkway junction at the town of Linville Falls. The parking area is 1.5 miles from the Parkway, beyond the campground (GPS: 35.954806 / -81.927835).

In winter, when the Parkway and the Linville Falls Spur Road to the falls can be closed due to snow, an alternative Forest Service trailhead can be used to reach these trails. Take the US 221 Parkway exit and go south on US 221 to the community of Linville Falls. Turn left onto NC 183, and in 0.7 mile turn right onto Wiseman's View Road (SR 1238, also called the Kistler Memorial Highway) where prominent signs direct hikers to the Linville Gorge. Even if that unpaved road has not been plowed, the Linville Falls trailhead is just a few hundred yards from well-maintained NC 183.

The Hikes

Just through the visitor center portico by the restrooms, go left at the junction onto the Duggers Creek Trail (the Linville Falls Trail goes right). The path wanders 0.2 mile along beautiful Duggers Creek, past plaques with inspiring sayings, to the end of the parking lot (return to your car via the lot).

For the Linville Gorge Trail, turn right away from Duggers Creek through inspiring hemlocks and rhododendrons. Turn right 0.3 mile from the visitor center for the easiest and best view of the falls at Plunge Basin Overlook. The path is level to a bench but then heads steeply down stone steps to a rock-walled perch above the falls for a 1-mile round-trip.

The perchlike stone vista spots at Linville Falls, like Chimney View at upper left, give hikers a bird's-eye view of the cataract.

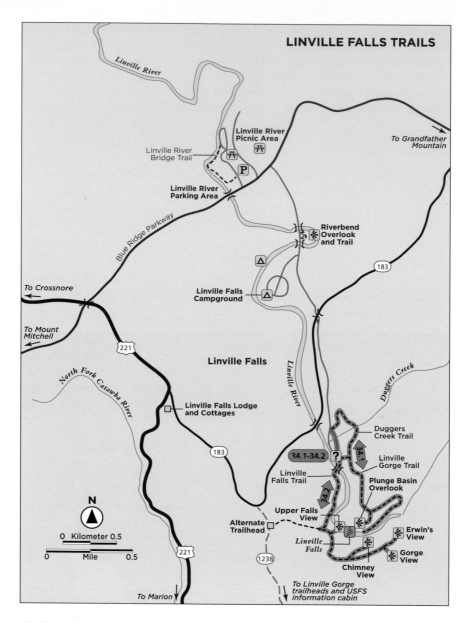

Linville River

To Grandfather
Mountain

Linville River
Picnic Area

Linville River
Bridge Trail

Linville River
Parking Area

Blue Ridge Parkway

Riverbend
Overlook
and Trail

183

To Crossnore

Linville Falls
Campground

To Mount
Mitchell

221

North Fork Catawba River

Linville Falls

Linville River

Duggers Creek

Linville Falls Lodge
and Cottages

183

34.1–34.2

Duggers
Creek Trail

34.1

Linville
Gorge Trail

Linville
Falls Trail

Plunge Basin
Overlook

34.2

N

Upper Falls
View

Alternate
Trailhead

Linville
Falls

Erwin's
View

Gorge
View

Kilometer 0.5

Mile

221

1238

Chimney
View

To Marion

To Linville Gorge
trailheads and USFS
information cabin

Back at the junction, go right; the gradual path has handrails as it skirts steep drops, descends a steep flight of steps, and turns sharply right at the bottom (the left is for the people who miss the turn). The trail follows the base of a towering cliff. When you hear river noise off to the left, keep right to the water's edge and rock-hop near the base of the thundering falls (this may be too icy in winter). The emerald water may tempt you—but swimming isn't allowed.

If you linger over lunch and scan the rock-hewn amphitheater, the start of Linville Gorge, you can imagine the hemmed-in feeling William Linville and his son must have felt near here in 1766 when confronted by Native Americans—who scalped them.

The round-trip hike to here is 1.4 miles, about 1.8 miles total with Plunge Basin Overlook.

Key Points

0.0   Leave visitor center.

0.3   Plunge Basin Overlook Trail branches from Linville Gorge Trail.

0.7   Linville Gorge Trail reaches base of falls.

1.4   Arrive back at parking area.

Option 2: Linville Falls Trail and Nearby Paths

Three hikes explore virgin forest and rugged scenery near Linville Falls, an impressive cataract that plunges into the Linville Gorge Wilderness. Two other walks—one on the access road from the Parkway, the other at Linville River Parking Area—also offer strolls.

See map on page 234.
Parkway mile: 316.4
Distance: Upper Falls View, 1.0 mile out and back; 2.0 miles out and back to Erwin's View
Difficulty: Easy for Upper Falls View; moderate for trail to Chimney, Gorge, and Erwin's Views

Elevation gain: Negligible for Upper Falls; about 200 feet to Chimney, Gorge, and Erwin's Views
Maps: *USGS Linville Falls;* Parkway Linville Falls map available at trailhead visitor center and campground and online at nps.gov/blri/plan yourvisit/linville-falls-trails.htm

---

Finding the trailhead: Leave the Blue Ridge Parkway between Mileposts 316 and 317 on the spur road to the trailhead, about 1 mile north of the US 221/Blue Ridge Parkway junction at the town of Linville Falls. The parking area is 1.5 miles from the Parkway, beyond the campground (GPS: 35.954806 / -81.927835).

In winter, when the Parkway and the Linville Falls Spur Road to the falls can be closed due to snow, an alternative Forest Service trailhead can be used to reach these trails. Take the US 221 Parkway exit and go south on US 221 to the community of Linville Falls. Turn left onto NC 183, and in 0.7 mile turn right onto Wiseman's View Road (SR 1238, also called the Kistler Memorial Highway) where prominent signs direct hikers to the Linville Gorge. Even if that unpaved road has not been plowed, the Linville Falls trailhead is just a few hundred yards from well-maintained NC 183.

The Hike

The level, road-width Linville Falls Trail crosses the Linville River on a footbridge to more distant and more popular views of the falls. Across the bridge, parallel the river; at 0.4 mile the spur trail from SR 1238 joins on the right.

There's a side trail left at 0.5 mile to the river's first big drop, Upper Falls View, a vista point substantially expanded and improved with new interpretive signs in 2015.

The Park Service and Blue Ridge Parkway Foundation installed signs that explain the Linville Falls Thrust Fault, a location where a one-billion-year-old layer of rock called Cranberry gneiss was thrust up and over a five-hundred-million-year-old layer of Chilhowee quartzite. The collision is a key element in the creation of the Grandfather Mountain window that explains the ruggedness of that mountain and the Linville Gorge. Evidence of such shifts in the Earth's crust is usually invisible underground.

The main trail rises and continues through towering virgin hemlock forest, with white pine, oak, and birches, then reaches the scrubbier vegetation and drier soils on crags overlooking the gorge.

At 0.6 mile from the visitor center, another junction splits the trail at a picnic/rain shelter. Left, steep steps reach Chimney View at 0.7 mile, an oft-photographed vista of the entire falls. At the shelter, continue away from the visitor center through piney forest to Gorge View, on the right, with an interpretive sign. The gorge appears again on the right; on the left at about 1 mile is Erwin's View, where the falls and gorge are both in sight from 3,360 feet (a 2-mile round-trip).

Key Points
0.0 Start at visitor center.
0.4 Forest Service spur trail from SR 1238.
0.5 Side trail left to Upper Falls View.
0.6 Junction left to Chimney View.
1.0 Erwin's View.
2.0 Arrive back at visitor center.

The Riverbend Overlook Trail
On the Linville Falls Spur Road, 0.4 mile from the Parkway, there's another short trail at Riverbend Overlook (GPS: 35.970263 / -81.930373). There's a bridge before and after this overlook, so here's the place to explore a big bend of the Linville River.

Linville River Bridge Trail
Just 0.1 mile south of the Linville Falls Spur Road on the Parkway (Milepost 316.5; GPS: 35.974452 / -81.936025), the Linville River Parking Area offers a leg-stretcher that arcs a gradual 0.1 mile down to the riverbank below the Parkway's largest stone structure (0.2 mile round-trip).

35 Linville Gorge Wilderness

Milepost 317.5

A 12,000-acre tract of designated wilderness, Linville Gorge lies between Jonas Ridge to the east and Linville Mountain to the west. The Blue Ridge Parkway skirts the head of the gorge on the northwest, where the Parkway's Linville Falls Recreation Area provides a nice glimpse into the chasm.

Peaks on the rim of the gorge tower over Morganton and Lake James. The wild canyon, up to 2,000 feet deep in places, was first protected as a primitive area by the USDA Forest Service in 1951. It became an "instant wilderness" area with the passage of the 1964 Wilderness Act. A subsequent wilderness bill in 1984 expanded the area.

Virgin forest and rugged, wild tangles of primeval density can be found in places where few people venture. Fire is an active part of the gorge ecosystem, and blazes in the past few years have blackened big parts of the wilderness. Linville Gorge is the most popular of North Carolina's wilderness areas, and only a limited number of permits are available for weekend camping between May 31 and October 31. Campers can remain in the area for only three days and two nights. Permits can be reserved in advance (for instance, June permits are available May 1) by calling the Forest Service office at (828) 652-2144. A limited number of first-come, first-served permits are available at the gorge's information cabin (see below).

The gorge funnels traffic into a narrow area, concentrating trail use. Those who want solitude should pursue a rugged off-trail adventure or go in late fall, winter, or spring—also the best times for bushwhacking to avoid timber rattlesnakes and copperheads, active in warmer months. If you must visit during peak season, go between Sunday and Thursday.

Except at trailheads, trails are unmarked and, in places, difficult to follow. Hikers get lost here every year. Other precautions include practicing zero-impact camping and wearing bright clothing during hunting season, late October to early January.

There is good news. A bridge now spans the river at the Spence Ridge Trail, built in 2006. In late 2009, Forest Service–funded crews reopened and stabilized the entire length of the Linville Gorge Trail along the river.

Even if you don't venture into the gorge, the 0.2-mile trail to Wiseman's View is a worthwhile side trip that will give you a feel for the gorge and its surrounding system of forest roads.

Parkway mile: Milepost 317.5
Distance: 0.2 mile out and back for the Wiseman's View Overlook Trail; 1.8 miles out and back for the Pine Gap Trail; about 3.0 miles for the Bynum Bluff–Pine Gap circuit; 9.0-mile circuit at the southern end of the gorge using the Pinch-In, Conley Cove, and Rock Jock Trails
Difficulty: Easy for Wiseman's View and Pine Gap Trails; moderate for the Bynum Bluff–Pine Gap circuit; strenuous for the Linville Gorge Trail circuit

Elevation gain: 520 feet for the Bynum Bluff–
Pine Gap circuit
Maps: USGS *Linville Falls* and *Ashford*. The
best map is the USDA Forest Service map of
the Linville Gorge Wilderness: www.national
forestmapstore.com/category-s/1844.htm.

Finding the trailhead: Leave the Parkway at the US 221 exit and turn left to the town of Linville
Falls (1 mile south of where the Linville Falls Spur Road joins the Parkway). In the community of
Linville Falls, turn left onto NC 183. In 0.7 mile from that junction, turn right onto Wiseman's View
Road (SR 1238, also called the Kistler Memorial Highway) where prominent signs direct hikers to
the Linville Gorge. The Linville Falls trailhead parking is a short distance on the left. The national
forest information cabin (GPS: 35.950450 / -81.933095) is 0.5 mile on the right (Apr through
Oct, primarily Thurs to Sat; 828-765-7550).

The trails descend from the left side of SR 1238 and are listed here by their distance south of
the NC 183/SR 1238 junction: Pine Gap Trail, 0.9 mile (GPS: 35.940283 / -81.930159); Bynum
Bluff Trail, 1.5 miles; Cabin Trail, 1.9 miles (GPS: 35.927766 / -81.925359); Babel Tower Trail,
2.7 miles; Wiseman's View Trail, 3.8 miles (GPS: 35.903189 / -81.907333); Conley Cove–Rock
Jock Trail, 5.3 miles; Pinch-In Trail, 8.2 miles.

Option 1: Wiseman's View, Pine Gap, and Bynum Bluff Trails

Trails here include a roadside view trail and a variety of other hikes into a wilderness chasm, varying from a down-and-back trip to the bottom of the gorge to a few
circuit hikes. Even if you don't venture into the gorge, the 0.2-mile trail to Wiseman's
View is a worthwhile side trip to get a feel for the gorge and its surrounding forest
roads.

The Hikes

A nice prelude to a hike from the western side of the gorge is a warm-up on the
Wiseman's View Trail. This easy, wheelchair-accessible, 0.2-mile trail is not a long
detour from the Parkway, and it will really give you the flavor of this primitive cleft in
the Blue Ridge. The parking area is only 3.8 miles from the paved road. The view is
spectacular, and you pass the Forest Service information cabin on the drive.

Unless you just hike to the river and back—which many people do to swim, fish,
picnic, or camp—you'll need to have cars at two trailheads to avoid a walk along
dusty SR 1238. Most hikers intent on a longer jaunt into Linville Gorge enter and
exit at two different western side trails and follow the river on the Linville Gorge
Trail between them. The easiest of these trails into and out of the gorge is the 0.7-
mile Pine Gap Trail. It drops on a rare gradual grade and descends to a junction with
the Bynum Bluff Trail. A left turn leads out to a crag with spectacular views of a
sharp bend in the river (avoid a right turn onto the Linville Gorge Trail on the way).
Retrace your steps for a day hike of about 2 miles.

The rugged terrain, virgin timber, and winding, boulder-studded stream of the Linville River make the gorge a challenge that routinely gets the better of the inexperienced.

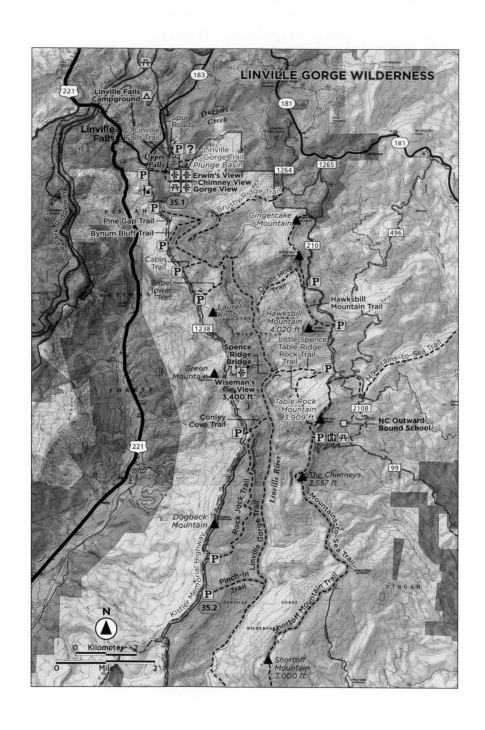

An easy circuit hike that requires just a 0.6-mile roadside walk pairs the Pine Gap Trail with the Bynum Bluff Trail. The Bynum Bluff Trail starts out gradually, reaches the point of a long promontory, then plummets down a sharp ridge to the Pine Gap Trail in 1 mile. Just beyond this junction, the Linville Gorge Trail goes right, downriver. Take in the views described above on the crag in a sharp bend in the river, or turn right for an out-and-back side trip along the river on the Linville Gorge Trail. Whichever you choose, make the easier climb out of the gorge on the Pine Gap Trail and walk the roadside for a 2.7-mile hike (if you don't go downstream).

Key Points for Bynum Bluff–Pine Gap Circuit

0.0 Start at Bynum Bluff trailhead.

1.0 Descend Bynum Bluff Trail to junction on left with Pine Gap Trail.

1.2 Viewpoint on river.

1.4 Right turn onto Pine Gap Trail.

2.1 SR 1238; turn left onto road.

2.7 Bynum Bluff trailhead.

Option 2: Linville Gorge Trail

It's hard to beat this classic route along the Linville River for wild scenery.

The Hike

Accessed from the Bynum Bluff or Pine Gap Trail, the Linville Gorge Trail descends along the west side of the river for almost 11.5 miles; the other trails that drop to join it afford other in-and-out options, many with obvious points of interest. The trail starts south around a sharp bend in the river on side-hill terrain, close under SR 1238. At just over 1 mile, the Linville Gorge Trail meets the Cabin Trail, a steep, strenuous 1-mile climb to SR 1238. On the left at the junction, a side trail juts out onto a bend in the river, reaching the peak of a 3,090-foot promontory. Continuing along the river another 0.8 mile, the trail switchbacks down, then slabs to a junction with the Babel Tower Trail at 2 miles. A side trail goes left to another summit, this one 3,035 feet, also encircled by the river. The popular Babel Tower Trail climbs a scenic ridge 1.2 miles to its trailhead on SR 1238.

From the junction, the Linville Gorge Trail switchbacks off a gap steeply down to the river. On the way to a junction with the Devils Hole Trail, on the left at 3.4 miles, there are great views of the gorge as it rises east nearly 2,000 feet to Hawksbill Mountain. The Devils Hole Trail climbs 1.5 miles to FR 210. At 3.9 miles on the Linville Gorge Trail, the terrain flattens and there are plentiful campsites and a spring.

The trail continues under Wiseman's View and intersects the Spence Ridge Trail at 4.5 miles. Spence Ridge is the most popular trail into the gorge from the east side. It leaves the Linville Gorge Trail, crosses the river on the only bridge in the wilderness, and climbs somewhat gradually in 1.7 miles to FR 210. A new bridge here, opened in 2006, expands your options.

Now the river flows directly down, the Linville Gorge Trail with it, to a junction on the right with the Conley Cove Trail at about 5.5 miles. This is a heavily used route, due largely to its lesser slope. From the junction, the Conley Cove Trail rises on a graded tread to a spring and a junction on the left with the canyon rim–running Rock Jock Trail at about 1 mile. It meets SR 1238 at 1.3 miles.

The Linville Gorge Trail passes this junction and runs for its greatest uninterrupted length along the river, about 3.5 miles. There are plentiful places to swim and nice views across the river at popular rock-climbing areas. The bulk of this section of trail flattens out.

At just more than 9 miles, the junction on the right is the Pinch-In Trail, a ruggedly steep, view-packed, 1.4-mile route to SR 1238. Below this trail junction, the Linville Gorge Trail gradually runs the next 2.4 miles beside the river, then fords it, to terminate. Savor the solitude and quiet at this point, then turn around and return to your vehicle along the river or the road. The true wilderness purist adventurer could concoct a wild circuit in this lower gorge area by climbing east to the Mountains-to-Sea Trail, or descending west from it.

Besides an out-and-back hike on this lesser-used portion of the lower Linville Gorge Trail, a southern circuit exists for the experienced hiker/backpacker. Parking at the Pinch-In trailhead, descend into the gorge and hike up the canyon, exiting at the Conley Cove Trail. Go left on the Rock Jock Trail. When it exits onto SR 1238, it's only about 0.5 mile downhill south to the Pinch-In trailhead. This is a rugged 9-mile hike in either direction, exploring an area recommended by the Forest Service as the least-used in the gorge.

Just south of Linville Falls at Milepost 333.4, the Little Switzerland Tunnel signals that you're close to dining and lodging in the longtime summer town of the same name.

36 Chestoa View Loop Trail

Milepost 320.8

From a popular roadside viewpoint, a quiet path leads to a nearby flat-topped knoll with a few good views.

Parkway mile: 320.8
Distance: 0.85-mile loop
Difficulty: Moderately easy

Elevation gain: Negligible
Maps: *USGS Linville Falls*; no Parkway map available

Finding the trailhead: The trail begins at the Chestoa View, just south of the US 221 entrance to the Parkway and the town of Linville Falls (GPS: 35.926731 / -81.954024).

The Hike

Before hiking the longer trail, take the short, steep descent on stone steps to Chestoa View, a clifftop semicircular rock outlook with a dramatic drop to the North Cove Valley. The square-topped crag of Table Rock on the horizon marks the crest of the Linville Gorge. Below, US 221 can be seen heading down to nearby Linville Caverns (North Carolina's only commercial cavern—open year-round), Marion, North Carolina, and I-40.

The airy formal observation point at Chestoa View is a classic of early Parkway stonework that still impresses in the twenty-first century.

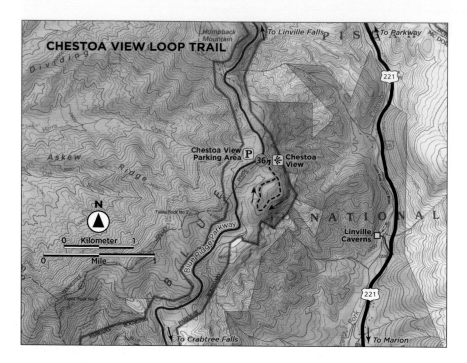

CHESTOA VIEW LOOP TRAIL

The dramatic drop from that first overlook is bordered by an impenetrable wire-mesh fence. Casual bushwhacking could easily become a free fall from unseen cliffs. If the macabre thought suddenly surfaces that a villain might do away with someone here—well, it's happened.

The lengthiest Chestoa hike begins at a sign, a once unmarked junction on the upper part of the paved viewpoint path. Don't be deterred by the sign. Look closely. It's 0.6 mile, not 6 miles. The decimal point was just pretty tiny in 2016. The trail dips gradually down through a flat gap and then rises again—the steepest part of the entire trail is the last 0.1-mile climb before the trail splits into its end loop. Go left at the split and the grade moderates to a fence-lined view on the left of Grandfather Mountain and Table Rock, the dominating presence to the east.

When the trail jogs back around toward the parking area, and there are no leaves on the trees, you get the full impact of how this side of the ridge drops through steep, gladed hillsides to sheer cliffs. Circling a marvelously flat-topped summit, you're again heading toward the parking area as the path dips gradually again to the junction of the loop.

Key Points

0.0 Leave the paved trail to designated view.

0.3 Trail splits; head left.

0.35 Nice view of Table Rock at Linville Gorge and Grandfather Mountain.

0.55 Return to loop split; head left.

0.85 Return to parking area.

37 Crabtree Falls Recreation Area

Milepost 339.5

Crabtree Falls Loop Trail is one of western North Carolina's best waterfall hikes—especially on a sunny spring day after significant rain. You'll also find a campground and picnic area. The area's snack bar and gift shop have been closed in recent years.

Parkway mile: 339.5
Distance: 2.5-mile loop from the campground, but now 3.1 miles round-trip with the recent relocation of the public trailhead to the former concession area parking area
Difficulty: Strenuous
Elevation gain: 600 feet

Maps: *USGS Celo*; Parkway handout map, available at the campground kiosk in season and online at nps.gov/blri/planyourvisit/crabtree-falls-trail.htm. At press time the map had not been updated to reflect the new trail parking by the concession buildings.

Finding the trailhead: The Parkway has closed the trailhead near the campground kiosk to reduce congestion for campers. Hikers should take the trail from the now-closed concession buildings past the amphitheater and keep right to the campground road at the contact station and trailhead. Take the northernmost entrance into the Crabtree Falls Recreation Area (Milepost 339.5) and bear left to park in the large lots beside the one-time gas station and restaurant/camp store buildings (GPS: 35.812686 / -82.143500).

The Hike

The former Crabtree Meadows Recreation Area was recently renamed as the meadows have become less prominent. Though only 253 acres, the spot now known as the Crabtree Falls Recreation Area is a small but compelling scenic enclave on the Parkway.

The Crabtree Falls Loop Trail now starts near the closed concession building, so enter the woods and pass the amphitheater at 350 feet. As you near the campground loops, bear right on a wide gravel trail to cross the campground entrance road at the kiosk into the old trailhead (a restroom lies off to the left in the campground loop). At the map sign board, about 0.3 mile, the trail descends on a wide gravel path to the loop junction. Turn right and wind down into a shady, often wet, hemlock-forested cove where steep stone steps mark two switchbacks.

At the base of the falls, about 1.2 miles, a bridge with embedded benches spans Crabtree Creek. This is one of the most picturesque falls in the Southern Appalachians—water dances down over ledges in a cascading fan of foam.

Continue across the stream and climb a sunny slope of switchbacks with great views of the falls. A bench marks the top of the climb to the crest of the cataract.

The trail then becomes intimate and easy as you wander under a hemlock forest through a tunnel of rhododendron and mountain laurel. Sunny openings in tall trees

Crabtree Falls' dancing fan of foam is a great destination for a spring hike on a sunny day just after the rain has stopped.

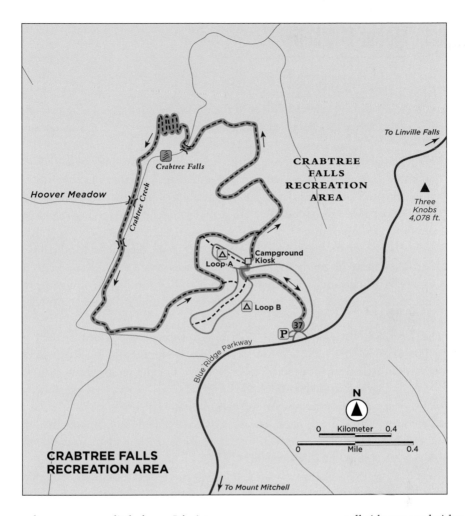

Hoover Meadow

Crabtree Falls

Crabtree Creek

CRABTREE
FALLS
RECREATION
AREA

To Linville Falls

Three
Knobs
4,078 ft.

Campground
Kiosk

Loop A

Loop B

37

P

Blue Ridge Parkway

N

0   Kilometer   0.4

0   Mile   0.4

CRABTREE FALLS
RECREATION AREA

To Mount Mitchell

reveal mossy, grassy little bogs. It's A+ scenery as you cross a small side stream bridge and then a bigger span where water cascades over ledge after ledge. The trail crosses a bridge at a bog beside a bench where northern white hellebore grows in late April. Side trails branch right to campground Loop B, then another branches to Loop A (see the map to shortcut back to your car near the concession building). But keep straight, go right at the loop junction, and return the way you started to the campground trailhead at 2.8 miles. Back at the concession area parking lot, it's a 3.1-mile hike.

Key Points

0.0 Park by the old concession building and take trail to campground kiosk.

0.3 Trail departs campground parking.

1.2 Wooden bridge across Crabtree Creek.

2.8 Campground.

3.1 Return to parking area.

38 Mount Mitchell

Mileposts 344.1–355.3

Mount Mitchell is the highest peak east of the Mississippi. It's a crowning part of the Blue Ridge Parkway experience—the only motorized access to the mountain is from the Parkway, at Milepost 355.3.

The 1,700-acre Mount Mitchell State Park—North Carolina's first—clings to the highest peak of the Black Mountains, a serrated string of summits that juts away from the Parkway. The mighty Blacks are frequently seen from the Parkway as a dark ridge crest rising above the clouds. The range includes six of the ten highest peaks in eastern North America.

Unlike that contrastingly named New England range, the White Mountains, the Blacks would have to be nearly 8,000 feet in height to create the treeless alpine zone found in New Hampshire at just under 5,000 feet. But the Black Mountains reign supreme, and high winds and deep snow (104 inches annually) yield a surprisingly severe climate.

The state park was established in 1915 largely through the efforts of then governor Locke Craig (1913–17) at a time when massive logging of the state's western mountains threatened to completely eradicate the last of the virgin forest.

Today, the park is a microcosm of the environmental factors that are destroying the world's high-elevation forests. An infestation by the balsam woolly adelgid, a pest introduced into the United States around 1900, has killed many Fraser firs. More recent studies suggest that red spruce trees have been damaged by acid rain, which inhibits a tree's ability to ingest nutrients.

Luckily, early 1990s changes to the Clean Air Act seem to be improving conditions in the evergreen zone. The Balsam Nature Trail is a nice introduction to this ongoing ecological issue.

The story of Mount Mitchell's crowning as the East's loftiest peak involves considerable controversy. Elisha Mitchell is acknowledged as the first to measure the preeminent peak, but that distinction was also claimed by North Carolinian Thomas Clingman, a congressman, senator, and Confederate brigadier general. Mitchell began measuring summits in the Black Mountains and arrived at the conclusion that one of the summits, then called Black Dome, was 6,476 feet high.

Clingman vaulted into what was apparently already a controversy in 1855, stating that Mitchell had not measured the loftiest peak and that he had; Clingman claimed 6,941 feet for the summit. Wishing to consolidate his advantage, the elderly Mitchell returned to the mountain in 1857.

Stopping his work near the end of June, Mitchell left his party to visit the homes of former guides, including Thomas "Big Tom" Wilson. Five days later, Mitchell's son reached Wilson's cabin to learn that his father had never arrived. Wilson remembered an obscure route over the mountain that he'd shown Mitchell years before. Following that route to the base of a 40-foot waterfall, the party found Mitchell, who had apparently stumbled in the fading light and drowned in a large pool.

A year after his burial in Asheville, he was laid to vindicated rest on "his" mountaintop. The peak officially became Mount Mitchell in 1858. His claim to the peak is enhanced by the fact that his final measurement of 6,672 feet is only 12 feet shy of the peak's true elevation.

The summit is still the site of Mitchell's grave. Various view towers have marked the peak. In 1959 a geometrical eyesore was built, but it was mercifully replaced in 2008 with a low-profile, wheelchair-accessible tourist tower.

Mount Mitchell State Park's ranger office is on the right immediately after the park entrance; next is a restaurant (open mid-May to late October). The park's small, nine-site tent campground is the East's highest (open May through October). Summit facilities include a snack bar (open June 1 through Labor Day and weekends through October) and restrooms beside the parking lot, where a noteworthy nature museum was dedicated during the summer of 2001.

In winter, motor access to the park varies depending on the absence or presence of snow. Call ahead, either to the state park or the Blue Ridge Parkway, before making the drive. Backpackers must register their vehicles on trailhead forms before camping (see the park's website).

These are good times for trails on Mount Mitchell. In 2010 local trail enthusiast Jake Blood and like-minded hikers launched the North Carolina High Peaks Trail Association to popularize the Black Mountain range and improve its overgrown trails. Their enthusiasm promises great things for hiking in the Blacks and tourism in adjacent counties. Check out their trail resources and group hikes at ncHighPeaks.org.

Option 1: Mount Mitchell Trail to Mount Mitchell

This spectacular part of the Mountains-to-Sea Trail climbs through virgin forest to the summit of Mount Mitchell. Its vertical rise is one of the great elevation changes in the East. A lower circuit on the same trails is a shorter hike.

Parkway mile: Reached from Milepost 344.1
Distance: Approximately 11.4 miles out and back; 5.7-mile loop
Difficulty: Extremely strenuous to the summit; moderate for the lower virgin forest hike

Elevation gain: 3,700 feet
Maps: USGS Old Fort and Mount Mitchell. Download the state park trail map at ncparks.gov/Visit/parks/momi/main.php. The USDA Forest Service South Toe River Trail Map is good too.

Finding the trailhead: Leave the Parkway at Milepost 344.1, going west on NC 80. In 2.2 miles, turn left onto FR 472. Black Mountain Campground is on the right at just more than 3 miles (GPS: 35.751719 / -82.221163).

The Hike

If only physically climbing a mountain earns the summit for you, this trail is your chance—nearly 4,000 vertical feet of it.

The blue-blazed trail quickly skirts the River Loop Trail (a recommended, yellow-blazed 3.7-mile streamside hike along the Toe River). You'll see white Mountains-to-Sea Trail blazes along much of this route. The trail climbs through impressive stands of hardwoods and evergreens. Stay on the Mount Mitchell Trail past the junction with the Higgins Bald Trail, on the left at 1.9 miles. The Higgins Bald Trail comes back in at 2.8 miles and climbs through virgin forest of red spruce and Fraser fir. At about 3.9 miles, join the Buncombe Horse Range Trail. Pass the Camp Alice Shelter site; in 0.1 mile the trail turns right and makes a rocky climb toward the peak. You'll join the Balsam Nature Trail near the Mitchell summit, where a left on the paved summit

Mount Mitchell's "newish" view tower is handicapped accessible and offers great views and plaques that identify distant peaks.

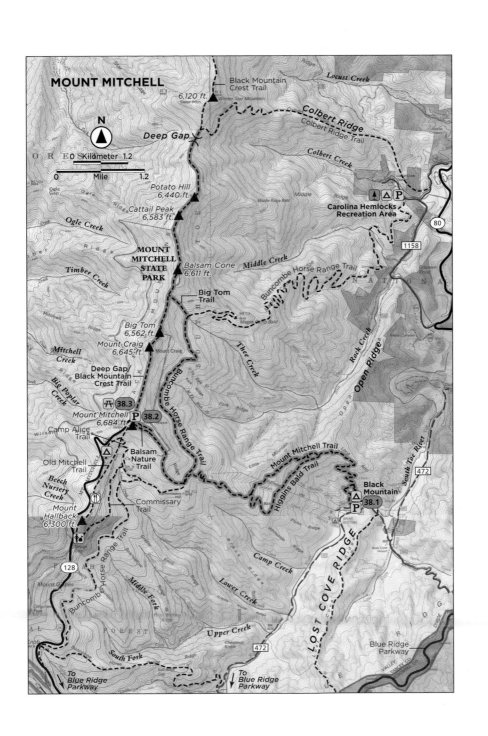

MOUNT MITCHELL

N

0 Kilometer 1.2

0 Mile 1.2

Black Mountain Crest Trail

6,120 ft.
Winter Star Mountain
Deer Mtn.

Locust Creek

Star

Ridge

Deep Gap

Colbert Ridge
Colbert Ridge Trail

Colbert Creek

Ogle Gap

Ridge

Ogle Creek

Potato Hill
6,440 ft.

Cattail Peak
6,583 ft.

Middle Ridge Bald

Middle Ridge

Middle Creek

Carolina Hemlocks
Recreation Area

P

80

1158

Timber Creek

MOUNT
MITCHELL
STATE
PARK

Balsam Cone
6,611 ft.

Big Tom
Trail

Buncombe Horse Range Trail

NATIONAL

Mitchell Creek

Big Tom
6,562 ft.

Mount Craig
6,645 ft.

Mount Craig

Thee Creek

Rock Creek

Open Ridge

Big Poplar Creek

Mitchell Creek

Deep Gap/
Black Mountain
Crest Trail

38.3

Mount Mitchell
6,684 ft.

P 38.2

Buncombe Horse Range Trail

Camp Alice
Trail

Balsam
Nature
Trail

Mount Mitchell Trail

South Toe River

472

Old Mitchell
Trail

Beech
Nursery
Creek

Commissary
Trail

Black Mountain
38.1

P

Mount
Hallback
6,300 ft.

Higgins Bald Trail

Camp Creek

128

Buncombe Horse Range Trail

Middle Fork

Lower Creek

LOST COVE RIDGE

Mount Gibbes

South Fork

Upper Creek

472

Blue Ridge
Parkway

To
Blue Ridge
Parkway

To
Blue Ridge
Parkway

FOREST

trail reaches the Mount Mitchell view tower at 5.6 miles. Consider taking a right on the white-blazed Higgins Bald Trail on the way down. It's only 0.3 mile farther than the Mitchell Trail and includes a nice waterfall.

The lower circuit of the Higgins Bald Trail is also a nice hike. Follow the hike as above, but turn left onto the Higgins Bald Trail at 2.8 miles. At 4.2 miles turn right onto the Mount Mitchell Trail and return to the campground for about a 6-mile hike. **Note:** Black Mountain Campground is a best-kept-secret camping spot with easy Parkway access. (See the Mileage Log for access at Mileposts 344.1 and 351.9.)

Key Points

0.0   Start at Black Mountain Campground.

1.5   Higgins Bald Trail goes left.

2.8   Higgins Bald Trail returns left.

3.9   Left on Buncombe Horse Range Trail.

4.0   Right off horse trail to climb Commissary Ridge.

5.6   Reach the summit tower.

11.4   Arrive back at the campground.

Option 2: Balsam Nature Trail

The Balsam Nature Trail is a self-guided interpretive trail that explains the spruce-fir forest and acid rain deforestation.

See map on page 251.
Parkway mile: Reached from Milepost 355.3
Distance: 0.8-mile loop
Difficulty: Easy
Elevation gain: Negligible

Maps: *USGS Mount Mitchell.* Download the state park trail map at ncparks.gov/Visit/parks/momi/main.php or grab one at summit facilities.

Finding the trailhead: Take NC 128, the state park access road, from Milepost 355.3 and go all the way to the Mount Mitchell summit parking area (GPS: 35.766254 / -82.265297). Walk past the concession stand/museum on the ascending now paved trail toward the summit tower. Go left when the Old Mitchell Trail branches right and then take the next left at the trailhead sign. (A right leads to the summit tower.)

The Hike

The white triangle–blazed Balsam Nature Trail explores the highest, most Northern climate in the South. Recently improved trailside interpretive exhibits feature the ecosystem, climate, plants, and animals that live in this rarefied evergreen zone, found this far south only at elevations above 5,500 feet.

In addition to coniferous species like Fraser fir and red spruce, the most prevalent deciduous species at this elevation is mountain ash. New England plants include

It's an easy stroll through Mount Mitchell's Canadian Zone on the Balsam Nature Trail.

hobblebush and mountain wood sorrel, or oxalis, a clover-like ground covering associated with boreal forests (early June bloom). The rhododendron here blooms in late June. In addition to the yellow birch trees found on the trail, you might notice a grove of mountain paper birch, similar to the white-barked birches so often associated with New Hampshire and Vermont. The small heart-shaped leaves are the giveaway. If, as some scientists speculate, this grove is actually a separate species of birch, then only about 400 specimens exist, all within this state park. The snapdragon-like purple turtlehead grows at damp seeps along the trail. The nice view north along the Black Mountain range shows Mount Craig beyond the summit parking lot.

The Balsam Nature Trail turns left where the Mount Mitchell Trail descends Commissary Ridge to Black Mountain Campground. The trail passes a small stream, likely the highest spring in eastern America (average temperature when not frozen: 36°F), then ends at the summit parking lot.

Key Points

0.0 Leave Mount Mitchell summit parking area. In about 250 feet, Old Mount Mitchell Trail goes right.

0.15 Tower trail goes right.

0.6 Balsam Nature Trail turns left from Mount Mitchell Trail.

0.8 Arrive back at summit parking.

Option 3: Black Mountain Crest Trail

An inspiring, out-and-back, summit-hopping hike/backpacking trip traverses a sparsely vegetated ridge well above 6,000 feet. Views plummet into adjacent valleys.

See map on page 251.
Parkway mile: Reached from Milepost 355.3
Distance: 11.3 miles one way to Bowlens Creek Trailhead. Round-trip day hikes vary: Mount Mitchell to Mount Craig, 2 miles; Mount Mitchell to Deep Gap, just under 8 miles. There's also a 6.6-mile loop of the summit.
Difficulty: Moderate to Mount Craig; strenuous for longer hikes

Elevation gain: 535 feet to Mount Craig and back
Maps: *USGS Mount Mitchell and Celo*, which intersect annoyingly on the trail's ridgeline location. The best map is the USDA Forest Service South Toe River Trail Map. Download the state park trail map at ncparks.gov/Visit/parks/momi/main.php.

Finding the trailhead: Take NC 128, the state park access road, from Milepost 355.3, and go all the way to the Mount Mitchell summit parking area. As you round the last curve into the summit parking area, the Black Mountain Crest Trail (also called the Deep Gap Trail on the way to that landmark notch) goes north on the left between log cabin picnic shelters (GPS: 35.767296 / -82.264453).

To reach the Bowlens Creek Trailhead, turn south from US 19E in Burnsville on NC 197. In 0.7 mile turn left onto Bowlens Creek Road (SR 1109). Go 2.4 miles to a hairpin curve, and take Watershed Road left a short distance to a five-car parking spot (GPS: 35.877137 / -82.284509). A sign warns of no turnaround and rough conditions ahead, so park here. The High Peaks Trail Association will likely have a new trailhead for this nationally significant hike in the next few years. If the lot is full, pass the hairpin turn and park by the small McClurd family cemetery, on the right.

The Hike

The first mile of the orange-blazed Black Mountain Crest Trail makes a wonderful out-and-back, 2-mile, round-trip day hike to Mount Craig. The plaque on the peak memorializes Locke Craig, the governor who helped secure creation of this first North Carolina state park.

Pass the picnic shelters and dip through spruces. At the 0.5-mile mark in the gap (about 6,330 feet), the land drops away west to Mitchell Creek and Mitchell Falls (4,400 feet), where Elisha Mitchell died. Then the trail rebounds to the open summit of Mount Craig (6,645 feet), the Blacks' second-highest peak. Looking back to the mountain you conquered by car, this view helps the peak gain in stature.

The trail dips to another gap then ascends to the summit of Big Tom (6,562 feet) at 1.2 miles. A plaque here memorializes Wilson.

The Black Mountain Crest Trail descends 0.4 mile to the Big Tom Trail, which drops east off the mountain (the return leg of the loop hike). Climb on to Balsam Cone (6,611 feet) at about 2 miles. The trail crosses Cattail Peak at 6,583 feet, then leaves the state park for national forest. Climb again briefly to Potato Hill (6,440 feet) then drop dramatically into Deep Gap at just under 4 miles. Deep Gap's shelter was torn down in 1995. A spring is 300 yards down the mountain to the east in front of the shelter site.

Deep Gap, the more than 700-foot cleft visible for miles in the ridge of the Blacks, is the next good turnaround point for a day hike (or backpack).

Key Points

0.0   Start at north end of Mount Mitchell summit parking area.

1.0   Summit of Mount Craig.

1.6   Big Tom Trail intersects right.

3.9   Deep Gap, a good turnaround.

7.8   Return to the parking area.

End-to-End Trek

The end-to-end adventure on this trail requires two cars and substantial driving. But the crest trail does continue, climbing out of Deep Gap to Winter Star Mountain (6,203 feet), where new switchbacks have tamed a dangerous rocky climb. The trail gains the lower ridge of the northern Blacks, with spectacular views. The trail goes left of the crest at about 6 miles, passing Gibbs Mountain and Horse Rock. At just more than 7 miles, the trail pitches up and slabs west of the final and most lofty of the northern Black Mountain peaks, Celo Knob (6,327 feet), at 7.5 miles. The next 4 or so miles go downhill on a switchbacking descent to the trailhead along rushing, beautiful Bowlens Creek near Burnsville at just over 11 miles.

You might try a summit circuit that uses the Big Tom Trail to return on the Black Mountain Crest Trail. Leave the summit parking area on the tower trail, then veer off left on the Balsam Nature Trail. When that trail bears left, go straight on the Mount Mitchell Trail down Commissary Ridge to the scenic and easy Buncombe Horse Range Trail, about 1.6 miles from the summit. This 15-mile, white-blazed horse trail parallels the ridge crest north to south. Go left on the old logging grade and follow the rocky but level trail north 3 miles to the Big Tom Trail. The horse trail descends right, but go left to make a steep 0.4-mile climb of about 560 vertical feet to the crest. Once on the ridge, turn left onto the Black Mountain Crest Trail at about 5 miles and prepare for a spectacular return to Mount Mitchell over Big Tom and Mount Craig for a 6.6-mile hike.

39 Craggy Gardens

Mileposts 364.1–364.4

How can names like Craggy Gardens, Craggy Dome, and Craggy Pinnacle not inspire hikers? Visible from all over northwest North Carolina, these barren crests offer awesome views.

As the Blue Ridge Parkway climbs from Asheville, the sun often disappears in a Craggies-caused microclimate. Summits and clouds coalesce, lending the area the feel of much higher mountains. You'd swear that the towering evergreen forests on the way by Mount Mitchell were straight out of the Pacific Northwest. During the coldest part of the year, the Craggy Gardens and the adjacent Mount Mitchell portions of the Parkway are often closed due to deep snow and severe weather.

This part of the Parkway possesses some of the high road's most dramatic scenery. You'll swear the treeless Craggies compare with Scotland. Craggy Gardens is one of the best places to savor the beauty of the seemingly alpine balds and the late-June rhododendron bloom. A visitor center (no phone) sits on the Parkway beside the start of the Craggy Gardens Trail; a nearby picnic area has restroom facilities and another trailhead.

It's a nice walk from the visitor center to the balds of Craggy Flats, views of Craggy Pinnacle, and a classic picnic shelter, courtesy of the Civilian Conservation Corps.

The Craggies' seemingly alpine, treeless environment is a one-of-a-kind ecosystem, and Craggy Gardens is one of the best places to experience the Southern balds. The balds come in two varieties—grassy and heath. Grassy balds may be best exemplified by the meadow-covered crest of Roan Mountain, on the North Carolina–Tennessee state line west of the Parkway There are grassy balds atop the Craggies, but you'll also see heath balds—extensive crests covered in rhododendron, mountain laurel, blueberries, and other plants of the heath community. The mountaineers called them "slicks," and "hells," which you would readily understand if you ever tried to bushwhack through one.

Craggy Gardens is a great spot to savor the "rhodo bloom" the third weekend in June. Try to confine your steps to designated paths to preserve the grasses, sedges, shrubs, and wildflowers. The Blue Ridge Parkway Foundation plans trail improvements here as 2017 dawns.

A visitor center sits on the Parkway beside the start of the Craggy Gardens Trail; a nearby picnic area has restroom facilities and a trailhead.

Option 1: The Craggy Pinnacle Trail

This trail offers one of the Parkway's most inspiring 360-degree views.

Parkway mile: 364.1
Distance: 1.4 miles out and back
Difficulty: Moderate
Elevation gain: 252 feet

Maps: USGS *Craggy Pinnacle*; Parkway handout map, available at the Craggy Gardens Visitor Center and online at nps.gov/blri/plan yourvisit/craggy-gradens-trail.htm

Finding the trailhead: The Craggy Pinnacle Trail begins in the Craggy Dome Parking Area at Milepost 364.1, north of the Craggy Gardens Visitor Center and the Craggy Pinnacle Tunnel. A spur road leads to the parking area (GPS: 35.704180 / –82.373658).

The Hike

At 5,892 feet, Craggy Pinnacle may be the Craggies' premier view. A veritable who's who of Southern Appalachian summits stand out on a clear day. The Mount Mitchell range dominates the northern horizon.

The path passes two resting benches and follows a level rhododendron tunnel then up stone steps on the way to a trail junction at 0.3 mile. A "Fragile Habitat Rare Plants" sign exhorts hikers to stay on the main trails and within the designated viewing spots. The sign

Craggy Pinnacle is the place for inspiring views and insight into the rare plants that grace these heath-covered crests.

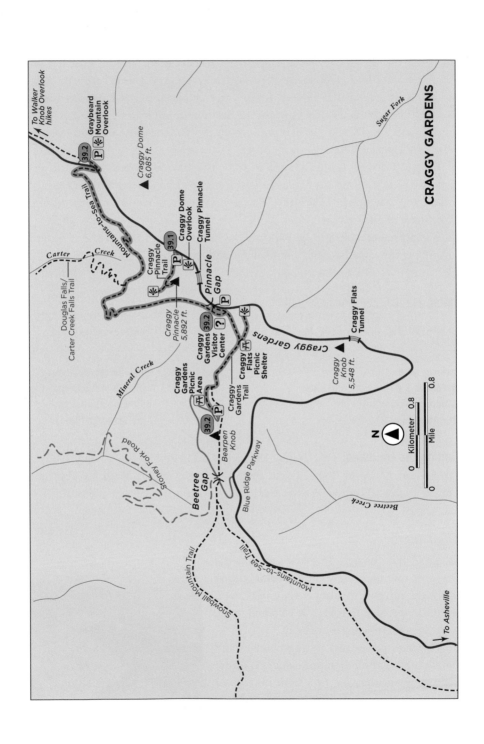

CRAGGY GARDENS

points right, to a lower overlook, and left, to the summit view. But first, turn right to a vista down on the visitor center. Back at the main trail, go right, to the top at 0.7 mile to four stone-encircled viewpoints with stunning 360-degree views. Even on a wildly windy or overcast day, it's worth the short walk to soak up the otherworldly aura of the peak. Return the way you came.

Key Points

0.0   Leave the roadside.

0.3   View trail goes right.

0.7   Summit view.

Option 2: Craggy Gardens Trail via Mountains-to-Sea Trail

Great views from spectacular mountaintop balds, with two shelters for picnics or if the weather threatens (as it can quickly at this elevation).

Parkway mile: 364.5
Distance: 0.8 mile out and back from the visitor center; 1.2 miles out and back from the Craggy Gardens Picnic Area; 6.2 miles via a third and longer route on the Mountains-to-Sea Trail

Difficulty: Moderate to strenuous
Elevation gain: About 145 feet
Maps: USGS Craggy Pinnacle; Parkway handout map, available at the Craggy Gardens Visitor Center and online at nps.gov/blri/plan yourvisit/craggy-gradens-trail.htm

Finding the trailhead: Craggy Gardens Visitor Center is at Milepost 364.5; the Craggy Gardens Trail begins on its south side (GPS: 35.699496 / -82.380005). To reach a Craggy Gardens Picnic Area trailhead, exit the Parkway at Milepost 367.6 onto unpaved Stoney Fork Road. Take the next right into the picnic area and continue to the end of the parking lot (GPS: 35.699842 / -82.391144). Start the Mountains-to-Sea Trail circuit at Graybeard Mountain Overlook (GPS: 35.710849 / -82.364220), Milepost 363.4; and a few other hikes at Walker Knob Overlook, formerly Balsam Gap (GPS: 35.748428, -82.333866), Milepost 359.8.

The Hike

From the visitor center, the trail climbs gently for 0.3 mile through a marvelously cylindrical rhododendron tunnel with benches. The trail leaves the woods in grassy Craggy Flats at a 1930s picnic shelter built by the Civilian Conservation Corps (CCC). A side trail leads from the shelter left up balds to a stone observation platform at 5,640 feet. The round-trip from the Parkway to this summit viewpoint is about 0.8 mile.

For a longer walk of just over 1 mile, start in the picnic area. The trail climbs gradually and at about 0.3 mile passes a short side trail to a gazebo shelter. The CCC picnic shelter is at about 0.5 mile. Include the summit view for a 1.2-mile round-trip.

Vistas look north from the Craggy Flats picnic shelter to Craggy Pinnacle (5,892 feet, left) and northeast to Craggy Dome (6,085 feet, right). The observation platform looks south over Craggy Knob (5,548 feet) and the Asheville watershed. Trail improvements on this hike are expected soon from the Blue Ridge Parkway Foundation.

A longer walk originates north of Craggy Gardens at Parkway Milepost 363.4. Take the white circle–blazed Mountains-to-Sea Trail from Graybeard Mountain Overlook south and across the road. Keep left around a ridge of Craggy Pinnacle when the Douglas Falls Trail goes right at 1.3 miles. When you arrive at the Parkway below the Craggy Gardens Visitor Center, turn on the Craggy Gardens Trail to reach the CCC shelter at Craggy Flats in about 3 miles. Include the summit for a round-trip of just more than 6 miles.

There are two more super hikes at Walker Knob Overlook, formerly Balsam Gap, just north of Craggy Gardens at Parkway Milepost 359.8 (also see the Mileage Log there). From the parking area (5,317 feet), on the west side of road, both the Big Butt Trail and Mountains-to-Sea Trail lead to superb views.

For rare close-in views of the Mitchell Range, take the Big Butt Trail left out of the parking area and follow the prominent ridge northwest. The trail eventually plummets down to NC 197, but the first 2.4 miles lead to campsites and especially great views at 1.6 miles and to Little Butt at 2.4 miles.

Take the right-hand trail from Walker Knob Overlook; the Mountains-to-Sea Trail traverses through the spectacular evergreen forests that clothe the intersection where the Black and Craggy Mountains collide. This hike runs above 6,000 feet for miles, and the trailheads are only 5 miles apart, so it's easy to spot a car on NC 128. (Go north to Milepost 355.3 and go left on NC 128; the trailhead is only 0.6 mile from the Parkway on the right.) From the gap, the hike climbs across the peak of Blackstock Knob and then dips through Rainbow Gap to great views at 3.6 miles from Promontory Rock. It's a 5-mile hike to NC 128. To Promontory Rock and back from Walker Knob Overlook is about 7 miles. The easiest hike to Promontory Rock is a 3-mile round-trip north from NC 128.

Key Points to Viewpoint from Picnic Area

0.0   Leave roadside.
0.5   Right turn at Craggy Flats picnic shelter.
0.6   Viewpoint.
1.2   Return to picnic area parking.

The Southern Appalachians

Mileposts 384.7 (US 74 at Asheville, NC) to 469.1 (US 441 at Great Smoky Mountains National Park, NC)

The loftiest part of the Parkway, the section from US 74 in Asheville (Milepost 384.7) to Great Smoky Mountains National Park (Milepost 469.1) is the perfect hikers' route through the mountains of southwestern North Carolina. Mount Pisgah starts a section of the Parkway that soars across the highest landmasses in the East. This is where the Blue Ridge meets the jumble of mountain ranges that make up the vast

From the Inn on Biltmore Estate, a meadow-traversing trail seems to lead to Asheville's glowing art deco skyline.

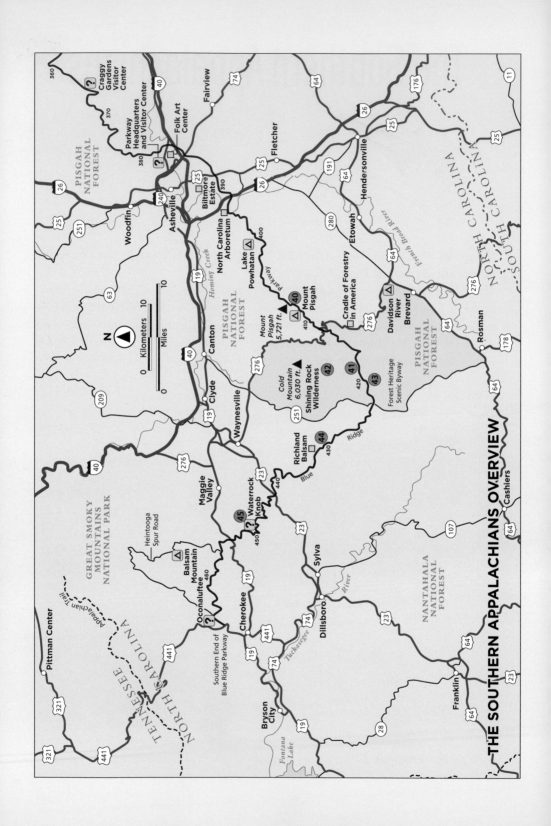

THE SOUTHERN APPALACHIANS OVERVIEW

heart of the Southern Appalachians. On your way to Cherokee and a memorable meeting with the massive wall of the Great Smokies, the road surveys some of eastern America's best scenery.

Despite a high and away-from-it-all experience that's second to none, off-Parkway options are close by in the Pisgah and Nantahala National Forests, including Looking Glass Rock and the Cradle of Forestry, the nation's earliest forestry school.

Classic mountain towns lie below and are at their liveliest during summer. Drop in (literally, from the Parkway) on Highlands, Cashiers, Franklin, Waynesville, Rosman, and Brevard (with its internationally known summer music festival, held June to August).

This area boasts the French Broad, Nantahala, and a raft of other rivers, and it is one of the East's best places for whitewater sports. One family-oriented trip in conjunction with the Great Smoky Mountains Railroad features a train ride up the river (which passes the location where the train wreck in the movie *The Fugitive* was filmed) and a rafting trip back down. Bryson City is a hot spot for the Nantahala Outdoor Center, known for watersports but a good stop regardless of your sport. They also offer great outdoorsy dining and lodging (noc.com).

The Forest Heritage Scenic Byway, near Mount Pisgah, passes by a number of these classic mountain towns, their inns, and restaurants. This 79-mile national forest circuit crosses the Parkway on both sides of Shining Rock Wilderness and follows US 276, NC 215, and US 64 in the vicinity of Brevard. The trip includes the Cradle of Forestry facility (see below).

The Brevard area is called the "Land of Waterfalls." The short stroll to Looking Glass Falls on US 276 is one of the roadside attractions of the Forest Heritage byway, as is the natural water slide, Sliding Rock. Many national forest campgrounds and picnic areas line the route.

Heading farther west brings you to Cherokee and the edge of the Smokies. The Oconaluftee Indian Village gives living-history insight into Cherokee culture at the time of European settlement. The Museum of the Cherokee Indian and the outdoor drama *Unto These Hills* are similarly worthwhile. Don't miss the Oconaluftee River Trail for insight into Cherokee culture.

Off-Parkway options are nearby and noteworthy but Asheville must lead that list. More Parkway visitors enter and exit the Parkway in Asheville than at any other place. Try the city's Urban Trail for an introduction to its vibrant downtown culture. (See Mileage Log 384,7.)

The biggest attraction is Biltmore House and Gardens, George W. Vanderbilt's 250-room summer place that is the United States' largest home. Its breathtaking gardens, interiors, and artwork are simply a must-see part of a Parkway experience. There are plentiful trails for hiking, mountain biking, and horseback riding, as well as kayaking. The Inn on Biltmore Estate is a perfect upscale platform for estate-raised foods and wines. The brand-new Village Hotel on Biltmore Estate is an affordable new accommodation next to Antler Hill Village and the estate's winery, the most visited in the nation.

Festivals are an Asheville forte, with crafts and music as a focus. August boasts the Mountain Dance and Folk Festival, the nation's oldest event focused on mountain music.

The literary heritage of the Appalachians and the increasing popularity of modern fiction about the mountains are most apparent here. Visit Thomas Wolfe's boyhood home before you, yourself, go home again. Both Wolfe and O. Henry (William Sydney Porter) are buried in Asheville's Riverside Cemetery. You can make the short side trip to Carl Sandburg's home, Connemara, at nearby Hendersonville. Later, from the Parkway, gaze at Cold Mountain, setting of the National Book Award–winning bestseller of the same name.

Parkway travelers can literally check into local literary heritage at the Grove Park Inn, among the most quintessential of Appalachian hotels. The preserved historic heart of the inn, with its massive fireplace, has a room that was frequently occupied by F. Scott Fitzgerald. It's a favorite with readers. The hotel is renowned for top-notch facilities, including a nationally significant spa.

Other tours from town include Handmade in America's seven craft heritage routes. From Asheville's eateries, with a focus on locally grown seasonal produce, to the Grove Arcade Market downtown, and on to out-of-the-way craft shops and galleries, these mountains are a hotbed of tradition. This is the city where the Southern Highland Handicraft Guild was born, and one of the Parkway's major facilities, the Folk Art Center, just north of the city, is a showcase for the work of its members. There are many, many other galleries all over town, some in unique shopping settings like Biltmore Village, a multiblock neighborhood of historic homes converted to distinctive shops.

Here also is the Parkway Visitor Center (Milepost 384). The new, primary visitor center for the high road was just in time for the Parkway's seventy-fifth anniversary in 2010. The environmentally green building has a meadow-covered roof and exhibits on the Parkway's vistas, history, geology, and culture. An interactive wall map covers the entire journey. And there's a large bookstore, theater, and restrooms.

Don't forget to check the Mileage Log for more detail about travel options in Asheville and Cherokee, and many outstanding trails and options in the Asheville area. Also see appendix B for relevant websites and contact information.

40 Mount Pisgah Area Trails

Mileposts 407.6–411.9

Mount Pisgah launches that southwestern mountain experience for hikers driving the Blue Ridge Parkway. On the way to Mount Pisgah from Asheville, it's humbling to realize that George W. Vanderbilt's Biltmore House and Gardens was just part of a 125,000-acre estate that today wraps the Parkway in the Pisgah National Forest.

Vanderbilt named this acreage Pisgah Forest after the mountain that dominates the area. Vanderbilt hired two of the United States' earliest foresters to restore and manage his lands. Following that effort, America's first school of forestry was located not far from Mount Pisgah. The aptly named Cradle of Forestry is a must-see stop for Mount Pisgah hikers.

From 5,000 feet at the Parkway's Mount Pisgah Recreation Area, the views over Pisgah National Forest are spectacular. So are the vistas from the rooms, front porches/balconies, and restaurant at Pisgah Inn. The campground is the Parkway's second highest, so expect cool nights. It's the only Parkway campground with showers (at publication time). A picnic area, camp store, and gift/craft shop round out the resources.

Vanderbilt built a 17.0-mile trail from his estate to a hunting lodge on the heights of what is now the Parkway's multifaceted Mount Pisgah Recreation Area (the lodge site is on the Buck Spring Trail and has new interpretive signs).

The trail to the site of Vanderbilt's hunting lodge is still in use; the Shut-In Trail was reclaimed and is now part of the Mountains-to-Sea Trail. Between that trail, other easy paths, and the notoriously steep ascent of Mount Pisgah itself, Vanderbilt's former forest domain endures as a place where hikers would do well to get out of the car.

Option 1: Mount Pisgah Trail and Picnic Area Connector

A heart-pumping climb leads to great views atop the conical summit of one of western North Carolina's landmark mountains.

Parkway mile: 407.6
Distance: 2.6 or 3.6 miles (from picnic area) out and back
Difficulty: Strenuous
Elevation gain: 726 feet

Maps: *USGS Dunsmore Mountain and Cruso*; Parkway Mount Pisgah map available in season at lodge, campground, and other facilities, and online at nps.gov/blri/planyourvisit/mt-pisgah -trails.htm

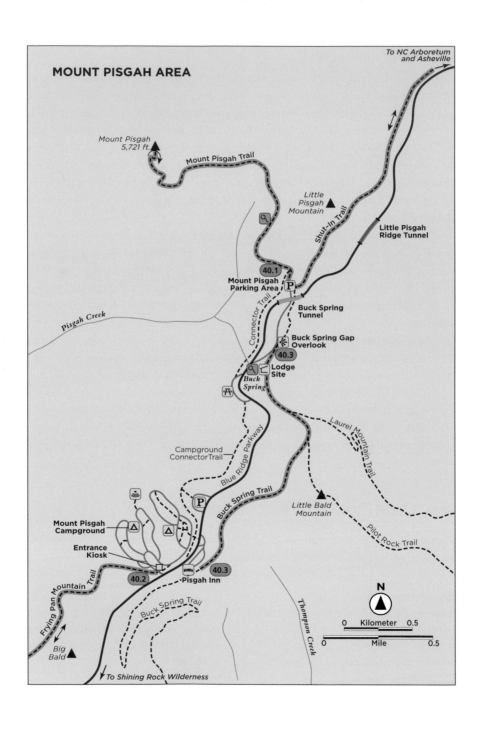

MOUNT PISGAH AREA

To NC Arboretum
and Asheville

Mount Pisgah
5,721 ft.

Mount Pisgah Trail

Little
Pisgah
Mountain

Shut-In Trail

Little Pisgah
Ridge Tunnel

Pisgah Creek

40.1

Mount Pisgah
Parking Area

P

Connector Trail

Buck Spring
Tunnel

Buck Spring Gap
Overlook

40.3

Lodge
Site

Buck
Spring

Laurel Mountain Trail

Campground
Connector Trail

Blue Ridge Parkway

P

Buck Spring Trail

Little Bald
Mountain

Pilot Rock Trail

Mount Pisgah
Campground

Entrance
Kiosk

40.2

40.3

Pisgah Inn

Frying Pan Mountain Trail

Buck Spring Trail

Thompson Creek

N

Big
Bald

To Shining Rock Wilderness

0   Kilometer   0.5

0   Mile   0.5

Finding the trailhead: Don't become befuddled trying to find this trailhead. Its location reflects an oddity of the Parkway's mileage system. South of the Parkway's Buck Spring Tunnel, turn into the Buck Spring Gap Overlook at Milepost 407.7. Follow the road extension back north to the Mount Pisgah parking area atop Buck Spring Tunnel at Milepost 407.6, but reached from Milepost 407.7 (GPS: 35.418723 / -82.747940). The trail from the picnic area leaves the northeast end of the lot at Milepost 407.8 (GPS: 35.413529 / -82.751283).

The Hike

Not far from the end of the lot, the trail connector to the picnic area goes left (see below). The trail slabs the northwest side of Little Pisgah Mountain, which forces the Parkway through two nearby tunnels.

Pass a spring at 0.4 mile, and rise along the ridge crest at 0.6 mile. The trail swings left of the ridge, and a few benches appear as the trail steepens to the 1-mile mark. As you ascend the summit cone, the trail switchbacks back to the right to emerge at the observation tower (5,721 feet) for one of the Parkway's best views. The Asheville Valley and Black Mountains lie north; the crest of the Shining Rock Wilderness and the Smokies are southwest.

You can add 1 mile (0.5 mile in each direction) to the Mount Pisgah hike by starting at the picnic area parking lot and going right on the connector, which makes sense if you're planning to hike after lunch. This is one of the "transportation" paths you'll find in developed Parkway recreation areas that lead picnickers or campers between their tents or RVs and other facilities. On the way, the trail passes Buck Spring Tunnel—a rare view from the roadside rather than through the windshield.

Another connector trail leaves the picnic area bound for the campground. (See the Frying Pan Mountain option for more on that hike.)

Key Points

0.0   Start at the Mount Pisgah Parking Area.

0.4   Pass a spring.

0.6   Ascend sharp ridge.

0.9   Trail steepens.

1.3   Summit tower. Return the way you came.

2.0   Arrive back at the parking area.

Option 2: Frying Pan Mountain Trail

A short, long, and longer way allow you to sample views of the Pisgah area from the base of a fire tower at about 5,260 feet.

Parkway mile: 408.8
Distance: 1.6, 4.2, and 6.6 miles out and back

Difficulty: Moderate to strenuous
Elevation gain: 410 feet

Maps: *USGS Dunsmore Mountain and Cruso*; Parkway Mount Pisgah map available in season at lodge, campground, and other facilities, and online at nps.gov/blri/planyourvisit/mt-pisgah-trails.htm

Finding the trailhead: Start near the campground entrance station (Milepost 408.8; GPS: 35.402900 / -82.757087) or at the picnic area via the campground connector trail (Milepost 407.8; GPS: 35.412397 / -82.750852) and head south.

The Hike

Any version of this hike reaches another great vista on a lofty section of the Parkway. But unlike the view from Mount Pisgah (Option 1), one of the focal points from Frying Pan Mountain is Mount Pisgah itself. There is no access to the fire tower atop the mountain.

Not far south of access to the Frying Pan Mountain Trail at Milepost 409.6, the Cradle of Forestry Overlook points out how easy it is to visit this worthwhile US Forest Service visitor center.

The trail leaves the roadside near the campground check-in kiosk and rises over the northwest ridge of Big Bald Mountain before swinging left to slab the mountainside. The Parkway is on the opposite side of the mountain, so this is a quiet stretch of trail through a scrubby forest that offers good winter views. At about the 0.5-mile mark, the trail begins a general descent into Frying Pan Gap (Milepost 409.6). This roadside pull-off, at 1.1 mile, marks the start of the portion of trail that follows a dirt road to the fire tower. Indeed, the last mile of the hike takes a big hairpin turn to the left and reaches the tower for commanding views. From Frying Pan Gap it's only a 1.6-mile round-trip hike—still a climb, but shorter. From the campground it's a 3.9-mile round-trip.

You could also make this a 6.4-mile hike by starting at the picnic area on the trail from the south side of the lot. The path dips quickly into a damp green corridor below the road through dense rhododendron and spruce forest. The first side trail to the left, at 0.8 mile, goes a few hundred feet to an unnamed parking area at Milepost 408.3. As the campsites appear off to the right at 1.0 mile, a trail goes right to the campground and left 0.1 mile to the Parkway across from the camp store. At 1.1 miles the trail joins and follows the campground loop road for 100 feet before heading back into the woods and arriving at the campground entrance kiosk at the 1.2-mile mark. Cross the road to the Frying Pan Mountain Trail. The round-trip from the picnic area to the peak makes for a 6.4-mile hike that's strenuous mostly due to distance.

Key Points

0.0 Start by the campground kiosk.

0.5 Trail begins descent to Frying Pan Gap.

1.1 Frying Pan Gap.

2.1 Summit tower.

Option 3: Shut-In Trail/Buck Spring Trail

A mostly graded trail makes for a pleasant walk from the Pisgah Inn to the site of George Vanderbilt's Buck Spring Hunting Lodge. A much longer but very easy section of the trail on Forest Service property is also inviting.

See map on page 266.
Parkway miles: 407.7, 408.6, and 411.8
Distance: 1.6 miles, 2.0 miles, or as much as 12.0 miles out and back
Difficulty: Easy to moderate
Elevation gain: About 480 feet from Pisgah Inn to hunting lodge site and back

Maps: USGS *Dunsmore Mountain and Cruso*; Parkway Mount Pisgah map available in season at lodge, campground, and other facilities, and online at nps.gov/blri/planyourvisit/mt-pisgah -trails.htm

Finding the trailhead: On the north end of the trail, park at Buck Spring Gap Overlook (Milepost 407.7; GPS: 35.415129 / -82.748549). On the south end (Milepost 408.6), park in the lot at the Pisgah Inn and start beside the trail map sign at the parking area's north end (GPS: 35.403640 / -82.753292). You can also walk between the lodge office and the restaurant, descend the stone steps, and follow the grassy path left to the map sign in the parking lot.

The Hike

Vanderbilt blazed a 17-mile trail from his estate to a hunting lodge in what is now the Mount Pisgah Recreation Area. The lodge site is on the easy-to-moderate Buck Spring Trail, which starts at Milepost 408.6 near the trail map sign on the north end of the Pisgah Inn parking area. It's 2 miles out and back to the lodge site and a mere 0.2 mile round-trip from the Buck Spring Gap Overlook at Milepost 407.7, the first parking area on the right heading out to the Mount Pisgah parking area.

New interpretive signage informs the site of Buck Spring Lodge. To the right of the woman, head across the grass and into the woods; the old spring house is just down the hill, then left.

The trail Vanderbilt took from Asheville to his hunting lodge is still in use too. The Shut-In Trail was reclaimed and is now part of the Mountains-to-Sea Trail. It runs from the right side of the Mount Pisgah parking area (Milepost 407.6) to near the North Carolina Arboretum at the French Broad Overlook (Milepost 393.8). Along that route, the Shut-In Trail is nice for short out-and-back hikes. Between those trailheads it's accessible from overlooks at Mileposts 396.4, 397.3, 398.3, 400.3, 401.7, 402.6, 403.6, 404.5, and 405.5. The Mileage Log will remind you of those access points as you drive the road.

The Buck Spring Trail sees most use as an untaxing walk to the site of Vanderbilt's hunting lodge for people starting from the Pisgah Inn. The trail leaves the inn area at the map sign, passes a junction on the right with the Thompson Creek Trail and then lodge employee housing on the left, gains a ridge at 0.3 mile, and at 0.6 mile passes the Pilot Rock Trail. That trail goes a bit more than 2.0 miles to Yellow Gap Road. (In that direction, the path reaches the summit of Little Bald Mountain 0.2 mile from the Buck Spring Trail—a nice side trip or turnaround point for a round-trip walk of 1.6 miles.)

Just 0.1 mile beyond that junction, the Laurel Mountain Trail also goes right, this time to Yellow Gap Road in 7.0 miles. Keeping to the Buck Spring Trail, you reach the lodge site at 1.0 mile (just 0.1 mile beyond is Buck Spring Gap Overlook). A new interpretive sign describes the history of buildings that were removed in 1963. Head straight down the grassy hill behind the sign, and a left below leads to the last remaining structure at the site, a springhouse. That's a 1.0-mile walk for a 2.0-mile round-trip (2.4 miles if you take in Little Bald Mountain's summit). Much of both these routes is part of the Mountains-to-Sea Trail.

The easiest route to the old lodge site is to start at the north end of the trail at the Buck Spring Gap Overlook. From there the lodge site is 0.1 mile. Along the way, informal paths lead left to the edge of the ridge—surely viewpoints in Vanderbilt's time. If you start here and descend to the springhouse, don't climb back up to the hilltop sign. As you leave the springhouse, bear left and walk along the stone wall back to the overlook.

Key Points

0.0 Start at Pisgah Inn lot beside trail map sign.

0.6 Pass Pilot Rock Trail.

0.7 Laurel Mountain Trail goes right.

1.0 Arrive at site of Buck Spring Hunting Lodge.

41 Graveyard Fields Loop

Milepost 418.8

This loop reaches three waterfalls and explores a high, alpinelike valley. A second circuit involves a portion of the Mountains-to-Sea Trail.

Parkway mile: 418.8
Distance: 2.3-mile loop, with 1.4-mile side-trip option
Difficulty: Easy to moderately strenuous; easy backpacking for beginners

Elevation gain: About 300 feet for the 2.3-mile loop; about 700 feet with the side trip to Upper Falls
Maps: *USGS Shining Rock.* Pisgah National Forest's Shining Rock–Middle Prong Wilderness map covers the area best.

Finding the trailhead: Graveyard Fields Overlook is at Milepost 418.8 on the Blue Ridge Parkway, 30 miles south of US 25 in Asheville (GPS: 35.320287 / -82.846936). The trail is about 7 miles south of the US 276 junction and about 4.5 miles north of the NC 215 junction.

The Hike

The big news here is that this very popular trailhead was greatly expanded and facilities significantly improved in 2014 with funding from the Blue Ridge Parkway, the USDA Forest Service, and the Blue Ridge Parkway Foundation. Solar restrooms were installed and many trail improvements went in, including sections of boardwalk and interpretive signing.

The most daunting part of the entire hike is the steep descent from the Blue Ridge Parkway. It's short, only a few tenths of a mile, but it is steep on the way back if you retrace your steps (the return described here climbs much more gradually). Otherwise, this hike is relatively easy.

The open fields here were named following a devastating 25,000-acre fire in 1925. The thousands of stumps remaining reminded some people of grave markers. The entire 50,000-acre watershed was consumed by wildfires again in the 1940s. There was a smaller fire in the late 1990s. These fires have given the Shining Rock area its largely treeless, alpine-like appearance.

This gentle stream valley makes the perfect place for a day hike, picnic, or backpacking trip, especially for beginners or those who want an easy walk to scenic camping. The area is very popular in summer and fall, though, so campers in this fragile area should observe scrupulous camping practices. (In 2016, camping was prohibited at times due to bear activity.) To find out-of-the-way sites for zero-impact camping, go during the week and off-season.

Leaving the edge of the Parkway overlook, the trail descends the steep paved path and then crosses Yellowstone Prong on a bridge. Go right on a side trail and down a long set of wooden steps to Second Falls (a spur of the Mountains-to-Sea Trail goes left on the way—more below). This lofty area—the trailhead is at 5,100 feet and the high point 5,400 feet—never gets too warm, but the pool below these falls is a great summer spot to cool off.

Retrace your steps to the bridge, about 0.5 mile, and continue. Soon the Graveyard Ridge Connector Trail branches right up a scenic rise of open fields and forest, a nice day hike or backpack to the summits. The Graveyard Fields Loop continues left along the stream through an open river valley. Fine campsites are just out of sight, where evergreens mingle with deciduous trees and blueberry bushes. Views reach up to the balds above.

Just past the 1-mile mark, the return part of the loop heads left across the stream. Hikers may continue on the right-hand trail, following a 0.7-mile side trail to the Upper Falls, a less frequently visited, more precipitous cascade with impressive views down the valley. This section of trail, a round-trip of about 1.4 miles, is steeper and rockier than the rest of the route. If you go, retrace your steps downstream and take a right turn across Yellowstone Prong.

The lofty valley of Graveyard Fields is a high-elevation setting popular as a day hike and easy overnighter when camping isn't off limits due to bear activity (but avoid busy times).

GRAVEYARD FIELDS LOOP

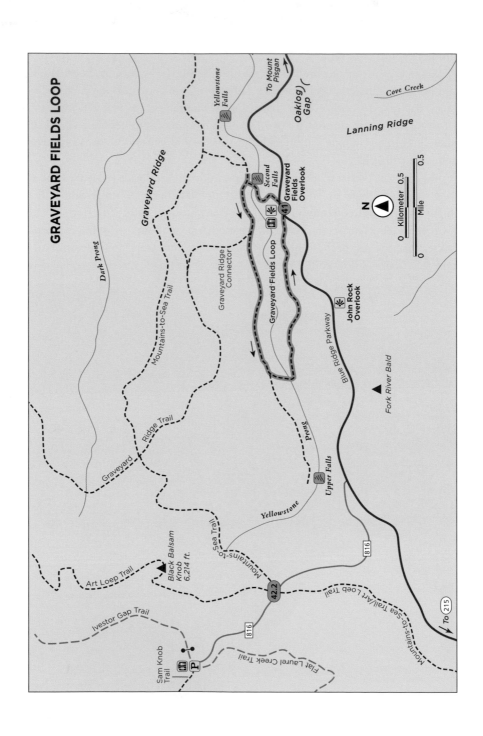

It's a quick side trip from the Graveyard Fields loop to impressive Second Falls (also called Lower Falls on trail signs).

The return route gradually ascends through a boggy area with a high–altitude feel. You'll cross a bridge and boardwalks on the way and be back at the parking lot after a moderate to moderately strenuous hike of just under 4 miles. Without the Upper Falls side trip, the loop is an easy 2.3-mile hike.

Key Points

0.0 Start from Graveyard Fields Overlook.

0.5 Return to bridge after side trip to Second Falls.

1.4 Return leg of loop goes left; side trail to Upper Falls goes right.

2.3 Return to parking area for hike without Upper Falls (just under 4 miles including side trip to Upper Falls).

42 Shining Rock Wilderness

Mileposts 411.8–423.2

Shining Rock—like the Craggy Mountains and Mount Mitchell just north of Asheville—is where the Parkway delivers some of the Southern Appalachians' most stunning scenery. The horizon peels back on an almost Western scale, and meadow-covered mountaintops march off to meet summits cloaked in evergreens and accented by milk-white crags of quartz—the area's namesake "shining rocks."

Unlike the "natural" balds of the Craggy Mountains, the meadows of the Shining Rock area were created by wildfires in the 1920s and 1940s. Few places in the South offer better views than the grasslands of the Art Loeb Trail that border the Blue Ridge Parkway. The area north and beyond the balds, the 19,000-acre evergreen-forested tract now designated as the Shining Rock Wilderness, was not as impacted by fire. In the middle of the wilderness, Shining Rock Mountain (5,940 feet) thrusts its crystal-covered crest above the trees. A more distant and appropriately named peak, Cold Mountain, rises to 6,030 feet near the northern boundary of the wilderness area. This is the isolated summit made famous in Charles Frazier's National Book Award–winning bestseller *Cold Mountain*.

Backpackers should avoid Shining Rock Gap, one of the most overused campsites in the wilderness. Regulations prohibit groups of more than ten persons, and all campfires are banned. Any backpacking plans for this area should include time to find a more-secluded site—and catch up with the current bear situation. In 2016, bear-proof food canisters were required.

Aside from the scenery, part of Shining Rock's appeal is the number of circuit hikes available from surrounding valleys (peruse the map while reading).

The beauty of the layout is that the Loeb Trail and its flanking paths form wonderful summit circuits reachable by no fewer than seven access trails from nearby valleys. You'd need a calculator to count the possibilities.

Option 1: Shining Rock Wilderness Circuits from the East Side

A variety of streamside hikes start on the east side and rise to the crest of Shining Rock Wilderness.

Parkway mile: 411.8
Distance: Major circuits ranging from 8.4 to 12.9 miles
Difficulty: Strenuous
Elevation gain: About 3,000 feet for all

Maps: *USGS Shining Rock.* The area is best covered by Pisgah National Forest's Shining Rock–Middle Prong Wilderness map: www.nationalforestmapstore.com/category-s/1844.htm.

Finding the trailhead: Trailheads for the Old Butt Knob, Shining Creek, and Greasy Cove-Big East Fork Trails are all located at the Big East Fork parking area on US 276, just under 3 miles north of the Parkway on the left (GPS: 35.365884 / -82.818010).

The Hikes

A trio of trails ascends the east side of the wilderness, and they all start at the same trailhead. The more northerly two, the Old Butt Knob Trail (3.6 miles) and the Shining Creek Trail (4.1 miles), terminate in Shining Rock Gap to form the shortest circuit to the heights (8.4 miles). This hike crosses Shining Rock.

The most southerly trail, a combination of the Big East Fork Trail (3.6 miles) and Greasy Cove Trail (3 miles), makes a 6.8-mile climb to the ridge at Ivestor Gap (which includes a 0.2-mile stretch on the Graveyard Ridge Trail). Heading north from there 1.8 miles on the ridgetop Art Loeb Trail to Shining Rock Gap creates much larger loops—12.7 miles with a descent of the Shining Creek Trail and 12.9

Hikers scrutinize the Forest Service signboard at the Big East Fork parking area on US 276 before making a loop over Shining Rock.

miles going down the Old Butt Knob Trail. The level Ivestor Gap Trail also links these access trails. The winding route it takes to slab west of the Art Loeb Trail adds 0.3 mile to each hike (see more down below).

To take the shortest circuit, leave the parking area on the Shining Creek Trail as it climbs away from the East Fork of the Pigeon River. At 0.7 mile, keep left in Shining Creek Gap where the Old Butt Knob Trail (your return route) goes right. The trail drops out of the gap to join Shining Creek above its confluence with the Pigeon River. From here most of the way up, the trail is within sight of the stream. Cross Daniel's Cove Creek at 2 miles and a stream rising right at 3 miles. High above, this branch starts as a trailside spring you might stop at when you pass through Beech Spring Gap on the Old Butt Knob Trail. The trail starts its steepest climb up out of the drainage and switchbacks across the headwaters of the North Prong of Shining Creek to Shining Rock Gap at 4.1 miles.

The gap is a popular camping area, and with tents and tall summer grasses, finding the Old Butt Knob Trail can be a challenge (not an issue if you climb it; see below). Turn right at Shining Rock Gap on the Old Butt Knob Trail and reach Shining Rock Mountain's crystal cap in 0.2 mile. Descend beyond to Beech Spring Gap at 4.7 miles (that spring is on the right). This next section of ridge—across Dog Loser Knob at 4.9 miles, to Spanish Oak Gap at 5.5 miles, back up to Old Butt Knob at 5.7, and even beyond, to the 6-mile mark, where the trail plummets—has gradual sections. Notice on the way down the steepest section—aptly named Chestnut Ridge—how the young American chestnuts still struggle up before falling victim to chestnut blight. There are plentiful campsites for the finding and fine views from outcrops on both sides of the trail. Then the trail drops very steeply for 1.5 miles to the Shining Creek junction at 7.7 miles. Take a left to the trailhead for an 8.4-mile circuit. If you're a baby boomer whose muscles are better on the uphill than your knees or ankles are on the way down, do this trip in reverse. (The Old Butt Knob Trail is the least-used trail on this side of the wilderness, but it's a punishing climb.)

Key Points on the Shortest Circuit
0.0 Leave Big East Fork parking area.
0.7 Keep left in Shining Creek Gap where Old Butt Knob Trail goes right.
4.1 Shining Rock Gap.
4.3 Shining Rock summit.
4.7 Beech Spring Gap.
5.7 Old Butt Knob.
7.7 Left on Shining Rock Creek Trail.
8.4 Arrive back at the parking area.

Option: Going down Shining Creek Trail or Old Butt Knob Trail is a nice way to form the largest loop from this side. That requires a start on the Big East Fork–Greasy Cove Trail combo to the south. Start by crossing the Big East Fork highway bridge from the parking area and heading right. This old railroad grade continues for miles

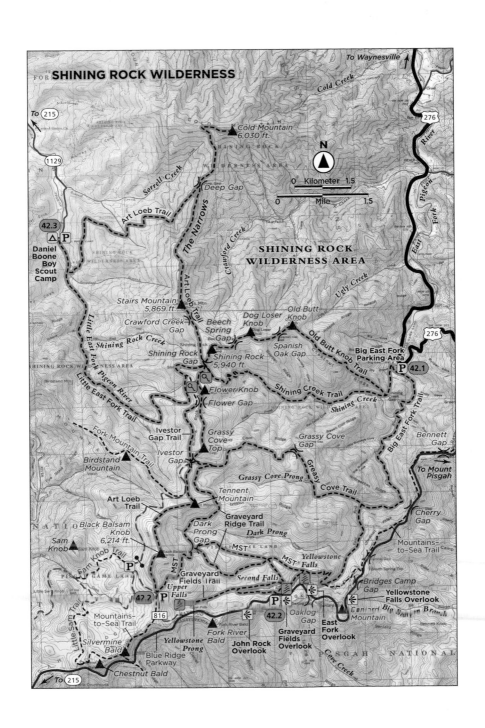

SHINING ROCK WILDERNESS

To Waynesville

Cold Creek

To 215

1129

Cold Mountain
6,030 ft.

N

0 Kilometer 1.5

0 Mile 1.5

Sorrell Creek

Deep Gap

Art Loeb Trail

The Narrows

Crawford Creek

SHINING ROCK
WILDERNESS AREA

Ugly Creek

276

42.3
P

Daniel Boone
Boy Scout
Camp

Art Loeb Trail

Little East Fork Shining Rock Creek

Stairs Mountain
5,869 ft.

Crawford Creek
Gap

Beech
Spring
Gap

Dog Loser
Knob

Old Butt
Knob

Old Butt Knob Trail

276

Shining Rock
Gap

Shining Rock
5,940 ft.

Spanish
Oak Gap

Big East Fork
Parking Area

42.1
P

Little East Fork Pigeon River

Little East Fork Trail

Flower Knob

Flower Gap

Shining Creek Trail

Shining Creek

Big East Fork Trail

Fork Mountain Trail

Ivestor
Gap Trail

Grassy
Cove
Top

Grassy Cove
Gap

Grassy Cove Trail

Bennett
Gap

Birdstand
Mountain

Ivestor
Gap

Grassy Cove Prong

To Mount
Pisgah

Art Loeb
Trail

Tennent
Mountain

Graveyard
Ridge Trail

Dark Prong

Cherry
Gap

Mountains-
to-Sea Trail

Sam
Knob

Black Balsam
Knob
6,214 ft.

Sam Knob Trail

Dark
Prong
Gap

MST

Yellowstone
Falls

MST

P

42.2
P

Graveyard
Fields Trail

Second Falls

Yellowstone
Falls Overlook

Bridges Camp
Gap

Mountains-
to-Sea Trail

Little Sam Trail

Silvermine
Bald

47.2
P

Upper
Falls

816

Yellowstone
Prong

Fork River
Bald

Graveyard
Fields
Overlook

Oaklog
Gap

John Rock
Overlook

East
Fork
Overlook

Coniard Mountain

Big Canyon Branch

NATIONAL

Blue Ridge
Parkway

To 215

Chestnut Bald

Cove Creek

COLD MOUNTAIN

Charles Frazier's 1999 National Book Award–winning bestseller *Cold Mountain* sparked increasing national interest in the rich literature of the Appalachians. Robert Morgan's *Gap Creek* rose on the bestseller list soon after. A wealth of other writers offers a deeper sense of the culture and setting of these mountains. Indeed, you won't go wrong reading *Cold Mountain* before a visit to Shining Rock (or the entire southern part of the Parkway, for that matter). That goes double if you're hiking into Shining Rock Wilderness.

The book, which became a motion picture in 2003, tells the story of a wounded Civil War veteran who escapes from the hospital and heads for home. He walks the length of North Carolina, then the route of the Blue Ridge Parkway from Grandfather Mountain to a farm on the flank of this evocatively named summit. Indeed, if you stand on Shining Rock and look north to Cold Mountain, you can see a tiny farm perched on the right flank of the peak far below the summit. It doesn't take much to imagine that this view could have inspired Frazier's plans for his protagonist.

You'll see far fewer people on this western side of Shining Rock, but if Cold Mountain is your destination, take a moment on the summit to revel in its notoriety as a literary landmark. The trail to the peak is a dead end—at least for everyone except author Charles Frazier.

up the drainage amid lush streamside scenery and plentiful campsites. Cross Bennett Branch at 1.3 miles; at 3.6 miles the old railroad grade goes left up the river.

Cross and continue up Greasy Cove Trail for the steepest part of the climb. The trail veers away from the stream at 4.5 miles and climbs steeply until 5.3 miles, when the grade slackens substantially at the crest of Grassy Cove Ridge. From here much of the way to the Graveyard Ridge Trail at 6.6 miles, the trail is only steep in spots; there are possible campsites where the ridge is broadest.

Go right on the Graveyard Ridge Trail, and at 6.8 miles turn right in Ivestor Gap on the Art Loeb Trail. The path switchbacks past the peak of Grassy Cove Top, dips across a gentle gap, and heads over the next rise to a sharp drop into Flower Gap at 8 miles. The path joins an old railroad grade there and slabs east of Flower Knob past a spring on the right at 8.4 miles. Shining Rock Gap is at 8.6 miles. The descent of the Shining Creek Trail makes a 12.7-mile route (the first streamlet you encounter on the way down is from the Art Loeb Trail spring you just passed); a descent of the Old Butt Knob Trail is 12.9 miles.

Option 2: Bald Summit Circuits on the Art Loeb Trail from the South Side

The Shining Rock area's most southerly summits are among the most spectacular balds in the South. The recommended circuits avoid the popular high-elevation trailheads and can be extended to include the namesake Shining Rock in the heart of the wilderness area.

Parkway mile: 418.8
Distance: Day or overnight circuit hikes across the area's southerly bald summits of 5.2 and 8.8 miles; longer circuits that include Shining Rock of 9.1 or 12.7 miles; a recommended out-and-back hike of 0.8 mile
Difficulty: Moderate to strenuous

Elevation gain: 1,674 feet
Maps: USGS *Shining Rock*. The area is best covered by Pisgah National Forest's Shining Rock–Middle Prong Wilderness map: www .nationalforestmapstore.com/category-s/ 1844.htm.

Finding the trailhead: Park at Graveyard Fields Overlook (GPS: 35.320287 / -82.846936). To reach the parking on FR 816 below Black Balsam Knob, turn right at Parkway Milepost 420.2. The trailhead is 0.7 mile on the right.

The Black Balsam parking area for the Ivestor Gap Trail (GPS: 35.325695 / -82.882024) is another 0.5 mile beyond (but that's the Shining Rock area's busiest trailhead, and that section of the trail isn't recommended), but modern privies are available at the parking area.

The Hikes

Descend from Graveyard Fields Overlook on the Parkway's loop trail, cross Yellowstone Prong, and head left. At about 0.3 mile take a right onto the Graveyard Ridge Connector Trail, then a left on the Graveyard Ridge Trail and follow this gradual logging railroad grade to a crossing of the Mountains-to-Sea Trail in a gap between Black Balsam Knob to the left and an unnamed peak to the right. These first 1.8 miles of the hike are rich with campsites, especially out of sight of the trail.

Turn left on the Mountains-to-Sea Trail as it swings north out of the gap at about 5,400 feet, rises abruptly to the 5,600-foot level, then climbs gradually past the upper edge of a large flat visible on the USDA Forest Service wilderness map. There are good campsites in this area and the remains of an old railroad camp used during logging days. The trail passes above the headwaters of Yellowstone Prong, follows an old railroad grade, and reaches FR 816 and a parking spot for the Art Loeb Trail just less than 3 miles from the start. See map on page 274.

Take an immediate right from FR 816 onto the Loeb Trail; ascend in 0.4 mile (3.2 miles from the start) to the open vistas and waving grasses of Black Balsam Knob (6,214 feet). North, the Mount Mitchell range bulks beyond Asheville, with the High Country resort area and Grandfather Mountain beyond that. The Smokies rise dramatically to the west. This is a 360-degree panorama worthy of binoculars and a camera.

Retracing your steps from here creates a round-trip hike of about 6.5 miles from the trailhead. Even if you don't have much time, this can be a quick 0.8-mile hike from the parking area you just left on FR 816.

Follow the Art Loeb Trail north along the open ridgetop into a shrubby gap at about 5,880 feet, and then back up to eye-popping views atop Tennent Mountain (6,046 feet) about 1.2 miles from Black Balsam Knob (4.4 miles from the Parkway). The 0.7-mile descent from Tennent Mountain brings you to the Ivestor Gap Trail and a right turn on the Graveyard Ridge Trail at 5.1 miles. Continue out of the gap; the Greasy Cove–Big East Fork Trail combo heads left to US 276 at 5.3 miles. After crossing the Mountains-to-Sea Trail, bear right on the Graveyard Ridge Connector and you'll reach the Graveyard Fields Loop at 8.5 miles. Ascend back to the trailhead at about 8.8 miles.

Key Points on the Art Loeb Circuit

- **0.0** Start at Graveyard Fields Overlook.
- **0.3** Turn right from Graveyard Fields Loop onto Graveyard Ridge Trail.
- **1.8** Turn left onto Mountains-to-Sea Trail.
- **2.8** Turn right from FSR 816 onto Art Loeb Trail.
- **3.2** Black Balsam Knob.
- **4.4** Tennent Mountain.
- **5.1** Turn right in Ivestor Gap onto Graveyard Ridge Trail.
- **8.5** Rejoin Graveyard Fields Loop.
- **8.8** Arrive back at the overlook.

Option: Keeping in mind that much of this hike is pretty gradual, if not flat, backpackers or well-conditioned walkers could extend the above circuit to include the ridgetop stretch of the Art Loeb Trail that continues north to Shining Rock Gap. From Ivestor Gap, that section of the Art Loeb Trail forms another loop with the nearly level Ivestor Gap Trail. The combination creates a big figure eight that adds another 3.9 miles to the hike, for a 12.7-mile walk from the Graveyard Fields Overlook.

If you have less time, start at the recommended spot on FR 816 and the first loop of the above circuit is about 5.2 miles (instead of 8.8 miles from the Parkway). Extend that to include Shining Rock Gap, and the hike is 9.1 miles (instead of 12.7). Either of these hikes will be 0.4 mile farther if you go to Shining Rock itself—a 0.2-mile hike out of Shining Rock Gap on the Old Butt Knob Trail.

Option 3: West Side Circuit and Cold Mountain

This hike includes a less-frequented circuit and an out-and-back option to Cold Mountain—the most isolated, least-visited part of the Shining Rock Wilderness.

See map on page 279.
Parkway mile: 423.2
Distance: 10.6 miles out and back to Cold Mountain

Difficulty: Strenuous
Elevation gain: About 2,790 feet to Cold Mountain from the trailhead

Maps: *USGS Shining Rock.* The area is best covered by Pisgah National Forest's Shining Rock–Middle Prong Wilderness map: www .nationalforestmapstore.com/category-s/1844.htm.

Finding the trailhead: The Daniel Boone Scout Camp trailhead for the Art Loeb and Little East Fork Trails is reached via NC 215. Leave the Parkway at Milepost 423.2 and go 13 miles north to turn right onto Little East Fork Road (SR 1129). Go 3.8 miles to parking just beyond the Boy Scout camp's main lodge (GPS: 35.387738 / -82.896297). To start the Little East Fork Trail, walk a little farther along the road, turn right across the bridge into the Scout camp, and then go left on a road that becomes the trail.

The Hikes

There's really only one circuit from the west side of Shining Rock—a 12-mile combination of the Little East Fork and Art Loeb Trails, which start at the same trailhead.

Not all Shining Rock area hikes are arduous overnighters. Whether day hiking or camping, start on FR 816 (see Finding the Trailhead for entry 42.2) and the short climb to Black Balsam Knob is an eye-popping emergence onto grassy summits of only a mile or less round-trip.

One of the area's best out-and-back hikes also starts there—the 10.6-mile hike to Cold Mountain.

The choice of which direction to hike this circuit will be arbitrary for most, as both trails gain the ridge at similar grades. Backpackers will surely decide based on where they want to camp. Starting on the Art Loeb Trail is the fastest route to the least-populated part of the wilderness—the Cold Mountain hike. It also approaches the highest terrain by climbing up the leading ridge. Taking the Little East Fork Trail descends that ridge and gets you to Shining Rock Gap sooner.

Leaving the roadside, the Art Loeb Trail switchbacks north and around a ridge-line at 1.1 miles. At 2 miles the trail crosses tumbling Sorrell Creek at the first good campsites. The trail continues to rise across the richly forested flank of the Shining Rock Ledge, weaving in and out of green drainages (the deepest of which is at 3.1 miles). Reach grassy Deep Gap at 3.8 miles.

Those intent on solitude should consider Cold Mountain. From the Art Loeb Trail at Deep Gap, take a left; the area's least-visited peak is just 1.5 miles north, a 5.3-mile hike from the valley. For backpackers, that plan puts Shining Rock within striking distance for day hikes.

Key Points to Cold Mountain

0.0　Start at the Daniel Boone Boy Scout Camp.

2.0　Sorrell Creek campsites.

3.8　Deep Gap. (***Option:*** Turn right for the circuit hike described below.

5.3　Cold Mountain summit. Return the way you came.

10.6　Arrive back at the Boy Scout camp.

Option: For the circuit, go right from Deep Gap across a rocky, knife-edge ridge called The Narrows. The ridge broadens then narrows again to Stairs Mountain (5,869 feet) at 5.9 miles. The trail enters an old railroad grade at 6.1 miles in Crawford Creek Gap and reaches Shining Rock Gap at 6.7 miles. Turn right here on the old railroad grade of the Ivestor Gap Trail; the Little East Fork Trail turns off right 0.4 mile ahead, at 7.1 miles. This old railroad grade switchbacks just below the Ivestor Gap Trail as it leaves the spruces and birches of the crest. It crosses the Little East Fork of the Pigeon River at 9.3 miles and follows the stream to emerge near the Scout camp at 12.1 miles.

43 Devil's Courthouse Trail

Milepost 422.4

A short, steep climb leads to a spectacular viewpoint with devices for sighting distant peaks. This is a popular peregrine falcon viewing area.

Parkway mile: 422.4
Distance: 1.0 mile out and back
Difficulty: Strenuous

Elevation gain: 258 feet
Maps: *USGS Sams Knob*

Finding the trailhead: Park at Devil's Courthouse Overlook (GPS: 35.305229 / -82.899348).

The Hike

Before you hit the trail, look across the drop-off east of the parking area and up to the crag of Devil's Courthouse at 5,720 feet. Chances are you can see a few tiny hikers enjoying the view.

Though steep, this largely paved path is rewarding. The rock wall–encircled overlook atop the courthouse offers great views. East is the plummet down into the Carolina Piedmont. West is the crest of the Shining Rock Wilderness, one of the loftiest, most alpine-appearing areas to abut the Parkway. Close in, you're likely to see the high-speed "stoops," or dives, of peregrine falcons or hawks.

Leave the parking lot and wander along the side of the Parkway toward the 665-foot-long Devil's Courthouse Tunnel. Enter the woods and breathe in the rich smells of a high-elevation, Canadian-zone forest of spruce, fir, and birch. The paved trail climbs steeply, with ribbed water breaks to divert the deluges. The pavement ends where a spur to the Mountains-to-Sea Trail veers left to cross the top of the tunnel on its way in 0.1 mile to the Sam Knob area. (See the map and below for more.)

The unpaved trail wanders to the right, ascending stone steps to a wall-enclosed viewing area that was refurbished and expanded in 2000. Rock gnome lichen grows on the crag; nearby you'll see Gray's lily and spreading avens.

The name Devil's Courthouse reflects the many folk tales about the peak. Some say there's a cave in the mountain where the devil holds court. Cherokee legend calls it a dancing chamber and dwelling of a slant-eyed giant named Judaculla. If you're ever on the peak when a thunderstorm rumbles nearby, you may understand the origin of such folklore.

Peregrines have been known to nest just under the overlook. The birds were reintroduced in the nearby Sam Knob area in the late 1980s. The birds have since returned to many places in the Southern Appalachians.

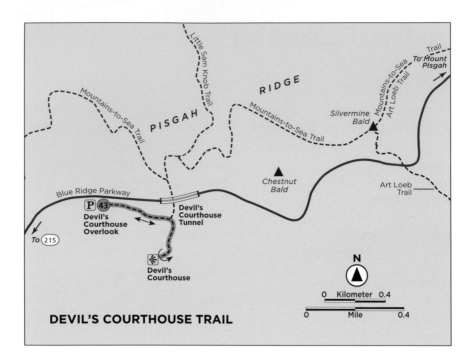

DEVIL'S COURTHOUSE TRAIL

Look west to see the area where the peregrines were reintroduced, and use the sighting device to locate the rocky summit of Sam Knob, 2.0 miles away.

Another option is to take the Mountains-to-Sea Trail over the tunnel; there are great views not far away. Take the spur across the tunnel to the MST and turn right (0.2 mile from the overlook). The Little Sam Knob Trail goes left at 0.4 mile, and there's a rocky crag at 0.5 mile that offers a vista of the alpinelike area that lies just south of Shining Rock Wilderness. The round-trip to the crag is 1.0 mile, for a 2.0-mile total hike including Devil's Courthouse.

Key Points

0.0 Leave Devil's Courthouse Overlook.

0.2 Mountains-to-Sea Trail spur goes left.

0.5 Summit viewpoint.

1.0 Arrive back at the parking area.

44 Richland Balsam Self-Guiding Trail

Milepost 431.0

Numbered posts keyed to an interpretive brochure describe the changing composition of a lofty spruce-fir forest at 6,410 feet—the highest elevation reached by a Parkway trail.

Parkway mile: 431
Distance: 1.4-mile loop
Difficulty: Moderate

Elevation gain: 390 feet
Maps: *USGS Sam Knob*; no Parkway map available

Finding the trailhead: The trail starts at the Haywood-Jackson Overlook (named for the boundary of the two counties), 9.2 miles south of NC 215 (GPS: 35.359901 / -82.986925).

The Hike

Here's an oddity—a kind of rough, rooty trail a lot like the backcountry tracks that wind everywhere in western North Carolina's national forests. The Richland Balsam

Upper-elevation evergreens blanket the slope of Richland Balsam. The loftiest part of the Parkway traverses the peak at 6,053 feet above sea level. Understandably, this overlook is a favorite place to document the achievement.

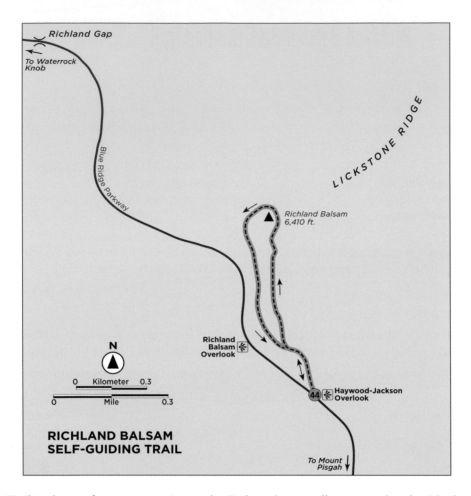

Richland Gap

To Waterrock
Knob

Blue Ridge Parkway

LICKSTONE RIDGE

▲ Richland Balsam
6,410 ft.

Richland
Balsam
Overlook

N

0   Kilometer   0.3

0   Mile   0.3

**RICHLAND BALSAM
SELF-GUIDING TRAIL**

44 Haywood-Jackson
Overlook

To Mount
Pisgah

Trail is the perfect counterpoint to the Parkway's generally groomed paths. It's also the Parkway's best path to experience the aromatic lushness of the dripping, cloud-dampened spruce-fir forest.

Before starting your hike, enjoy the fine view of the Shining Rock Wilderness on the overlook's skyline. Prominent peaks run from Cold Mountain on the left, to the gentle pyramid of Mount Pisgah, the white-quartz summit of Shining Rock, and on to Devil's Courthouse on the far right.

Just up the paved first 100 yards of the trail is a brochure box with laminated trail brochures to borrow for your hike. The theme here, as it is at Mount Mitchell State Park's Balsam Nature Trail, is a Fraser fir forest in decline. The brochure's twenty-plus interpretive stops explore the topic.

Where the loop splits after the pavement ends, go right at the first two of many benches. The trail passes an odd mileage sign (3,100 feet to the summit) then winds around through dense summer growths of sedge grasses and briers.

The trail passes rich Canadian-zone vegetation and a sign reading "1,600 Feet to Summit." It rises over a series of small peaks to a bench at 0.6 mile where the Parkway's summit sign reads 6,410 feet. The path drops off the back of the peak, descending flights of stone steps amid evergreens and grasses.

The evergreen needle–carpeted trail levels off and glides through a very scenic fir forest full of ferns. A faint side trail goes right to the top of the road-cut with views of the Richland Balsam Overlook, the next view south on the Parkway (highest point on the motor road). You'll pass another few benches at about 1.2 miles, the second with the trail's best view—a look along the Parkway to the next overlook heading north, the Cowee Mountain Overlook. The trail passes through more spruce forest and ferns to the loop junction and a right back to the parking area at about 1.4 miles.

Even on a warm, dry day, the summit shade is cool, which explains the seemingly drunken bumblebees fighting to do their summer duty amid the gusty chill. It's that evergreen forest feeling that recommends this trail. If that experience and not the summit is your goal, just go left when the loop starts for a short, easy, and atmospheric out-and-back walk to the last few benches. (And please return your brochure to the box.)

Key Points

0.0 Leave overlook. In about 800 feet, the loop branches; go right.

0.6 Summit bench.

1.2 Bench with good view.

1.3 Loop junction.

1.4 Return to parking lot.

Red spruce, Fraser fir, and plentiful ferns reflect the Canadian zone climate of the Richland Balsam Trail.

45 Waterrock Knob Trail

Milepost 451.2

This steep-paved path climbs from one of the Parkway's small visitor centers to a designated must-see viewpoint. A rougher path continues on to the wilder summit of Waterrock Knob (6,292 feet).

Parkway mile: 451.2
Distance: 1.2 miles out and back
Difficulty: Moderate to strenuous

Elevation gain: 472 feet
Maps: *USGS Sylva North*; no Parkway map available

Finding the trailhead: Park in the Waterrock Knob Visitor Center parking lot and ascend the paved path (GPS: 35.460042 / -83.140527).

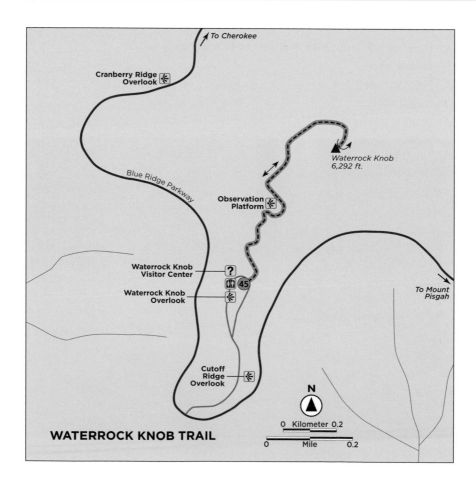

The Hike

Waterrock Knob is one of the key viewpoints that recommend the high-altitude southernmost section of the Blue Ridge Parkway. Luckily there are two sides to this steep and strenuous trail that make it a suitable walk for less-than-serious hikers.

The trail soars out of the parking area as a steep paved path, and on the way up, the Mountains-to-Sea Trail veers off left for the Smokies. Take your time; a bench appears just where the grade slackens to nearly level.

The trail ascends past another bench before switchbacking up two flights of stone steps to a rock wall–encircled observation point. The mountains ripple away; below, the Parkway arcs across a mountainside. This is the place to head back if you're tired or unsure of foot.

Above the viewpoint, the trail rises over steps, becomes rocky then gravel covered, and levels out as it leaves the evergreens and enters an open meadow of filamentous ferns where northern white hellebore still grows in July. There's a bench in this clearing. Farther on, the trail gets rougher, eroded in some spots, and ascends steeply, at times over crags and up one flight of steep stone steps. The trail winds around the back of the peak on switchbacks with stone steps to a nice view into Maggie Valley. The trail climbs again and, after a last flight of steps, reaches an evergreen-bordered bench on the largely open top of Waterrock Knob at 6,292 feet.

More than 80 percent of mature firs on this part of the Parkway have died from the balsam woolly adelgid, and the destruction is evident here and in many places on the way up.

Key Points

0.0 Start the steep paved climb.

0.2 Developed viewpoint.

0.6 Summit bench.

Blue Ridge Parkway Mileage Log

This mileage log is your guide to the Parkway, its overlooks and parking areas, picnic spots and campgrounds, visitor centers and geographic features. That includes entrances and exits, and the resources just off the road, including nearby towns and attractions. Consult it frequently on your trip—in fact consult it first when you decide where you want to travel on the Parkway. It contains frequent referrals to hikes featured in the body of the book, but it also includes trails that may just make a nice out-and-back stroll, such as sections of the Appalachian and Mountains-to-Sea Trails. **Boldface** entries highlight noteworthy destinations along the way, and the ones with parentheses refer you inside the book to featured hikes on and along the Parkway.

Parkway Milepost 0 promises a half thousand miles of smiles. It's located on the bridge that links the Blue Ridge Parkway to Shenandoah National Park's Skyline Drive, a stellar 100-mile addition to a Parkway trip.

Appalachian Trail access from the Blue Ridge Parkway: See Mileage Log, pages 293 to 300, between Mileposts 0 and 97, specifically 2.2, 6.0, 8.5, 9.2, 9.6, 13.1, 13.7, 15.4, 34.4, 51.7, 71.0, 74.7, 74.9, 76.3, 78.4, 80.5, 91.0, 91.8, 92.5, 93.1, 93.2, 94.9, 95.3, 95.8, 97.0

Mountains-to-Sea Trail access from the Blue Ridge Parkway: See Mileage Log, pages 309 to 336, between Mileposts 235.7 and 458.2, Heintooga Spur Road (Spur Road mile 8.9, Heintooga Ridge Picnic Area, page 337). See individual mileposts 235.7, 238.5, 241.1, 242.4, 243.4, 243.7, 244.7, 260.3, 294.0, 296.1, 296.9, 297.2, 299.0, 299.9, 302.4, 302.8, 303.6, 304.4, 304.8, 305.2, 344.1, 345.3, 359.8, 361.2, 367.6, 374.4, 374.5, 375.6, 377.4, 381.0, 382.0, 384.4, 384.7, 386.0, 388.1, 388.8, 392.1, 393.6, 396.4, 407.6, 407.7, 408.6, 408.8, 412.5, 414.5, 415.0, 415.6, 417.0, 418.8, 420.2, 425.4, 426.5, 427.6, 435.3, 435.7, 436.8, 451.2, 455.5, 458.2

0.0 Note Milepost 0 in the middle of the stone bridge that links Shenandoah National Park to the Blue Ridge Parkway across the highways below.

0.0 Rockfish Gap • Elevation: 1,909 ft. (582m) • Signboard: history of Rockfish Gap • Facilities: Tourist Information Center (9 a.m. to 5 p.m. daily).

0.0 US 250/I-64 underpass • Access to US 250 and I-64 West; 4 miles to Waynesboro, VA (west); 16 miles to Charlottesville, VA (east).

0.2 Afton Overlook, east • Elevation: 2,054 ft. (626m).

1.5 Rockfish Valley Overlook, east • Elevation: 2,148 ft. (655m).

2.2 VA 610 access, west • Trail: Appalachian Trail crossing.

2.9 Shenandoah Valley Overlook, west • Elevation: 2,354 ft. (718m) • Wayside panel: Virginia's profile.

4.4 VA 609 crossing • Access VA 610, west.

5.8 **Humpback Rocks Visitor Center and Pioneer Farm Exhibit, west (Hike 1, Option 1)** • Elevation: 2,353 ft. (717m) • Facilities: great exhibits, restrooms, water, self-guiding trail • Trail: **Mountain Farm Self-Guiding Trail,** 0.5 mile (Easy).

6.0 **Humpback Gap Parking Area, east (Hike 1, Option 2)** • Elevation: 2,360 ft. (719m) • Cars: 20 • Facilities: picnic table • Wayside panel: pioneer methods of clearing fields • Trail: Appalachian Trail access.

8.5 **Humpback Rocks Picnic Area, east (Hike 1, Option 2)** • Facilities: 91 sites, water, restrooms • Trails: **Catoctin Trail.** This short path reaches a lofty perch over the Shenandoah Valley. Go to the end of the Humpback Rocks Picnic Area and take the trail to the right. (The path to the left reaches the Appalachian Trail.) Appalachian Trail access.

8.8 **Greenstone Overlook, west (Hike 2)** • Elevation: 3,007 ft. (916m) • Cars: 8 • Signboard: old stone fences • Trail: **Greenstone Self-Guiding Trail,** 0.2 mile (Easy).

9.2 Laurel Springs Gap, east • Trail: 300 yards to Appalachian Trail on east.

9.6 Dripping Rocks Parking, east • Trail: Appalachian Trail access. 2.8 miles north to Humpback Mountain, 5.6 miles round-trip.

10.4 Rock Point Overlook, west • Elevation: 3,113 ft. (949m) • Cars: 5 • Lift-top easel: Catoctin greenstone (geologic formation).

10.7 Raven's Roost Overlook, west • Elevation: 3,200 ft. (975m) • Facilities: picnic table • Interpretive device: orientation • Recreation: hang gliding, rock climbing.

11.7 Hickory Spring Parking, east • Facilities: picnic table • Hunter access west during hunting season only.

13.1 Three Ridges Overlook, east • Elevation: 2,697 ft. (822m) • Facilities: picnic table • Trail: Appalachian Trail access.

13.7 Reids Gap • Elevation: 2,637 ft. (804m) • Trail: Appalachian Trail access.

13.7 **VA 664 crossing (Hikes 3 and 4; Hike 5, Option 2)** • West to VA 814; east to US 29. Access to Wintergreen Resort, east, and Sherando Lake Recreation Area, west. Devils Backbone Brewing Company's Basecamp Brewpub, 5.6 miles east, permits free camping to AT thru hikers (dbbrewingcompany.com/locations/basecamp/). This valley below Wintergreen makes an excellent side tour for vineyards, breweries, a cidery and distillery (nelson151.com).

15.4 Love Gap • Elevation: 2,597 ft. (792m) • Trails: Appalachian Trail access—fire road to Maupin Field Shelter on Three Ridges Wilderness circuit.

16.0 VA 814 staggered crossing • Right to Love Maintenance Area; left to Massies Mill, VA.

16.0 Love Maintenance Area • Elevation: 1,700 ft. (518m).

17.6 **The Priest Overlook, east (Hike 7, Option 1)** • Elevation: 2,695 ft. (821m) • Cars: 10 • Wayside panel: hickory trees • Facilities: picnic table • Trail: **The Priest Trail,** 0.2 mile (Easy). This easy walk terminates 100 yards from the parking area at a roadside hilltop and a bench.

  The prominent summit and leading ridges of The Priest, 4,026 feet, rise in the distance. Other peaks of the adjacent Religious Range include The Cardinal and The Friar. The Appalachian Trail crosses The Priest's summit and makes a nice hike from the area of **Crabtree Falls.**

  Note the Parkway interpretive easel about hickory trees at this overlook. You will see many hickories on your hikes—mockernut, pignut, bitternut, and shagbark. Just a minute with this exhibit and you'll be able to recognize the long, gray bark strands of the shagbark—at 100 feet, one of the tallest hickories. Fifteen of the twenty known species of hickory are found in the United States.

18.5 **White Rock Gap Parking Area (Hike 5)** • Elevation: 2,549 ft. (777m) • Trails: White Rock Gap Trail to Slacks Trail circuit and USDA Forest Service (USFS) Sherando Lake, west; **White Rock Falls Trail,** east (Moderate).

19.0 20 Minute Cliff Overlook, east • Elevation: 2,715 ft. (827m) • Signboard: story of 20 Minute Cliff.

19.9 **The Slacks Overlook, west (Hike 5)** • Elevation: 2,800 ft. (853m) • Trails: **White Rock Falls Trail,** east, to falls, 1.3 miles (Moderate) and on to Slacks circuit • Slacks Trail circuit access, west, past picnic table.

22.1 **Bald Mountain Parking Area, west (Hike 6)** • Elevation: 3,250 ft. (991m) • Facilities: picnic table.

22.1 USFS road access, west.

23.0 **Fork Mountain Overlook, east (Hike 6)** • Elevation: 3,294 ft. (1,004m).

24.3 Federal Aviation Administration (FAA) road access (to radar site), east.

25.6 Spy Run Gap • Elevation: 3,033 ft. (924m).

25.6 VA 686 access, east.

26.4 **Big Spy Overlook, west** • Elevation: 3,185 ft. (971m) • Trail: **Big Spy Mountain Overlook Trail,** 0.1 mile (Easy). Many of the Parkway's best views are from roadside meadows. This grassy trail reaches a wonderfully breezy hilltop with a bench and views west to the Shenandoah Valley across the ridgetops of the **Saint Mary's Wilderness Area (Hike 6).** The prominent more-pointed peak with the boulder-covered scree slopes is Big Spy—so named because it served as a lookout for troop movements in the Shenandoah Valley during the Civil War. To the east, the grassy, high fields of adjacent farms lend a pastoral feel to the scene.

27.2 Tye River Gap • Elevation: 2,969 ft. (905m).

27.2 **VA 56 crossing, underpass (access east, north of crossing) (Hike 7)** • Right to Vesuvius, 4 miles, and Steele's Tavern, VA, 6.5 miles; left to Montebello, VA, 0.75 mile • Trails: access left to Crabtree Falls Trail, AT trailhead for Three Ridges Wilderness circuit • AT hikes to The Priest and Spy Rock.

29.0 Whetstone Ridge • Elevation: 2,990 ft. (911m) • Facilities: restrooms and picnic tables, west.

29.0 VA 603 access, east.

29.5 VA 603 crossing, underpass (no access).

31.4 Stillhouse Hollow parking, east • Elevation: 3,000 ft. (914m) • Facilities: picnic table.

31.9 VA 886 crossing.

33.0 Fence exhibit, west.

34.4 **Yankee Horse Ridge Parking Area, east (Hike 8)** • Elevation: 3,140 ft. (957m) • Facilities: picnic table • Trails: **Yankee Horse Trail,** 0.2 mile (Easy); Appalachian Trail access • Signboard: old logging railroad • Exhibit: 200 feet of railroad track, trestle • View: Wigwam Falls.

34.8 Yankee Horse Ridge.

37.4 Irish Gap • Elevation: 2,200 ft. (671m).

37.5 US 60 access, east.

37.5 VA 605 crossing, underpass (access east, north of crossing) • Right to Irish Creek and Buena Vista, VA; left to US 60 and Amherst, VA (maintained dirt road).

38.8 **Boston Knob Parking Area, west** • Elevation: 2,508 ft. (764m) • Facilities: picnic table • Trail: **Boston Knob Trail,** 0.1 mile (Easy; 5-minute leg-stretcher). Leave the overlook to the right; the trail rises on a grassy tread and circles left around a small tree-topped hummock. It's an often-breezy wander, with limited views down into a grove of white pines before the trail dips back to the center of the overlook.

40.0 Clarks Gap • Elevation: 2,177 ft. (663m).

40.1 USFS road access, east.

40.9 USFS road access, east (gated, with "Foot Travel Welcome" sign).

42.0 Gravel pull-off, west.

42.2 Irish Creek Valley Parking, west • Elevation: 2,665 ft. (812m).

44.2 USFS road crossing • (Old Jordan Road).

44.4 Whites Gap Overlook, east • Elevation: 2,567 ft. (782m) • Facilities: picnic table.

44.9 Chimney Rock Mountain Overlook, west • Elevation: 2,485 ft. (757m).

45.6 Humphries Gap, east • Elevation: 2,312 ft. (705m).

45.6 US 60 crossing, underpass (access east, north of crossing) • Right to Buena Vista, VA, 4 miles, and Lexington, VA, 11 miles; left to Amherst, VA, 22 miles.

45.7 Buena Vista Overlook, west.

47.5 **Indian Gap Parking Area, east (Hike 9)** • Elevation: 2,098 ft. (639m) • Facilities: picnic table • Trail: **Indian Gap Trail,** 0.3 mile (Easy; 10-minute trail to Indian Rocks).

48.9 Licklog Spring Gap • Elevation: 2,481 ft. (756m).

49.3 House Mountain Overlook, west • Elevation: 2,498 ft. (761m). Great view of the square-topped peak towering over Lexington and the Great Valley.

50.5 Robinson Gap • Elevation: 2,412 ft. (735m).

51.1 USFS road access, west (gated) • To Bluff Mountain/Punch Bowl area.

51.7 Appalachian Trail crossing and parking area. Hiking south on AT, Punchbowl Mountain Shelter is 0.4 mile.

52.0 Punch Bowl Mountain Overlook.

52.8 Bluff Mountain Overlook, east • Elevation: 1,850 ft. (564m) • Signboard: George Washington National Forest's multiple resources.

53.1 Bluff Mountain Tunnel • Length: 630 feet • Max height: 19 feet, 1 inch • Min height: 13 feet, 7 inches.

53.6 Rice Mountain Overlook, east • Elevation: 1,755 ft. (535m). • Facilities: picnic table.

53.8 USFS road access, east (gated).

55.1 **White Oak Flats Overlook, west** • Elevation: 1,460 ft. (445m) • Facilities: picnic table • Trail: **White Oak Flats Trail,** 0.1 mile (Easy). From White Oak Flats, at 1,460 feet, south to the James River, at 650 feet, the Parkway descends for nearly 9 miles through a rich streamside environment of beautiful evergreen and deciduous forests. There are streamside "flats" all along the way.

White Oak Flats is the loftiest, and it leans to its namesake white oak trees, with a scrubby understory of mountain laurel and young white pines. A formal trail is difficult to discern. You can wander past the picnic table to the right and reach the stream. Or go left at the table and stroll the greater distance to the creek, where rocks invite you to hop across and head up the side drainage.

Driving south, you'll want to stop and savor a few other flats, especially along Otter Creek, with its extensive trail system. Otter Creek Flats Overlook (Milepost 58.2) is a nice place to pause; on the way, be sure to notice the chimney standing off the right side of the road at Milepost 58.

55.9   Dancing Creek Overlook, west • Elevation: 1,300 ft. (396m) • Facilities: picnic table.

56.1   USFS road crossing (gated, with "Foot Travel Welcome" sign).

57.0   USFS road crossing (gated).

57.6   Upper Otter Creek Overlook, east • Elevation: 1,085 ft. (331m).

58.2   Otter Creek Flats Overlook, east • Elevation: 1,005 ft. (306m) • Facilities: picnic table.

59.7   Otter Creek Overlook, west • Elevation: 885 ft. (270m).

60.4   The Riffles Overlook, east • Elevation: 822 ft. (251m).

60.8   **Otter Creek Recreation Area, east (Hike 10, Option 1)** • Elevation: 777 ft. (237m) • Campground: 42 tents, 26 trailer sites • Facilities: water, restrooms, campfire circle (restaurant, gift shop closed in 2016). • Trails: Otter Creek Trail trailhead, 3.4 miles (Moderate).

61.0   Otter Creek Bridge #6.

61.4   **Terrapin Hill Overlook, west (Hike 10)** • Elevation: 760 ft. (232m) • Facilities: picnic table • Trails: Otter Creek Trail access.

61.4   VA 130 access • Right (west) to US 501, 2 miles, Glasgow, VA, 8 miles, and Natural Bridge, VA, 15 miles; left (east) to US 29, 15 miles, and Lynchburg, VA, 20 miles.

61.6   VA 130 crossing, underpass (no access) • Right to US 501, 2 miles, Glasgow, VA, 8 miles; left to Elon, VA, 12 miles, Lynchburg, VA, 20 miles.

62.5   **Lower Otter Creek Overlook, east (Hike 10)** • Elevation: 685 ft. (209m) • Facilities: picnic tables across trail bridge to left • Trail: Otter Creek Trail access.

63.1   **Otter Lake Overlook, east (Hike 10, Option 2)** • Elevation: 655 ft. (200m) • Parking: additional parking on west side • Trail: Otter Lake Trail, 1.0 mile (Moderate; lake loop).

63.2   Lowest elevation on Blue Ridge Parkway, 646.4 ft. (197m).

63.6   **James River Overlook, east (Hike 10, Option 1; Hike 11)** • Elevation: 668 ft. (204m) • Facilities: visitor center, restrooms, water • Trails: James River Trail, 0.4 mile (Easy; trail to Kanawha Canal lock exhibit); Trail of Trees, 0.5 mile (Moderate; self-guiding nature trail) • Exhibits: Kanawha Canal locks •

Signboard: James River Visitor Center and trails; Trail of Trees. Also Otter Creek Trail.

63.7   James River Bridge.

63.7   C&O Railroad crossing, underpass.

63.9   **US 501 crossing, underpass (access east; south of crossing) (Hike 12, Option 1)** • Right (south) to Big Island, VA, 2 miles, and Lynchburg, VA, 11 miles; left (north) to Glasgow, VA, 9 miles, and Natural Bridge, VA, 15 miles.

69.1   James River Valley Parking Area, east • Elevation: 1,874 ft. (571m) • Facilities: picnic table.

69.1   FSR 951 access, east (Battery Creek Road).

71.0   **Petites Gap (Hike 12, Options 2 and 3)** • Elevation: 2,361 ft. (720m).

71.0   FSR 35, west • Trails: Appalachian Trail access parking (50 yards west); Sulphur Spring, Belfast, and Gunter Ridge Trails • Cave Mountain Lake Recreation Area, 8 miles. Taking AT south, Thunder Ridge Trail and view is 3.3 miles (6.6 round-trip).

72.6   Terrapin Mountain parking, east • Elevation: 2,885 ft. (879m).

74.6   National Park Service road, west (gated).

74.7   **Thunder Ridge Parking Area, west (Hike 13)** • Elevation: 3,485 ft. (1,062m) • Facilities: picnic table • Trails: **Thunder Ridge Trail,** 0.2 mile (Easy; 10-minute loop trail to pedestrian overlook; view of Glasgow and Natural Bridge); Appalachian Trail access. Via AT, Thunder Hill Shelter is 1.4 miles south.

74.8   Thunder Hill • Elevation: 3,510 ft. (1,070m).

74.9   Appalachian Trail crossing • Right to Thunder Ridge Parking Area • Left to Thunder Hill Shelter (USFS), 1.4 miles south. • Trails: Hunting Creek Trail (USFS); AT access 150 feet east to FSR 45.

75.2   Arnold Valley Parking (north), west • Elevation: 3,510 ft. (1,070m) • Cars: 5 • Hunter access east and west during hunting season.

75.3   Arnold Valley Parking (south), west • Elevation: 3,700 ft. (1,128m) • View: Devil's Hopper and Snake Den Ridge, west.

76.2   US Air Force access road, east (gated).

76.3   Appalachian Trail crossing • Right to Apple Orchard Mountain • Left to Thunder Hill Shelter, 0.3 mile north.

76.5   Apple Orchard parking, east • Elevation: 3,933 ft. (1,199m) • Signboard: Apple Orchard Mountain.

76.7   Highest point on the Blue Ridge Parkway in Virginia • Elevation: 3,950 ft. (1,204m).

76.7   US Air Force access road to Apple Orchard Mountain, west (gated).

78.4   **Sunset Field Overlook, west (Hike 14)** • Elevation: 3,472 ft. (1,058m) • Trails: **Apple Orchard Falls Trail;** Appalachian Trail access as it crosses Apple Orchard Falls Trail (NPS–USFS), west • Gated entrance to former Camp Kewanzee, east.

78.4   FSR 812 access, west • Parkers Gap Road to Apple Orchard Falls; North Creek Campground (USFS).

79.7   **Onion Mountain Overlook, east** • Elevation: 3,145 ft. (959m) • Facilities: picnic table • View: Suck Mountain, east • Trails: **Onion Mountain Loop Trail,** 0.2 mile (Easy; 6-minute loop). The Onion Mountain Loop circles the little summit that sits just south of the parking area. A few stone steps lead to a split in the trail. Take the right fork, then bear left at a second, heavily trodden trail. The trail weaves around and down among rocks, dipping significantly off the back of the crag. Heading left on a flat section, there are views down into the surrounding forest. Then the trail rises over stone steps, sloping rocks, between crags, and over a final few flights of steps to the top. A right turn steps down to the parking lot. Though easy, the climb back to the parking area and rocky footing make this leg-stretcher a bit more challenging. For some it could take longer than the 6 minutes noted on the sign.

79.9   Black Rock Hill Parking, west • Elevation: 3,195 ft. (974m).

80.5   FSR 190 crossing • Right: gated • Left: open to public; to VA 640 • Trails: Appalachian Trail access to Cornelius Creek Shelter (USFS), west • Appalachian Trail leaves Parkway, heading down into Middle Creek (USFS).

81.9   View Head Foremost Mountain, east • Elevation: 2,860 ft. (872m) • Wayside panel: tulip poplar tree.

83.1   **Falling Cascades Parking Area, west (Hike 15, Option 1)** • Elevation: 2,557 ft. (779m) • Trail: **Fallingwater Cascades Trail,** 1.6-mile loop (Moderate; to cascades).

83.1   USFS road access, west (gated).

83.4   Wilkerson Gap • Elevation: 2,511 ft. (765m).

83.5   **Flat Top Parking Area, east (Hike 15, Option 2)** • Elevation: 2,610 ft. (795m) • Trail: **Flat Top Trail,** 4.4 miles (across Flat Top Mountain, elevation 4,001 ft., to Peaks of Otter Picnic Area).

85.2   Peaks of Otter Maintenance Area, west • Trail: Road to Johnson Farm (4 historic buildings—house restored to 1930s).

85.6   **Peaks of Otter Lodge, east (Hike 15, Option 3)** • Elevation: 2,525 ft. (770m) • Facilities: lodge—58 rooms/3 suites; restaurant with lounge, coffee shop, gift shop, parking areas • Abbott Lake: 24-acre lake, east; managed for smallmouth bass • Trail: **Abbott Lake Trail,** 1.0 mile (Easy, now designated a TRACK Trail) • Feature: Polly Woods Ordinary.

85.9   **Peaks of Otter developed area, east (Hike 15, Option 4)** • Elevation: 2,875 ft. (876m) • Facilities: Nature Center, restrooms, bus station for concession bus up Sharp Top Mountain (bus goes to within 1,500 feet of summit) • Campground: 90 tents, 53 trailer sites • Picnic Area: 62 sites • Signboards: Big Springs, weather at work; boulders of Sharp Top, Sharp Top summit, Elk Run Trail • Wayside: Sharp Top Mountain, Polly Woods Ordinary, Johnson

Farmhouse • Trails: **Sharp Top Trail,** 1.5 miles (Strenuous); Sharp Top Summit Trails (Strenuous), with spur trail to Buzzards Roost.

85.9 **Peaks of Otter Visitor Center, west (Hike 15, Option 5)** • Elevation: 2,550 ft. (777m) • Facilities: visitor center, gift shop, district ranger office, restrooms, water, amphitheater • Trails: **Johnson Farm Loop Trail,** 2.1 miles (Easy); **Harkening Hill Trail,** 3.3 miles (Moderate); **Elk Run Self-Guiding Trail,** 0.8 mile (Easy).

85.9 VA 43 access, east • Straight to Bedford, VA, 15 miles; left to public road (VA 614) by bus station to Sheep Creek; private road right off public road (VA 614) and R.A. Church Camp.

89.1 Powell Gap, west • Elevation: 1,916 ft. (584m).

89.1 VA 618 access, west • To Arcadia • North Creek Campground (USFS).

89.4 Upper Goose Creek Valley Overlook, east • Elevation: 1,925 ft. (587m).

90.0 Porter Mountain Overlook, east • Elevation: 2,100 ft. (640m) • Lift-top easel: different types of oak.

91.0 Bearwallow Gap • Elevation: 2,258 ft. (688m) • Trails: Appalachian Trail crosses under Parkway bridge and parallels and traverses the Parkway for the next 7 miles.

91.0 VA 695 crossing, underpass (access east and west) • West to VA 43, Buchanan, VA, 5 miles; east to US 460 at Montvale, VA, 10 miles.

91.8 Mills Gap parking, west • Elevation: 2,435 ft. (742m) • Facilities: picnic table. Access to Appalachian Trail.

91.9 Mills Gap • Elevation: 2,425 ft. (739m).

92.1 Purgatory Mountain parking, west • Elevation: 2,400 ft. (731m) • Wayside panel: hawk migration.

92.5 Sharp Top Parking, east • Elevation: 2,415 ft. (736m) • Trail: Appalachian Trail crossing • Wayside panel: Appalachian Trail.

93.1 Bobblet's Gap Overlook, west • Elevation: 2,150 ft. (655m) • Facilities: picnic table • Trail: Appalachian Trail access (0.7 mile south to Bobblet's Gap Shelter).

93.2 Bobblet's Gap • Elevation: 2,148 ft. (655m) • Trail: Appalachian Trail near Parkway.

93.2 VA 617 crossing, underpass (no access) • Right to I-81; left to US 460.

94.9 USFS Hammond Fire Trail access, west • On Appalachian Trail north for 250 paces then Fire Trail down mountain to VA 645.

95.2 Pine Tree Overlook, east • Elevation: 2,490 ft. (759m).

95.3 Harvey's Knob Overlook, west • Elevation: 2,524 ft. (769m) • Trail: Appalachian Trail crossing (2.4 miles north to Bobblets Gap Shelter); excellent scenery in fall and winter • Wayside panels: hawk migration and identification.

95.9 Montvale Overlook, east • Elevation: 2,441 ft. (744m) • Trail: Appalachian Trail accesses overlook, east (3 miles north to Bobblet's Gap Shelter) • Facilities: picnic table • Wayside panel: Appalachian Trail.

96.0 USFS Spec Mine Fire Trail access, west • To VA 645, 2.8 miles; 5.6 miles round-trip. A downhill hike with a strenuous return on the same trail.

96.2 Iron Mine Hollow parking (north), west • Elevation: 2,364 ft. (720m).

96.4 Iron Mine Hollow parking (south), west • Elevation: 2,372 ft. (723m) • History: pre–Civil War iron mining (low-grade ore).

97.0 Taylors Mountain Overlook, east • Elevation: 2,340 ft. (713m) • Trail: Appalachian Trail crossing. Bid adieu to the AT when driving south—the trail departs the Parkway heading west.

97.7 Black Horse Gap • Elevation: 2,402 ft. (732m).

97.7 FSR 186 access, west (gated) • Goes down to Wilson Creek (USFS) to Camp Bethel and VA 640.

97.7 Abandoned Virginia Forestry Service road, east (gated) • 0.3 mile to old Black Horse Tavern site.

99.6 The Great Valley Overlook, west • Elevation: 2,493 ft. (760m) • Facilities: picnic table • Interpretive sign: the Great Valley. Super view of this storied route of mass migration and scenic settlements.

100.9 The Quarry Overlook, east • Elevation: 2,170 ft. (661m).

101.5 Curry Gap • Elevation: 1,985 ft. (605m).

101.5 FSR 191 crossing • Right to Fullhardt Knob, Shay Hollow at access 1 mile; left to US 460.

105.0 Interpretive board.

105.8 US 460 crossing, overpass (access west and east) • Right (west) to Roanoke, VA, 9 miles; left (east) to Bedford, VA, 21 miles.

106.9 N&W Railroad Overlook, east • Elevation: 1,161 ft. (354m).

107.0 Coyner Mountain Overlook, west • Elevation: 1,150 ft. (350m).

109.8 Read Mountain Overlook, west • Elevation: 1,163 ft. (354m).

110.6 **Stewarts Knob Overlook, east (Hike 16, Option 1)** • Elevation: 1,365 ft. (416m) • Trail: **Stewarts Knob Trail,** 0.1 mile (Easy).

112.2 VA 24 crossing, underpass (access west and east) • Right (west) to Roanoke, VA, 5 miles, and Vinton, VA, 2 miles; left (east) to Booker T. Washington National Monument, 33 miles, and Stewartsville, VA, 4 miles.

112.9 Roanoke Basin Overlook, east • Elevation: 1,250 ft. (381m).

114.7 Roanoke River Bridge • Elevation: 825 ft. at river (251m) • Other: N&W Railroad bridge, 0.25 mile long.

114.9 **Roanoke River Parking Area, west (Hike 16, Option 2)** • Elevation: 985 ft. (300m) • View: Appalachian Power Dam • Trails: **Roanoke River Trail,** 0.4 mile (Easy; 20-minute trail to river level and patio; angler trail to river edge; loop trail).

115.0 Access to Explore Park, a Roanoke county park that is undergoing a master-planning process that locals hope will guide it toward renewed vitality as a living-history and recreation area. A Parkway visitor center and museum is open on a seasonal basis and there are a variety of trails available. The 0.7-mile

Society of American Foresters Trail is a nice leg-stretcher that focuses on interactions between man and the natural environment (GPS: 37.237216, –79.852468). Before visiting, update the park's status at explorepark@roanoke countyva.gov.

115.1   Pine Mountain Parking Area, east • Elevation: 1,002 ft. (305m).

118.0   Horse trail crossing.

119.8   Roanoke Mountain Loop exit, east.

120.3   **Roanoke Mountain Loop entrance, east (Hike 16, Option 3)** • Length: 4-mile loop road • Restrictions: no recreational vehicles over 20 feet • Overlooks: 5 • Trail: **Roanoke Mountain Summit Trail** (10-minute trail) • View: Excellent views of City of Roanoke, Roanoke Valley, Mill Mountain, and surrounding areas.

120.4   **Mill Mountain Spur Road, west (Hike 16, Options 4 and 5).**

0.1   Gum Spring Overlook • Elevation: 1,445 ft. (440m) • Trail: Horse trail crossing.

0.4   Welcome Valley Road/(VA 672) crossing (no access).

1.1   **Chestnut Ridge Overlook** • Elevation: 1,465 ft. (446m) • Interpretive: map and access to 5.4-mile **Chestnut Ridge Trail (Hike 16, Option 4).**

1.3   Roanoke Mountain Picnic Area • Facilities: scattered picnic table sites in former campground, some barrier-free • Trail: access to Chestnut Ridge Trail

1.4   View of back side of Mill Mountain Star.

2.5   **End Blue Ridge Parkway jurisdiction • Left to Mill Mountain Park, (Hike 16, Option 5)** • Playhouse, and zoo • Begin J. B. Fishburn Parkway down Mill Mountain to Roanoke, VA (2 miles).

120.6   Horse trail crossing • Trail: Roanoke Valley Horse Trail, 18.5 miles (Moderate).

121.4   US 220 crossing, underpass (access west and east) • Right to Roanoke, VA, 5 miles; left to Rocky Mount, VA, 21 miles.

123.2   **Buck Mountain Overlook, east (Hike 17)** • Elevation: 1,465 ft. (446m) • Trail: **Buck Mountain Trail.**

126.2   Masons Knob Overlook, east • Elevation: 1,430 ft. (436m).

128.7   Metz Run Overlook, west • Elevation: 1,875 ft. (571m) • View: Cascade Falls, east (no access).

128.8   Circular bridge crossing Metz Run (creek).

129.3   Poages Mill Overlook, west • Elevation: 2,035 ft. (620m) • View: Roanoke Valley.

129.6   Roanoke Valley Overlook, west • Elevation: 2,100 ft. (640m) • View: Roanoke Valley 1,100 feet below.

129.9   Lost Mountain Overlook, west • Elevation: 2,200 ft. (671m).

132.0   Dividing Springs • Elevation: 2,800 ft. (853m).

132.9   Slings Gap Overlook, east • Elevation: 2,817 ft. (859m).

133.0   Slings Gap • Elevation: 2,825 ft. (861m) • VA 612 crossing (no access).

133.6   Bull Run Knob Overlook, east • Elevation: 2,890 ft. (881m).

134.3 Lancaster Gap • Elevation: 2,786 ft. (849m).

134.9 Poor Mountain Overlook, west • Elevation: 2,975 ft. (907m).

135.9 US 221 access, west • Right to Roanoke, VA, 19 miles.

136.0 Adney Gap • Elevation: 2,690 ft. (820m).

138.5 Sweet Annie Hollow • Elevation: 2,889 ft. (881m) • Trail to Smith Tract.

139.0 Cahas Knob Overlook, east • Elevation: 3,013 ft. (918m).

143.5 Cemetery, east (Confederate soldier buried here).

143.9 Devils Backbone Overlook, east • Elevation: 2,687 ft. (819m) • Cars: 22 • View: Western Piedmont of Virginia.

144.3 Pine Spur Gap.

144.8 Pine Spur Overlook, east • Elevation: 2,703 ft. (824m) • Cars: 10.

145.3 VA 610 access, west.

145.7 VA 791 crossing.

146.4 VA 642 staggered crossing.

148.1 VA 641 crossing.

148.2 Honeytree Development.

148.4 VA 663 crossing.

149.1 VA 640 crossing.

149.5 Cannady Woods.

150.5 VA 639 crossing • Right to VA 221 to Roanoke, VA; Payne Creek Church.

150.8 Kelley Springhouse, east (no sign).

150.9 Public road crossing • Right to VA 681 (Floyd-Franklin Turnpike); left to VA 640 (Five Mile Mountain Road) and Ferrum, VA.

152.0 VA 888 staggered crossing.

153.6 VA 993 crossing.

154.1 Smart View Overlook, east • Elevation: 2,560 ft. (780m).

154.5 **Smart View Parking Area, east (Hike 18)** • Trail: **Smart View Loop Trail** • Signboard: describing Trails Cabin; brief history of log cabins • Facilities: picnic area (42 sites), 2 comfort stations, picnic shelter, 8 tables, fireplace; first-come, first-served basis.

155.3 VA 793 crossing • Left to Endicott, VA, 4 miles; right to VA 680.

156.3 VA 635 crossing.

157.6 Shortts Knob Overlook, east • Elevation: 2,806 ft. (855m).

158.9 VA 637 crossing • Right to Floyd, VA, 6 miles; left to Endicott and Ferrum, VA (Shooting Creek Road).

159.3 VA 860 crossing • Right to Floyd, VA, 6 miles; left to Endicott and Ferrum, VA (Shooting Creek Road).

161.3 VA 615 crossing.

162.1 VA 711 crossing.

162.4 Rakes Mill Pond Overlook, west • Elevation: 2,477 ft. (755m) • Signboard: history of Rakes Mill Pond.

162.6 Staggered road crossing.

.9   VA 710 crossing.

3.2   VA 797 crossing • Thomas Grove Baptist Church, east.

63.5   VA 709 crossing.

165.3   Tuggle Gap • Elevation: 2,752 ft. (839m).

165.3   **VA 8 crossing, underpass (access west, north of crossing) (Hike 19, Option 1)** • Right to Floyd, VA, 6 miles, and I-81, 28 miles; left to Stuart, VA, 21 miles, and Fairy Stone State Park, 30 miles. Tuggles Gap Restaurant and Motel lies just south of the Parkway on VA 8 (tugglesgap.biz; 540-745-3402).

167.1   **Rocky Knob developed area, west** • Facilities: campground (81 tent sites, 28 trailer sites, 150-person capacity campfire circle), restrooms, trailer dumping station • Trails: **Rock Castle Gorge Trail,** 10.6 miles (Strenuous); 3 miles to Rock Castle Gorge and Rock Castle Creek • CCC camp for backcountry camping (backcountry permit required).

168.0   **Saddle Overlook, east (Hike 19, Option 2)** • Trails: access to Rock Castle Gorge Trail; old AT shelter; 1.0 mile to Rocky Knob Picnic Area; 0.7 mile to Rocky Knob Campground, east.

168.2   Rocky Knob, east (no sign) • Elevation: 3,572 ft. (1,089m).

168.8   Rock Castle Gorge Overlook, east • Elevation: 3,195 ft. (974m) • Trails: access to Rock Castle Gorge Trail • Views: Brammer Spur, Rock Castle Gorge, Western Piedmont • Wayside panel: Rock Castle Gorge.

169.0   **Rocky Knob Picnic Area, west (Hike 19, Options 3 and 4)** • Sites: 72 • Facilities: Rocky Knob Contact Station, comfort stations, phone, picnic shelter • Trails: **Black Ridge Trail,** 3.1 miles (Moderate); **Rocky Knob Picnic Loop Trail,** 1.3 miles (Easy).

169.1   Twelve O'Clock Knob Overlook, east.

169.2   Pump House Road access, west.

170.4   VA 720 crossing.

171.3   VA 720 crossing.

171.7   VA 726 crossing • Elevation: 3,471 ft. (1,058m) • Highest motor road elevation between Apple Orchard and Doughton Park. Turn right onto VA 726, then immediately left on VA 777 and in a short distance reach Chateau Morissette Winery and Restaurant.

172.7   Belcher Curve (no sign).

174.0   Rock Castle Gap • Elevation: 2,970 ft. (905m).

174.0   VA 799 access, west • Right to Willis, VA; Hubbards Mill.

174.1   VA 758 access, east (Woodberry Road) • Left to Meadows of Dan and Rocky Knob Cabins (8 CCC-built housekeeping cabins, closed in 2016).

175.9   VA 603 crossing • Entrance to Mabry Mill overflow parking area.

176.2   **Mabry Mill, east (Hike 20)** • Elevation: 2,855 ft. (870m) • Facilities: coffee shop, gift shop, restrooms, and phone; water-powered sawmill, carpenter shop, and working gristmill • Trail: **Mountain Industry Trail,** 0.5 mile (Easy;

self-guiding Pioneer Industry Trail, including blacksmith and whee
shop exhibit and whiskey still) • Signboard: rural life in Appalachia • W
panel: whiskey still, mill challenges/mill operation.

176.3   VA 603. Entrance to Mabry Mill overflow parking area.

177.7   Meadows of Dan • Elevation: 2,964 ft. (903m).

177.7   US 58 crossing, underpass (access west, north of crossing) • Right to Hillsville
VA, 21 miles; left to Stuart, VA, 16 miles, and Cochran's Mill, 3 miles.

Access to Primland Resort / Like Wintergreen Resort in Virginia
and Biltmore Estate in North Carolina, Primland is an upscale, many thousand acre private preserve by the Parkway with top-notch lodging, fine dining, resort amenities (golf, tennis, spa, hunting) and even trails (primland.com;
866-960-7446).

Though certainly a massive tract of "Prime Land," the resort name actually honors the beautiful, Blue Ridge–straddling property of founder Didier
Primat. From a stunning, celestial observatory–equipped lodge beside a
spectacular summit golf course, the resort enclave plummets below the Blue
Ridge, offering all kinds of outdoor adventures, from ATV tours, to sporting
clays, kayaking, mountain biking, horseback riding, guided hunts, and trout
fishing. Great hikes leave the lodge, including a stretch of the original Appalachian Trail. Accommodations include fairway cottages, mountain homes, and
what the resort calls treehouses.

Just 7 miles off the Parkway at Meadows of Dan, Primland's more distant
main lodge is about 25 minutes from the high road. From Milepost 177.7,
take US 58 east 0.9 mile to a right on US 58. In 3.8 miles, turn right on VA
610, and the resort's north gate is another 2 miles (2000 Busted Rock Rd.;
GPS: 36.688202 / -80.354375).

178.8   VA 744 crossing.

179.2   **Round Meadow Overlook, west (Hike 21)** • Elevation: 2,800 ft. (853m)
• Views: excellent mountain cove with large hemlocks.

179.4   Round Meadow Viaduct • Elevation: 2,800 ft. (853m) • Creek elevation:
2,690 ft. (Round Meadow Creek).

180.1   VA 600 crossing • Mayberry Presbyterian Church and Cemetery.

180.5   VA 634 crossing • Mayberry Crossing; 0.1 mile to Mayberry Trading Post,
country store.

180.6   Mayberry Gap.

180.7   Mayberry Creek • Elevation: 2,775 ft. (846m).

183.4   Pinnacles of Dan Gap • Elevation: 2,875 ft. (876m).

183.9   VA 614 access, east • To Mount Airy, NC.

187.7   VA 639 crossing.

188.8   **Groundhog Mountain Picnic Area, east** • Elevation: 3,025 ft. (922m)
• Facilities: picnic area (26 sites), one comfort station, trail from parking area
to observation tower (leg-stretcher) • Views: excellent 360-degree view from

Catch the view from the log tower, and learn about different kinds of fencing, at Groundhog Mountain Picnic Area.

tower • Cemetery in parking area island • Wayside panel: different types of rail fences • Exhibits: 4 types of rail fences • Trail: **Groundhog Mountain Observation Tower,** 300 feet (Easy). Parkway motorists can see this hilltop observation tower long before they reach it. And the easy 100-yard stroll that leads to the amazing log structure means that even if you don't climb the tower, no one should miss exploring the hilltop. Like other key exhibits along the Parkway, this one truly informs—this time about fences. The variety and elegance of the ways mountaineers used logs to fence animals in and out is nothing short of amazing. The exhibit explores many of the fence types you'll see being maintained by the Park Service along the road—or rotting on the forest floor in remote trail locations.

188.9 VA 608 crossing, underpass (no access).

189.1 Pilot Mountain Overlook, east • Elevation: 2,950 ft. (899m) • Views: excellent view of Pilot Mountain State Park, with its distinctive North Carolina Piedmont summit. The Saura Indians called the mountain Jomeokee, or "Great Guide," and Native Americans and settlers used the mountain as a travel landmark visible for miles.

189.2 VA 608 crossing, underpass.

189.9 **Puckett Cabin Parking Area, west** • Elevation: 2,848 ft. (868m) • Wayside panel: history of Puckett Cabin • Trail: Puckett Cabin, 150 feet (Easy). Pause at this roadside cabin where Orelena Hawks Puckett spent the second half of a 102-year life. The rude cabin and outbuilding sit beside a fenced garden space. Puckett was married at sixteen and lived her entire life near Groundhog Mountain. She turned to midwifery in midlife and helped deliver more than 1,000 babies—the last in 1939, the year she died. None of "Aunt" Orelena's own twenty-four children lived beyond infancy. A photo of the woman during the last year of her life appears on the roadside interpretive easel.

190.0 Crossing to Puckett Primitive Baptist Church.

190.6 VA 910 crossing.

191.4 VA 608 crossing.

192.2 VA 648 crossing • Left to Willis Gap (VA 771); Mount Airy, NC.

193.2 Volunteer Gap crossing • Elevation: 2,672 ft. (814m) • Access: Old Volunteer Road.

193.7 Orchard Gap • Elevation: 2,675 ft. (815m).

193.7 VA 691 crossing • Right to Hillsville, VA; left to Mount Airy, NC.

194.7 VA 608 crossing.

195.5 Wards Gap • Elevation: 2,750 ft. (838m).

196.4 VA 682 crossing, underpass (Guynn Town Bridge).

197.7 Cascade Mountain Development, east • Access from VA 608 only.

198.4 VA 685 crossing • Left to VA 608.

198.9 VA 608 access, east, start of staggered crossing.

199.1 Fancy Gap Maintenance Area, west.

2
2
20

206
207.
208.
209.3
209.8
211.1
213.0

p
H
Tr

213.3 VA
215.3 VA
215.6 VA 7
215.8 VA 8
      7 mile
216.9 Virgin
217.1 North
217.3 NC 18
      NC, 15 1
217.5 **Cumber**
      parking, p
217.8 Leaving C

Appalachian Spring on the Parkway. At Heffner Gap (Milepost 325), cross the road and hike a historic stretch of the Overmountain Victory National Historic Trail.

327.5 Public road crossing, underpass (access west, south of crossing; Altapass Road)
• Right to Spruce Pine, NC, 5 miles; left to US 221, 10 miles. Access to trailhead for lower section of Rose River Trail hike from Heffner Gap is 0.5 mile west toward Spruce Pine.

328.3 **Orchard at Altapass (Access on Orchard Road).** This popular old-time attraction features apples, all kinds of local foods, not to mention mountain music, country dancing, and more. The nonprofit enterprise offers heritage programming of many kinds and a variety of trails, including a Kids in Parks TRACK Trail. One brochure features "apples and animals" and another recounts the story of the nearby Overmountain Victory Trail, route of colonial patriots who won the pivotal battle of Kings Mountain in 1780. Visit kidsinparks.com/orchard-altapass and altapassorchard.org.

328.6 The Loops Overlook, east • Elevation: 2,980 ft. (908m) • Wayside panel: Carolina, Clinchfield, and Ohio Railway. This major railroad breached the Blue Ridge here in an engineering marvel of railroad construction using eighteen tunnels in 13 miles of track. One panel describes that, and another panel features mountain music easily heard at the neighboring Orchard at Altapass.

329.5 Swafford Gap • Elevation: 2,852 ft. (869m).

329.5 NC 1113 crossing.

329.8 Table Rock Overlook, east • Elevation: 2,870 ft. (875m) • Trail: a 1.3-mile, moderate section of the Overmountain National Historic Trail leads from this overlook to the Museum of North Carolina Minerals (2.6 miles round-trip).

330.9 Gillespie Gap • Elevation: 2,819 ft. (859m).

330.9 NC 226 crossing, underpass (access west, north of crossing) • Right to Spruce Pine, NC, 4 miles; left to NC 226A, Little Switzerland, NC, 4 miles, and Marion, NC, 14 miles. East, worthwhile dining and views recommend Mountain View Restaurant (mvrestaurant.com/).

330.9 **Museum of North Carolina Minerals** • Extensive interpretive/informational displays in a top-notch museum devoted to the richness of North Carolina's geology and the local importance of mining in the Spruce Pine area. • Open year-round; the Mitchell County Chamber of Commerce maintains an information station in the museum that can direct visitors to the area's extensive gem mining attractions and to attractive Spruce Pine restaurants.

330.9 Gillespie Gap Maintenance Area • Facilities: ranger and maintenance offices.

332.6 Lynn Gap (Dale Road) • Elevation: 3,109 ft. (948m).

333.4 Little Switzerland Tunnel • Length: 542 feet • Min height: 14 feet, 4 inches.

333.9 Public road crossing, underpass (access east, north of crossing) • Elevation: 3,490 ft. (1,064m) • Left to NC 226A; Little Switzerland, NC. Dining/lodging at Switzerland Inn (switzerlandinn.com) on the Parkway with easy access to Switzerland Café and General Store (switzerlandcafe.com) and Little Switzerland Books and Beans (lsbooksandbeans.webs.com).

335.4 Bearwallow Gap • Elevation: 3,490 ft. (1,064m).

336.3 Gooch Gap • Elevation: 3,360 ft. (1,024m).

336.3 Public road crossing (access east; Wild Acres Road).

336.8 Wildacres Tunnel • Length: 330 feet • Min height: 13 feet, 1 inch.

337.2 Deer Lick Gap Overlook, west • Elevation: 3,452 ft. (1,052m) • Facilities: 2 picnic tables • Wayside panel: groundhogs.

338.8 Three Knobs Overlook, west • Elevation: 3,875 ft. (1,181m).

339.5 **Crabtree Falls Recreation Area (Hike 37)** • Campground: 71 tent and small RV sites, 22 large RV sites, 3 comfort stations, amphitheater • Trail: **Crabtree Falls Loop Trail,** 3.1 miles (Strenuous) • Crabtree Falls, total drop 90 feet • Facilities: former restaurant, gift shop/camp store have been closed for a number of years.

340.2 Picnic area, east • Facilities: 82 sites, 1 comfort station.

342.1 Public road crossing (Victor Road access).

342.2 Black Mountains Overlook, west • Elevation: 3,892 ft. (1186m) • Wayside panel: Black Mountain Range (identifies named peaks). From this dramatic perch, the peaks of this massive mountain range stand out in grandeur.

344.1 Buck Creek Gap Overlook, east • Elevation: 3,355 ft. (1023m) • Trail: access to Mountains-to-Sea Trail. Heading south on the Parkway, here the MST

About the Author

Randy Johnson is an award-winning travel writer and editor who has lived in the Southern Appalachians most of his life and written widely on travel and the outdoors for newspapers and ski and travel magazines. He is the author of the acclaimed new book *Grandfather Mountain: The History and Guide to an Appalachian Icon*, as well as the classic *Southern Snow: The Winter Guide to Dixie* (due out again in 2018), *Hiking North Carolina, Best Easy Day Hikes Blue Ridge Parkway,* and *Best Easy Day Hikes Great Smoky Mountains National Park*. For years he was editor-in-chief of United Airlines' *Hemispheres*, the United States' most award-winning airline magazine (named world's best in-flight magazine in 2006).

Randy has a unique history with the Parkway. He proposed and implemented the trail management program at Grandfather Mountain as the Parkway was being completed on the mountain. He reclaimed the mountain's trails, built new paths, and helped lay the groundwork for the mountain's designation as a United Nations Biosphere Reserve. He was a trail design consultant for the Parkway's Tanawha Trail on Grandfather and helped create the system of state park and national park trails found on the mountain today. Previous editions of this book have recommended hikes that were later formalized by the National Park Service.

He's currently the task force leader for the Grandfather Mountain portion of the Mountains-to-Sea Trail and a member of the Grandfather Mountain State Park Advisory Committee. Randy has hiked and skied all over the world and is a member of the Society of American Travel Writers and the North American Snowsports Journalists Association. He invites you to visit his website (randyjohnsonbooks.com) to send him an e-mail or read more about his books.